ORGANIZATIONAL ETHICS

By addressing ethical environments in health care and business organizations this book examines a new era – research in organizational ethics. This book will help decision-makers to develop and sustain organizational ethics in their firms and to think more critically about the issues that emerge within contemporary organizations.

This book develops the themes that ethics is good business; that developing and sustaining ethics relates directly to assessing ethics in organizations through research, evaluation or audit; and that decision-makers perform the role of ethical advocate in their organizations. Justice is explored as an underlying component in the development of an ethical environment. The book concludes with the role of decision-makers as ethical advocates in their organizations. Discussion is complemented by cases and examples, thereby addressing the intersection of theory and application.

ASHGATE STUDIES IN APPLIED ETHICS

Scandals in medical research and practice; physicians unsure how to manage new powers to postpone death and reshape life; business people operating in a world with few borders; damage to the environment; concern with animal welfare – all have prompted an international demand for ethical standards which go beyond matters of personal taste and opinion.

The *Ashgate Studies in Applied Ethics* series presents leading international research on the most topical areas of applied and professional ethics. Focusing on professional, business, environmental, medical and bio-ethics, the series draws from many diverse interdisciplinary perspectives including: philosophical, historical, legal, medical, environmental and sociological. Exploring the intersection of theory and practice, books in this series will prove of particular value to researchers, students, and practitioners worldwide.

Series Editors:

Ruth Chadwick, Head of Centre for Professional Ethics & Professor of Moral Philosophy, University of Central Lancashire, UK
Dr David Lamb, Honorary Reader in Bioethics, University of Birmingham, UK
Professor Michael Davis, Center for the Study of Ethics in the Professions, Illinois Institute of Technology, USA

Organizational Ethics
Research and Ethical Environments

CHARLOTTE McDANIEL
Emory University, USA

ASHGATE

Published by
Ashgate Publishing Limited
Gower House
Croft Road
Aldershot
Hampshire GU11 3HR
England

Ashgate Publishing Company
Suite 420
101 Cherry Street
Burlington, VT 05401-4405
USA

Ashgate website: http://www.ashgate.com

British Library Cataloguing in Publication Data
McDaniel, Charlotte
Organizational ethics : research and ethical environments. – (Ashgate studies in applied ethics)
1. Organizational behavior – Moral and ethical aspects
2. Business ethics 3. Employee motivation
I. Title
174.4

Library of Congress Cataloging-in-Publication Data
McDaniel, Charlotte, 1942-
Organizational ethics : research and ethical environments / Charlotte McDaniel.
p. cm. – (Ashgate studies in applied ethics)
Includes bibliographical references and index.
ISBN 0-7546-3447-7 (alk. paper)
1. Business ethics. I. Title. II. Series.

HF5387.M414 2004
174'.4—dc22

2004000850

ISBN 0 7546 3447 7

Printed and bound in Great Britain by MPG Books Ltd, Bodmin, Cornwall

Contents

Contents

Preface

Ethical situations are desirable employment places for health care and business workers. Respect, honesty, and justice are compelling ethics dimensions of work life for workers, as are places affirming diversity in social groups; meaning in work is also important. Rather, recent corporate scandals illustrated by Enron decrease employee satisfaction and rob them of a sense of purpose in work; employees respond to these unsavory activities with decreasing loyalty and lack of confidence in leadership. The accompanying constancy of organizational change, profit maximization, and technological advances exacerbate these ethics challenges, while heightening the importance of ethics in work, primarily due to exorbitant costs resulting from *un*ethical activities. Despite ethics challenges faced daily at work and less than appealing examples from high profile cases, many employees try to do the right things, work well and productively, and engage with their coworkers in deliberations to resolve ethics disagreements. Creating positive workplaces is also important for employers in health care and business as they search for ways to utilize this human resource, to enhance employee commitment resulting in retention, and to increase abilities to work effectively resulting in productivity. The search continues for ways to understand workplaces and enhance employees' work.

The purpose of this book is to provide leaders and decision makers in health care and business organizations with information to aid them in their pursuit of enhancing the ethical environment of organizations.[1] It does so with an examination of issues related to organizational ethics from a theoretical approach in Part One and an applied approach in Part Two.

As with any work, there are certain assumptions that one makes in developing and presenting material. Five assumptions are made here. The first assumes managers, workers, health care providers, as well as customers and patients, prefer an ethical to a less ethical environment. Preference for applied ethics, rather than metaphysical or philosophical ethics, is the second assumption; the approach emphasizes the practice of ethics.

The third assumes there is no one—and only one—solution to resolve an ethical dilemma, or only one applicable theory. There are, in fact, few agreed upon right and wrong solutions or approaches in applied ethics, which is why we focus predominantly on critical analysis. Since we are concerned with leaders who make decisions, we are concerned with how to analyze and resolve ethical concerns in a manner consistent with the values, codes, and mandates of the organization, as well as how to retain quality service that is ethical. We are concerned with the advancement of knowledge regarding ethics and ethics as foundational for decisions and activities resulting in quality work settings for providers and employees and services for customers, patients, and their families.

The fourth assumption pertains to measurement. Measurement poses a challenge. What is an assessment? Assessment implies a systematic collection of information. That still begs the question, nevertheless, of what we understand as organizational ethics and its relevance for measurement, explored in this work. The final assumption is that organizations are open systems, implying the need to consider the ecology of the organization. External situations influence the health care or business endeavor. System approaches provide an analytical framework with a macro perspective for organizational analysis; it also allows one to explore how the various features of the organization relate to one another, and how they influence one another.

To address its aims, the book is divided into two parts. Part One begins with four theoretical issues emerging as one examines ethics in organizations. Building upon empirical research conducted in organizational ethics, with an applied approach, attention is turned in Part Two to the issues and strategies for developing organizational ethics in both health care and business endeavors. The second part follows the organizing framework of examining, assessing, developing and sustaining the ethical organization to establish the ethics initiative.

Chapter *One* examines the issue of measuring ethics, including the challenges inherent to measuring ethics empirically. While few persons deny that ethics is measurable, authors do attest to the challenges in measuring ethics empirically. Aguilar (1994:70), for instance, notes that ethics 'suffers by comparison' to quantitative assessments. Instructors in professional education also cite the need for stronger measures and a need to evaluate the influence of imparting ethics (Bebeau, Rest, and Yamoor, 1985; Hébert, Meslin, and Dunn, 1992). Research results can direct preventive and follow-up activities. Thus empirical clues about the ethical puzzle contribute to developing a positive ethical environment. These issues will be given significant attention in Chapter One, including conceptual problems to avoid. This work does not renounce qualitative approaches; however, since limited attention has been given to empirical analyses, it will emphasize quantitative assessments.

Chapter *Two* addresses the challenge of instilling ethics in employees. Underlying this question is the lingering question of whether we can instill ethics. If employers want to instill good conduct and appropriate behaviors in the workplace, whether it is in health care or business, how do they do so? Even more fundamental to this issue is whether employers can positively influence the behaviors of employees. If current popular literature is correct, significant proportions–50 per cent–of employees cheat at work (Greengard, 1997). Chapter Two extends the dialogue to address instilling ethical behaviors, and examines errors and reporting.

The distinction between ethics and compliance is explored in Chapter *Three*. One of the contextual issues surrounding contemporary organizations is an increasing emphasis on compliance. Lawsuits in health care, news accounts about corporate fraud, and whistleblowing provide a plethora of examples suggesting compliance in the workplace is a growing concern for health care and business. A trend in the U.S. is to subsume ethics under compliance for institutional ethics committees, or, likewise, to assume that if an organization is compliant it is, therefore, ethical. Is this is a global trend? Because there are distinct and unique contributions that compliance and ethics offer, the two concepts are examined for their differentiation and complementarity.

Chapter *Four* begins by exploring empirical research conducted in organizational ethics. As the Conference Board concludes (1994:1), '...companies need to incorporate well-defined ethics investigative processes into their policies.' Among several studies explored are those revealing the manner in which enhancement of ethics in health care and industry is related to employee retention (Singhal, 1994; McDaniel, 1998c). Ethics is key to maintaining appropriate relationships and behaviors, as well as preventing unethical and fraudulent activities. Ethics builds trust (Conference Board, 1994). It also supports employees' willingness to report improper conduct. A significant ethical issue for some employees is sustaining diversity. Research results, presented here as summary reviews rather than detailed reports, shed light on this important employment issue.

Part Two introduces the application of ethics and begins with Chapter *Five*. This chapter provides a detailed discussion of the first step, assessing, of the three-part ethics initiative in organizations. It explores the parallel need for evaluation procedures that are consistent with ethics. Examples and cases illustrate problems emerging when these two aspects are *in*consistent. Emphasis in Chapter Five is on the first of the three interactive steps and the need to include evaluation in any *program* addressing ethics.

Developing ethics in organizations is the focus of Chapter *Six*. Following an initial assessment, procedures need to be implemented to change organizations toward enhanced ethics in the system. This chapter examines those strategies, providing enough detail so health care and business leaders of systems can use them in developing their own ethics programs.

The last of the three-part steps is explored in Chapter *Seven*. Sustaining programs once developed is an important consideration. Chapter Seven explores the interactive feedback loop foundational to building and sustaining a strong system ethics. Linking the sustainment efforts to outcomes and the mission, and back to evaluation is a significant aspect explored in this chapter. Several cases illustrate creative ways managers in health care and business have used program sustainment to advantage.

Chapter *Eight* discusses the central role of CEOs as ethics advocates. While the centrality of the CEO role is highlighted, roles of other decision makers— managers, directors, ethics committee chairs, or clinical unit administrators, for instance—are also explored in this chapter. The important role they play in communicating the mission (Aguilar, 1994), in modeling good conduct and appropriate behavior, and in monitoring the features of a system enhancing an ethical domain are included.

Hans Wolf, former Vice Chairman of Syntex Corporation located in Mexico City, confirms the need to offer the right example in the role of CEO (Conference Board, 1994). Respect, trust, honesty, and fair treatment are all critical issues to maintain in the organization. In addition, the ethos of the firm is addressed. The conduct of the ethics project may contribute to a new culture in which integrity and openness in assessment, for instance, are being introduced.

The book concludes with Chapter Eight that provides an overview of important issues examined in organizational ethics, as well as suggestions for sustaining ethics in health care and business organizations. The emphasis is upon applied ethics as a way to instill ethics in organizations and the role leaders play in making it evident in their organizations.

Several cases are interwoven into each chapter. These cases, while attempting to capture the reality of work in health care and business settings, are not based on real situations. Any resemblance of or similarity to an actual situation, either in health care or business, unless so noted, is coincidental. Cases requiring permission are cited in notes and references.

It is impossible to extend appreciation for and acknowledgements to all the persons who so considerately and generously contributed, directly and indirectly, to this work. Allow the following, alphabetical list, to suffice as a small token of my appreciation for their kind contributions to this manuscript: Holley Butkovich, Craig Cleland, Maryjeanne Crawford, Sarah Doeppner, Karen Esterl, Nick Fotion, the Fulbright Commission for my 2002-03 Fulbright Scholar Award allowing some advance time for reading and writing, Jamila Garrett-Bell, Patrick Graham, Robert Hall, Hinton Rural Life Center for quiet and reflective time, Brooks Holifield, Joyce Hoskings, Corey Keyes, Alice Miller, Regina Pyke, Mary Rorty, and my wonderful family, Kirk and Kristian. Special acknowledgement goes to the editors and staff at Ashgate Publishing, especially Paul Coulum and Emma Williams, for a productive and collaborative process.

Note

1   Although some argue health care is a business, for our purposes health care is one type of organization, and business, here referring to another type, includes the corporate businesses illustrated by insurance, car, food, or retail industries, but not health care.

References

Aguilar, F. J. (1994). *Managing corporate ethics.* New York, NY: Oxford University Press.

Bebeau, M., Rest, J., and Yamoor, C. (1985). Measuring dental students' ethical sensitivity. *Journal of Dental Education 49*:225 ff.

Conference Board. (1994). *Business ethics: Generating trust in the 1990s and beyond* (Report #1057-94-CH; S. J. Garone, Ed.). New York, NY: Author.

Greengard, S. (1997, October). 50% of your employees are lying, cheating and stealing. *Workforce 76*:44-53.

Hébert, P., Meslin, E., and Dunn, E. (1992). Measuring the ethical sensitivity of medical students: A study at the University of Toronto. *Journal of Medical Ethics 18*:142-150.

McDaniel, C. (1998c). Ethical environments: Reports of practicing nurses. *Nursing Clinics of North America 33(2):*363-372.
Singhal, S. (1994). *Senior management: The dynamics of effectiveness.* London, UK: Sage Publications, Inc.

Introduction

Background

Ethical environments as ambiences for daily work are preferred as places for employees to work. Workers in various types of organizations, but especially in health care and business, desire to work in surroundings that support clear organizational values; offer them respect, justice and fairness, honesty, and trust. In their work *In Search for Excellence*, Tom Peters and Richard Waterman (1982:280) note that excellent companies offer clear values and take the process of shaping values seriously. As contemporary workers face an increasing number of morally challenging situations they seek ethical places in which to perform their tasks. Health care and business employees seek situations where discrimination is absent and fairness prevails, and in settings in which they can explore ethically troublesome situations with coworkers and supervisors in order to arrive at positive resolutions. Positive work sites also exhibit features illustrating ethical environments.

Scholars and researchers have historically understood the importance of employees' work environments. To more clearly understand and identify positive places to work, journal articles and scholarly manuscripts focus on organization and work design, satisfaction of workers, patient and provider interactions, leadership and organizational strengths, organization of managed care, or concepts approximating ethics such as dignity and justice in organizations. Few of these important works, however, draw attention to and directly focus on ethical dimensions of the work setting.

Because ethics is rarely the central focus of organizational studies, this book explores organizational ethics in health care and business. The aim is to provide decision makers in health care and business endeavors with information to aid them in sustaining ethics in their organizations. It develops three themes. One is that organizational ethics is critical in today's systems. Indeed, applied ethics as evidenced in organizational ethics is good business. The second theme is that evaluation is an integral part of developing and sustaining organizational ethics; the third is that leaders as ethical advocates play a critical role in these developments.

Why is ethics so important to organizations, whether health care or business? What is it about ethical environments that employers and employees find attractive? Instilling ethics in organizations is becoming increasingly important for health care and business and is attracting the attention of their executives. The past few decades have witnessed a resurgence of interest in ethics, especially applied ethics, and the emergence of organizational ethics. Several developments are contributing to this focus. In the previous century European countries experienced evolutions in the organization of health care systems and medical reimbursement, illustrated by advancements in the health care systems in Finland and the U.K. Similar changes have followed in the U.S. The recent signal event in the U.S. is the development of managed care in the later part of the 1900s.

What influence does managed care have? Managed care re-focuses attention from the physician-patient relationship to the relationships between physicians and other providers and patients, but within the context of the organization. This shift in emphasis is illustrated by attention to the reimbursement of patient care, the patients' access to adequate care, and the manner in which the organization influences the delivery of health services. Rather than analysis at the micro level, managed care implies analysis of macro issues. These developments also raise a number of complex moral issues requiring examination for their ethical implications. From an ethical perspective these organizational evolutions highlight issues regarding resource allocation, access to care, provider and patient accountability and control, and just and fair treatment of patients and providers. In 1987, for instance, Larry R. Churchill explored the relationship between managed care and rationing, yet allocation is even more turbulent in today's environment. All these issues involve organizational ethics.

The corporate sector is also witnessing heightened emphasis on organizational ethics (Aguilar, 1994). Unfortunately much of this emphasis is the result of litigation emanating from errors, scandals, and fraudulent business management. Lawsuits resulting from harassment between employer and employee or the perception of a ceiling effect by workers suggest unfair practices. The ethical issues raised by the Enron debacle in the U.S. highlight the need for preventive approaches. An increasingly turbulent and competitive work world is leading to tensions, and in some cases to a contentious work environment. These in turn have led to lessened consumer trust in corporations and in some instances their products. High employee turnover only exacerbates this growing mistrust regarding corporations. Employees as well as consumers suspect ethics is a missing component.

Why is identifying desirable workplaces important? While it appears straightforward—that a desirable workplace is preferred—it is helpful to establish why good places are important for organizations. Desirable workplaces attract and retain employees, important because good employees contribute to the productivity of the endeavor. The average corporate cost per employee in hire, training, and turnover is more than $30,000, with higher estimates for health care turnover (Reidenbach and Robin, 1989:8-10). Multiplied by the millions of employees who change jobs for whatever reason, the cost is exorbitant. Attractive workplaces, however, reduce turnover costs. Studies reveal that companies judged good places to work also outperform other companies. In the past decade, companies listed as 'good places to work' outperformed the Standard and Poor 500 (Levering, 2000:259). Two aspects of desirable places are respect and fairness, both ethical dimensions of work. Measured by stock appreciation and earnings per share, the 'best places' stocks grew at three times the rate of comparable Standard and Poor 500 companies. Summary results note '…evidence is strong that companies that treat their workers well benefit on the bottom line' (Levering, 2000:259). A similar study from the U.K. reveals that ethical sites also benefit shareholders (IBE Survey, 2003).

Good workplaces are less stressful places, thereby leading to decreases in the health care costs that are of increasing concern to companies. Desirable places are places in which workers exhibit pride in their work, thus extending the perception of a positive site for patients and customers. Another reason to seek desirable workplaces is that studies reveal time spent at work is more productive if working is pleasant rather than unpleasant, resulting in higher quality of work and linked to the business 'bottom line' (Keyes, Hysom and Lupo, 2000). For a number of reasons desirable workplaces are thereby less costly sites.

It is extremely difficult to measure precisely the consequent cost of undesirable or unethical behaviors. But lack of control and participation at work (Petterson and Arnetz, 1995), unsupportive leadership (Landeweerd and Boumans, 1988), and low social support (Bourbonnais and Mondor, 2001), are all correlated with poorer health outcomes among employees. Undesirable places exacerbate stress and its related problems. Workers in undesirable places may not leave, but they 'call in' sick and take extra time off, leading to decline in productivity. Reports show employees in *un*desirable situations are frequently the same workers who steal, create work slow-downs, and behave in other disruptive ways in order to get back at their employers, behaviors explored in more detail in Chapter Three. It has been estimated, for instance, that more than 50 per cent of employees steal on the job (Greengard, 1997). These undesirable activities reduce organizational profits. Costs due to unethical and illegal behaviors are between 40 to 300 billion dollars per year (Reidenbach and Robin, 1989:9). Unethical behaviors also result in fines and increased litigation. Add to these increased costs for hiring legal teams to protect an organization, and the costs of unethical or illegal activities escalate quickly.

The loss of reputation of a company when illegal activity and its consequences become public is another significant, albeit difficult to measure, cost. Any sage leader knows it takes years to build a reputation and seconds for it to be lost, as was illustrated by the sale of Arthur Andersen in the early 21st century. The stigma of poor products is yet another loss. Related to these is the difficult to measure loss of morale on the part of a corporation's or hospital's employees, and the parallel loss of confidence among their customers or patients when unethical and illegal activities are revealed or products are poor. These are all reasons why undesirable places to work are costly to organizations and less productive and attractive to employees and customers, resulting in employee stress, burnout, and illness. Workplace quality influences the organization and work results. Ethics is rarely addressed as a variable in analyses, but is negatively related to undesirable activities. As ethics moves to center stage in the aftermath of Enron and similar corporate scandals, we find that despite the quest for understanding good work sites, ones supporting values, seldom is ethics the focus of scholarly work examining employment. However, in spite of the lack of attention to ethics in research, a growing number of CEOs and managers are exploring constructive options to the illegal and unethical behaviors occurring in their organizations, thereby increasing the consideration of organizational ethics.

Themes

Ethics as Good Business

Corporate executives and hospital directors are turning to applied ethics. Why? The seminal exploration of the hospital as a moral institution serves as a basis for today's discussions, highlighting the organizational and aesthetic dimensions of patient care (Pellegrino, 1979). In part, these initiatives are spurred on with relatively recent developments by the Joint Commission on Accreditation of Healthcare Organizations (1994) or the guidelines enacted in the U.S. by the Federal Sentencing Commission in 1991.[1] Ethical guidelines are a means to improve employee retention, enhance consumer trust, and increase the productivity of their corporations. Executives are exploring organizational ethics as a means of instilling good conduct or equitable employment practices and enhancing the ethical environment of their firms. They are discovering that ethics is good business. Indeed, organizational ethics is good business for corporate and health care systems.

Are there reasons then why ethics is good business? There are cogent reasons for viewing ethics as good business. Managers and leaders of organizations discover systems with a positive ethics or a high value on ethics garner the attention of employees. Corporations become listed in the popular literature as good places to work, illustrated by *Business Ethics'* (2001) best organizations and *Fortune Global 500*'s (2000) annual listing of the best large global corporations. Organizations with regard for good relationships with employees, justice and good conduct in the workplace are desirable places for employees. Corporations are also listed with specific notations on their ability to recruit and attract female or minority employees because they attend to issues of employee diversity (Kahn, 2001). Corporations of excellence foster creativity and innovation in the workplace (Hart, 1997). The word gets around. The ability to hire and retain valued employees is parallel to the employees' opinions about their work settings. These impressions of the work setting are influenced by public awareness and exemplify extant justice.

In 2000, the Coca-Cola Corporation headquartered in Atlanta, GA, U.S., with numerous international locations, settled a billion-dollar lawsuit with its employees. The central issue was discrimination on the job and employee harassment. Although Coke does not acknowledge wrongdoing, the employees feel vindicated. Their central issue: Coke was not a *just* place to work. However, recent listings of 'Best Places to Work' now include Coke. New attention to diversity and fairness in the workplace paid off for Coke, and may serve to prevent similar losses. Other companies are taking note (See: 'Coke settles,' 2000).

What difference does it make if a corporation is listed among the best? Retention of valued employees is a high priority for a productive and growing endeavor. Paramount among these issues is the need to prevent the expense inherent in employee turnover. Employee turnover lessens productivity, and turnover of employees—especially those in positions requiring extensive training or on-the-job experience—becomes extremely expensive for the employer. Managers and supervisors who have high levels of employee turnover themselves become less attractive to the firm; they are costly to the corporation if their behaviors and work values are not conducive to retaining high quality employees (Hart, 1997).

These issues then begin to affect what corporations and health care systems refer to as the bottom line. When the bottom line reflects higher costs or fewer profits than anticipated, management begins to look for ways to decrease costs. Managers or supervisors with high employee turnover and its associated lower productivity become expendable in most systems. Thus, ethics as exhibited in good conduct and positive relationships with employees is a factor that enhances productivity and prevents liability concerns. Ethical behavior is sought and nurtured by good management. It is an international concern supported by managers worldwide (Conference Board, 1994:18).

As these organizational experiences gather momentum they are building an emerging area for scholarly attention. They contribute to the continued development of organizational ethics with attention to research. Organizational ethics attends to the moral or ethical concerns pertaining to and emerging from the interactions, linkages, and relationships of the organizational whole. It subsumes those relationships between particular individuals, reaching beyond them to the framework in which those specific interactions occur. Organizational ethics thus initiates a new paradigm, illuminating a new set of relationships by shifting from a micro-oriented analysis to one focused on the macro level. This changes the level of abstraction and alters the paradigm, modifying the worldview through which one perceives the situation (Kuhn, 1996).

What does this change in emphasis mean? What implications emerge from these alterations? Paradigm shifts result in different foci. Earlier foci included the relationships between individual patients and their physicians. In business the relationships between supervisors and employees were germane for discussion. These foci exemplify major accomplishments in ethics, especially when considering applied ethics. Earlier work provided an important foundation and explored critical areas for the advancement of ethics. Organizational ethics, however, expands this analysis to include collectivities of patients and employees in their health care or corporate environments and focusing on the organization as a whole. As health system and the business organization experience turbulence, they raise new and challenging issues of a moral nature. These issues in turn demand new and creative ethical examination reflecting the organizational whole.

Change not only requires critical reflection on the whole, but it also highlights an important aspect of organizational ethics: justice. Justice is a fundamental component of organizational ethics, and thus one way to approach the ethical nature of organizations is to explore concerns related to justice. Inherent in these moral challenges is the related issue of justice in the workplace. For a system to exhibit organizational ethics, there must be good conduct, equitable treatment, and fair behavior among employees and between them and their employers; providers and patients in health care expect no less. These behaviors provide extant illustrations of justice and application of ethics.

Classic explorations of justice (*e.g.*, Rawls, 1971; Kant, 1988; Mill, 1993), have tended to discuss relationships between individuals reminiscent of the micro level of analysis. Organizational ethics, however, implies that examination of the entire system is under consideration. This revision in paradigm implies new applications of these important explorations, searching for guides to instill moral and ethical behaviors in the work setting. Using these important classic discussions in application to the work environment is one of the challenges facing organizational ethics. These issues lead directly into the second theme, the evaluation of ethics in organizations.

Evaluation: Toward an Ethical Environment

How do CEOs know their organizations are ethical? Is it enough to have an ethics code or a mission statement? What measures are available for ethically accountable organizations to use? In order to address these questions, the discussion explores evaluation processes and (need for) empirical research in organizational ethics.

To date there are few guidelines for the development of organizational ethics in business or health care. Although guidelines are emerging from federal and regulatory systems, they, too, grapple with the plethora of ethical concerns developing in today's organizations. Even the development of organizational ethics as a domain is relatively new. Employers ask, what do we mean by organizational ethics? Students in ethics courses ask, how, if any, does it differ from ethics or applied ethics? CEOs ask, what are the criteria for a well-designed and implemented program instilling organizational ethics? Leaders want to know how to develop organizational ethics in their firms and sustain an ethical environment over time. Even more important is the consideration that needs to be given to these questions in order to think critically about the moral implications and their results for all concerned.

Even if the corporation is interested in ethical behavior and policy, how will it know if and when its efforts have succeeded? What are the corporate marker points? As these developments gather international momentum and organizational ethics garners more attention, there are few guidelines regarding ways to proceed. Yet, fewer are the tools to measure of ethics in organizations. An ethics audit, while attractive, seems beyond the reach of most health care and business organizations because there are so few quality measures of ethics. Although many executives and managers in the corporate world at first glance would argue that ethics is too abstract and removed from their daily activities, they are finding that ethics is very relevant to their endeavors (Rosenthal and Buchholz, 2000). Philosophers, ethicists, and researchers working in applied ethics have much to say and offer organizations, whether in health care or business. They can aid business and health care leaders in thinking critically about important ethical situations emerging in their daily endeavors. This book gives significant attention to these concerns.

The lingering question then is, how do the parts interact and fit together? As one initiates a program to instill organizational ethics, it is helpful to break the steps into easily understandable parts. In quality systems, however, these steps become so frequent, interrelated, and complex they become melded into one comprehensive program. It is thus artificial to think in terms of outcomes without evaluation, and assessment without an eye to the organization's mission and its future. For the purposes of this book, the three steps of assessing, developing, and sustaining are treated separately. But this division should be appreciated as a heuristic distinction to provide an organizing framework for this discussion.

If CEOs want to instill ethics in their organizations where should they start? What directions would leaders give to their employees? In order to understand the current status of ethics in an organization, an assessment needs to be conducted serving as the plan for the next step. The first step gathers information leaders need in order to make informed decisions. Audit, appraisement, assessment, or evaluation, terms used synonymously for the purposes of this work, gives management a clear picture of the current situation. Sometimes called an ethics audit or an organizational ethics assessment, this evaluation is essential for obtaining a comprehensive view of the organization's current ethics status. This initial assessment is the foundation on which other decisions are based.

Indeed, any assessment of ethics involves not only issues of ethics but meta-ethical issues as well.[2] Ethics evaluation itself must be conducted in an ethical manner. The processes must parallel the content. The procedures for conducting the ethics analysis and implementing the resulting program are central to the integrity of the program and the quality of the results. Such a program also conveys very important messages from the management to the employees of the firm. These concerns hold true in contemporary organizations worldwide.

Sheldon Smith is the new CEO of Products Corporation. He is eager to instill a more positive environment in his new concern, based on reports from the prior management. To that end Smith's assistant implemented an ethics audit. Careful attention was given to the parameters in which the audit would be conducted in order to obtain a useful response rate: confidentiality, informed consent, replies to an outside concern, and so forth. Employees were told in writing that replies would be kept anonymous. After the audit was complete, it was possible to identify areas that needed attention but not the specific personnel of sub-units. Nevertheless, the team conducting the audit received a phone call wanting information about the managers of several 'problematic' units. The researcher declined to reveal this information, reminding the person about the agreed-upon parameters; other information allows the firm to implement appropriate training and support in the areas of concern. The caller was not pleased.

What difference does ethical consistency make? Critical to the initiation is the manner in which the project itself is framed; it needs to exhibit extant ethics in how it is conducted. When the Sheldon Smiths of corporations initiate an ethics audit, employees are watching the procedures and implementation for commitment to the pre-arranged process. Although it is not clear from this case that CEO Smith knew about the telephone call, a breech in protocols along the way would be quickly communicated throughout the organization. The result sends a message to the employees. Significant features for any successful ethics evaluation, for instance, are informed consent, confidentiality, and full disclosure regarding the way results are used. The same thoughtful and careful procedures employed with patients need to be implemented with employees. Doing otherwise is a practice potentially resulting in loss of confidence in management, as well as unreliable data. The procedures serve as meta-ethical statements about the ethics audit.

A system exhibiting justice, typically, can also prevent *unjust* activity. Indeed, uncovering poor conduct, discrimination, and harassment are tantamount to the foundational assessment management conducts to obtain a depiction of the firm. Developing a system of accountability so responsibilities can be examined is fundamental to ethical procedures and practices. Conversely, looking the other way or making excuses (McDowell, 2000) for inappropriate behavior, or tolerating traditional yet unsuitable conduct leading to unfair employment practices can often be avoided with fair policies and procedures. Even though authors report widespread use of excuses, an organization exhibiting justice in its practices has ways to support accountability and avoid making excuses.

Research provides important information for organizational leaders. As a relatively new area of attention, empirical studies in organizational ethics are assuming more importance and emerging in greater numbers. These various studies offer clues to important facets of organizations aiding in developing and sustaining ethics in endeavors (Victor and Cullen, 1988). Not surprisingly, employees working in organizations where they perceive the situation to be ethical 'love their work,' and their retention rates and work satisfaction confirm those opinions; the obverse is also true (McDaniel, 1998c). Reports reveal that male and female employees perceive their ethical environments differently, as do employees occupying various positions in the firm (McDaniel, Schoeps, and Lincourt, 2001; McDaniel and Schoeps, 2003a). Critical to employees desiring a positive ethical environment is a supportive supervisor or an opportunity to discuss perceived ethical breaches occurring at work.

Additionally, employees who report access to an ethics committee in health care have a quite different view of their workplaces than employees in systems lacking such avenues of discussion (McDaniel, 1998c; McDaniel and Schoeps, 2003a). For example, workers in corporate sites have expressed a desire for similar structures with their ensuing conversations. While CEOs or managers, especially in business, may gloss over these central committees they are critical to employees' perceptions of a work environment sustaining organizational ethics. This is one point on which business leaders may learn from health care executives: health care organizations frequently have an ethics committee as one structure offering access to dialogue about ethical issues. While not conclusive, these research results provide important directions for leaders and other decision makers to consider in their attempts to enhance ethics in their organizations. Evaluation is central to establishing an ethical environment.

Leaders as Ethics Advocates

Leadership is key to establishing an ethical organizational environment. Leaders—executives, managers, directors, and other decision makers—in health care and business serve as moral leaders. They are the ethical advocates of their firms. Leaders can be models of good conduct and ethical behavior in their organizations.

Why are leaders so important? Are not other employees also important? Leaders create the environments and set the tone for others to emulate (Aguilar, 1994). Organizational leaders play a key role in supporting others in their ethical work. Inherent in this assumption is its corollary: managers affect other employees in the company, in particular their fellow employees, and managers in turn are affected by others in their work settings. Nowhere is this more evident than in descriptions of Synovus, where the CEO, Jim Blanchard, is repeatedly recognized as an excellent leader at the forefront of developing a value-oriented workplace (Levering, 2000). As Blanchard knows, modeling ethical conduct, honesty, and integrity on the job and development of policies and procedures supporting these behaviors also influence employees. Creating an ethical environment is tantamount to supporting ethical behavior in the workplace. Leaders play an essential role in developing and sustaining this ethos in their organizations. The leader, therefore, is the organization's conscience (Darr, 1991:2), a role that can be developed and sustained throughout the organization and taught to other employees.

If CEOs desire a stronger ethical workplace, how would they go about it? What would he/she do? Strong leaders make statements in their mission about the integrity of their endeavors. A clear statement from 'the top' goes a long way in instilling an ethical environment in the health care or business system. The lack of such statements is conspicuous by its absence. However, merely stating a strong mission is not enough in today's corporate environment, whether health care or business. Policies, procedures, and other guides need to be developed to support employees' behaviors. Realistically, these procedures also need to include ways in which employees may redress unfair practices: grievance procedures and structures for deliberation. Systems developing strong ethical environments are systems with clear mission statements followed by policies supporting them (Kitson and Campbell, 1996:107). They provide strong models for behavior.

While the CEO is central for conveying the corporate message, the various managers and directors, or clinical unit and service administrators also support the ethical environment of the system. What happens, then, if mid-level managers diverge from the mission, if supervisors do not support and enact the ethical values of the firm? Managers enhance, or detract, from the ethical nature of the organization. In studies of employees desiring a more ethical work setting, having a supervisor who supported them was central to employees' perceptions of a good work setting and an ethical environment (McDaniel and Schoeps, 2003a). Because employees rarely interact directly with the CEO, or even the top management of a concern, it is important that mid-level managers and supervisors convey clear messages regarding values. Confusion, obfuscation, or mixed messages create a situation in which unethical behavior is more likely to occur. Consistency is a critical feature of ethical environments. Thus, in addition to the top management, mid-level decision makers become central as supporting ethics advocates, promoting the objective of a more ethical work setting. These three themes of ethics as good business, the centrality of evaluation in ethics, and CEOs as ethics advocates, are further explored and expanded in the following chapters. These issues, however, raise several questions of a conceptual nature briefly outlined and forming the basis for continuing discussion.

Conceptual Issues

The themes noted above and explored in detail in the following chapters, raise conceptual questions important to ethics. Each chapter in Part One, in part, responds to a larger theoretical issue central to ethics.

When a CEO inquires about how well his/her organization is doing, or how ethical it is, it raises the question of measurement or, minimally, obtaining information to address the question. How is my firm doing in terms of ethics? How would the CEO expect to obtain information in a responsible manner, here implying indicators of the organization's ethical status? Can we measure individual employees in organizations? This is the primary issue addressed in Chapter One.

But measurement, too, raises further questions, which are explored in Chapter Two. If the CEO decides to obtain indicators of the ethical status of his/her firm, it raises a fundamental question of how one understands the organization *qua* organization. How is the organization conceptualized? Is the organization merely a whole or is it composed of parts? Which is primary? Is the corporate nature or individual nature the unit of analysis in which we are interested, or both? How do we understand the organization in relationship to individuals? Considering the question of the organization as a whole raises the vexing question of whether the organization is a moral entity. Can we hold organizations responsible for their ethical—and unethical—actions?

The question of responsibility continues in the discussion in Chapter Two: instilling ethics among employees. As CEOs and other decision makers address the results of their first question—how are we doing—questions follow of how to take action on the results. Following on the discussion in Chapter One, if CEOs desire more ethical organizations, it raises the conceptual issue for Chapter Two of how one instills more ethical behaviors among employees.

As CEOs explore the prospect of instilling more ethical behaviors among the firm's employees, the question arises regarding desirable behaviors, and the occurrence of *un*desirable behaviors. What are the parameters for acceptable actions, and what do mangers do with unacceptable ones? Distinguishing compliance and ethics focus this issue in Chapter Three. While distinctions are the fundamental issues, they, too, cohere on the foundation laid in the previous chapter on the relationship between the corporate and individual. Likewise, the issues in Chapters Two and Three raise questions pertaining to the context surrounding employees, here limited to those of the organization rather than examination of relationships between corporate and community or society. This fundamental question regarding the influence of others is age-old, with Aristotle initially focusing the issue by discussion on the community. We continue the debate today.

Lastly, in Chapter Four these issues lead to the question of indicators of desirable employment sites, understanding that preferable workplaces retain employees and are sites with more ethical environments. Here again, it raises the concern of how one identifies ethical places, returning to indicators of ethical organizations and continuing assessment and monitoring. Implied in the discussion in Chapter Four is the question of how one is to understand ethics in corporations in order to enhance it, and, as explored in Chapter Eight, how to lead these ethical organizations.

The fundamental questions of what is meant by ethics and measurement, how we understand the corporate and individual and the relationship to each other, and changing behaviors for more ethical actions, are conceptual issues addressed in the first part of this work. In addition to the examination of desirable workplaces for employees, they provide a foundation and set the stage for the continuing discussion in Part Two on achieving more ethical environments for leaders and workers in health care and business.

Notes

1   The Federal Sentencing guidelines provide some indicator for organizations with regard to 'doing the right thing.'
2   The term meta-ethical as used here does not reference the technical term, *metaethical*, in ethics. Rather it pertains to a similar term meta-communication referring to the over arching or more abstract ethical issues.

References

Aguilar, F. J. (1994). *Managing corporate ethics*. New York: Oxford University Press.
Bourbonnais, R., and Mondor, M. (2001). Job strain and sickness absence among nurses in Province of Quebec. *American Journal of Industrial Medicine 39:*194-202.
Business Ethics. (2001). The 100 best corporate citizens, Corporate social responsibility report. *Business Ethics 15*(2):12-16.
Churchill, L. R. (1987). *Rationing of health care in America: Perceptions and principles of justice*. Indianapolis, IN: Notre Dame Press.
Coke settles lawsuit with employees. (2000, July 1). *Atlanta Journal Constitution* p. A5.
Conference Board. (1994). *Business ethics: Generating trust in the 1990s and beyond* (Report #1057-94-CH; S. J. Garone, Ed.). New York, NY: Author.
Darr, K. (1991). *Ethics in health services management* (2nd ed.). Washington, DC: Health Professions Press.

Federal Sentencing Commission. (1991). *Federal guidelines*. Washington, DC: United States Government.

Fortune Global 500. (2000). The world's largest corporations. *Fortune Global 500 142*(3):232-312.

Fortune's Best. (2002). Listing of best companies in U.S. *Fortune 154*(2):111.

Greengard, S. (1997, October). 50% of your employees are lying, cheating and stealing. *Workforce 76:*44-53.

Hart, J. (1997). *Ethics and technology: Innovation and transformation in community contexts*. Cleveland, OH: The Pilgrim Press.

IBE Survey. (2003, May 12). *Ethics Today Online* (Vol. 1(9). Washington, D.C.: Ethics Resource Center. Web page access from: http//www.ethics.org/today.

Joint Commission on Accreditation of Healthcare Organizations (JCAHO). (1994). *Accreditation Manual*. Oakbrook Terrace, IL: Author.

Kahn, J. (2001). Special report: America's 50 best companies for minorities. *Fortune 144*(1):114.

Kant, I. (1988). *Fundamental principles of the metaphysics of morals* (T. K. Abbott, Trans.). Buffalo, NY: Prometheus Books (Original work published 1785).

Keyes, C., Hysom, S., and Lupo, K. (2000). Positive organization: Leadership legitimacy, employee well-being, and the bottom line. *Psychologist-Manager* Journal *4*(2):143-153.

Kitson, A., and Campbell, R. (1996). *The ethical organization*. London, UK: Macmillan Press, Ltd.

Kuhn, T. S. (1996). *The structure of scientific revolution* (3rd ed.). Chicago, IL: The University of Chicago Press.

Landeweerd, J. A., and Boumans, N. (1988). Work satisfaction, health, and stress: A study of Dutch nurses. *Work Stress 2*:17-26.

Levering, R. (2000). *A great place to work: What makes some employers so good (and most so bad)*. New York, NY: Great Places to Work Institute, Inc.

McDaniel, C. (1998c). Ethical environments: Reports of practicing nurses. *Nursing clinics of North America 33*(2):363-373.

McDaniel, C., and Schoeps, N. (2003a). Ethics in corporations: Employee position and organizational ethics. In process.

McDaniel, C., Schoeps, N., and Lincourt, J. (2001). Organizational ethics: Perceptions of employees by gender. *Journal of Business Ethics 33*(3):245-256.

McDowell, B. (2000). *Ethics and excuses: The crisis in professional responsibility*. Westport, CT: Quorum Books.

Mill, J. S. (1993). Utilitarianism. In G. Williams (Ed.), *Utilitarianism; On liberty; Considerations on representative government: Remarks on Bentham's philosophy* (pp. 1-43). London, UK: J. M. Dent (Original work published 1910).

Pellegrino, E. (1979). *Humanism and the physician*. Knoxville, TN: University of Tennessee Press.

Peters, T. J., and Waterman, R. H. (1989). *In Search of Excellence*. New York, NY: Harper and Row.

Petterson, I-L., and Arnetz, B. B. (1997). Perceived relevance of psychosocial work site inter-ventions for improved quality of health care work environment. *Nursing Science 18:*4-10.

Rawls, J. (1971). *A theory of justice*. Cambridge, MA: Harvard University Press.

Reidenbach, R. E., and Robin, D. (1989). *Ethics and profits: A convergence of corporate America's economic and social responsibilities*. Englewood Cliffs, NJ: Prentice Hall.

Robin, D., and Babin, L. (1997). Making sense of the research on gender and ethics in business: A critical analysis and extension. *Business Ethics Quarterly* 7(4):61-90.

Rosenthal, S., and Buchholz, R. (2000). *Rethinking business ethics: A pragmatic approach.* New York, NY: Oxford University Press.

Victor, B., and Cullen, J. (1988). The organizational bases of ethical work climates. *Administrative Science Quarterly 33:*101-125.

PART I
THEORETICAL ISSUES IN
ORGANIZATIONAL ETHICS

Chapter 1

Measuring Ethics: Conceptual and Methodological Challenges

Introduction

This chapter focuses on the foundational issues at the intersection of ethics, organizations, and the leadership of organizations. It addresses the enhancement of organizational ethics in health care and business endeavors and provides conceptual background in order to assess, develop, and sustain organizational ethics in those settings. The central aim of this book is attaining an ethical environment. This chapter contributes to that aim by exploring measurement and its implications for organizational ethics. In particular, this first chapter examines the fundamental conceptual relationship between the organization *qua* organization and its members, the various individuals who comprise the system.

Background Concepts of Organizational Ethics

Let us turn now to the central concepts of this discussion, concepts foundational to our work. We begin with the terms basic to organizational ethics. What is organizational ethics? This is a relatively new term that was introduced in the U.S. in the late 20th century. Use of the term in Finland, other Nordic countries, and Europe began in the middle of the late 1990s and it is now used relatively widely across the globe. The term, organizational ethics, however, is actually reliant upon understanding the two foundational terms: *organization* and *ethics*.

Organization

There are various ways to understand an organization, with extensive discussion, but the fundamental definition used here is: an organization is a collectivity of three or more individuals who identify with a shared, acknowledged mission. It may be thought of as a social system involving collaboration '...designed to enhance individual effort aimed at goal accomplishment' (Hodge, 1988:7). Another way of thinking about organizations is to say that in some manner they are a heuristic design for human beings; they are a way of accomplishing functions humans could not do, or do as well, and as efficiently, by themselves. For our discussion we also focus on structured and formal organizations in contrast to informal ones. Collectivities, in addition to hospitals and businesses, are social clubs, informal work groups, or churches. Gathering persons together in a common task, a shared goal, is a way of understanding organizations.

> Let us consider a very simple example: Fifteen Finnish graduate students from a local university are gathered on the street corner in the city center. They are all enrolled in the school and are talking excitedly about their courses, professors, and school year. Are these students an organization?
>
> To pursue this further: These 15 students agree they will all try to cross the street together, otherwise none of them will cross. Are they an organization? The latter example serves to illustrate an organization, albeit a very loosely developed, even temporary, one. Nevertheless, because they all share a common goal and have agreed upon it, they serve to illustrate one form of an organization, an informal or *ad hoc* system.

In contrast to the very informal, even tenuous, nature of the organization posed above, contemporary health care systems offer another illustration. Hospitals have been referred to as physicians' workplaces, referring to the manner in which hospitals, as organizations, make it easier for health care providers to offer their services collectively, rather than going individually to a family home or an individual's workplace. It is more effective and efficient to collect the health care providers—physical therapists, physicians, and registered nurses, among others— in one place and have patients come to them. There is, of course, a down side to this structure, but from the standpoint of functionality the hospital as organization is preferable. Thus another way of examining organizations is through the concepts of effectiveness and efficiency. Organizations, theoretically, allow individuals to be more efficacious.

According to Argyris (1953:131), an organization involves six sets of identifiable tasks: (1) awarding, (2) authorizing, (3) communicating, (4) identifying, (5) sustaining, and (6) 'workflow.' Organizations ignoring any of these will experience adverse influence in the whole system. An organization '...exists when all the ...processes are being performed simultaneously and exist in a sea of interdependence' (Argyris, 1953:131-2). Understanding organizations as open systems is therefore another way of construing organizations; organizations constitute a set of interdependent parts forming a whole (Charns and Schaefer, 1983:8). Furthermore, complex systems, of which health care organizations or major corporations offer examples, have within them sub-parts.

Boundary is another way to explore organizations. Organizations construed as open systems (von Bertalanffy, 1968) are surrounded by boundaries. Boundaries may be understood as permeable or semi-permeable to organizations, differentiating the internal and external aspects. Through the boundary the environments interact with the facets existing external to the system. Boundaries also designate organizational membership and the manner in which employees as members come and go, and the relationship between the internal and external environments of the system. Full-time employees, for instance, are considered part of the internal dimension; they are inside the boundary compared to those external to the system boundary. Anyone whether full- or part-time—paid or volunteer—who contributes to the goal accomplishments may be considered within the internal boundary (Charns and Schaefer, 1983:38), however, typically they are regarded as paid employees of the system.

Different organizations also have different aims, complexities, etiologies, forms, histories, sizes, and types. As long as a system meets the six prior requirements, it may vary in these respects, including how often it gathers. Organizations may gather intermittently, as do churches, or continuously, as do hospitals. Given the variety of their missions, organizations by definition include a range of features, here limited to health care and business endeavors. The key to understanding an organization is to understand that the members involved in the referenced gathering all share a common focus on the mission of the system, and through varied tasks, members collected together to address the stated mission contribute in some manner to its goal attainment. Organizations thereby represent collectivities of three or more persons whose members share common and acknowledged goals and have the varying dimensions noted above (*e.g.*, aim, complexity) within a boundary.

Ethics

We also need to ask the question: What do we mean by ethics? Ethics is an 'endeavor'; it is a system of inquiry in which the primary concern is the advancement of the understanding by individuals, or by groups, regarding what they 'ought' to do in particular situations (Baier, 1992). Ethics is generally an examination of the moral life, and pertains to the numerous thoughtful but independent decisions, which in this instance, leaders and employees will make in the daily functions of their work (Beauchamp and Childress, 1994). Ethics also refers to a way of thinking. It concerns analytical approaches or critical analyses regarding situations arising.

Clarity about the definition of ethics is essential as we begin to discuss not only measurement but also the assumption of responsibility and accountability in the organization. For instance, ethics as critical analysis and application to events and situations emerging in work life also frames the discussion of the examination of the responsibility and accountability of actions taken. When decisions are made in organizations and actions are taken on them, we need to understand what we assume to be ethics, and ethical and unethical behavior, as well as the implications and consequences of those decisions and behavior. Thus we are focused on thinking about how best to understand and to resolve ethical challenges in terms of what we ought to do in those particular and yet confounding situations. We are concerned with the many ethically troubling and challenging situations providers of health care and employees in business face in the daily enactment of their work. What is the best ethical solution, and how does one respond?

No single approach for ethical discernment is assumed in this book. However, it would be remiss to ignore ethical decision making. While this discussion is delimited in scope, a brief overview of concerns for decisions in organizations is undertaken. Common approaches to ethical discernment rely upon well-known ethical theories, of which the most common are utilitarian, deontological, stakeholder, and values assessment. Although used frequently, there is no one approach used by all leaders in all organizations, especially for both health care and business firms. Hall (2002) suggests two models used in health care, but these may not be as useful to business firms. Examination of business approaches reveals that most leaders approach ethical theory from the perspective of values for business (Driscoll and Hoffman, 2000).

Among those values, there is no consensus on which values comprise the list, but several frequently emerge: respect, honesty, integrity, and fairness, with the latter often referenced as justice, reflecting the work of John Rawls (1971). The Woodstock Conference on ethics considering the business aspects of health care outlines a similar set of principles (Woodstock, 1995:9-14) suggesting respect and compassion, honesty, confidentiality, and good stewardship among others. Beauchamp and Childress' (1994:38) work in biomedical ethics reveals concepts used today as principles for consideration: autonomy, beneficence, nonmaleficence, and justice.[1] The principles, applied to health care, intersect with values leaders in business articulate or ones that are similar. Respect for persons is indebted to the work of Immanuel Kant (1964), who provided important influential reflection upon the individual as a person worthy of respect. The Kantian perspective implies treating other persons as we, too, would want to be treated, with consideration and respect. Fundamental to this perspective developed as a categorical imperative, is the treatment of other persons as ends unto themselves, rather than as means to an end (Chadwick, 1992). Thus respect and justice continue to emerge among the various lists both health care and business firms applaud.

There are reasons why no one model or list of concepts is used in both health care and business organizations. The most obvious reason is that health care and business endeavors share many features in common. However, the two types of organizations also differ thereby creating a different requirement for implementation. The very nature of the decisions within health care in terms of life threatening issues, and those of business with a mandate for profit, reveal a fundamental distinction.[2] Within the organization are also differences that alter the need for sundry approaches. The contextual nature of decision making imposes its own restraints as the circumstances surrounding a case or situation change and evolve over time. Even if leaders of these organizations affirm and thereby implement a 'pure' ethical theory, such as Rawlsian justice (1971), utilitarianism advocated by Adam Smith (1995), or deontological methods (Kant, 1964), from a practical approach no one theory will be used consistently and it may not be fruitful for the organization over time. Leaders, too, evolve, as does the leadership of organizations.

With these caveats in mind, the suggestion here is to retain explicit codes or a set of core concepts that each organization articulates for its own endeavor. These might be construed as core values, key principles, norms, or virtues for the firm. The Woodstock Conference articulated a foundational concern for organizations, noting the issue of how the organization lives out its 'covenant of trust' with the general public (1995:1), and denoting the foundational set of responsibilities any organization has with society. Duty, borrowing from the deontological perspective, might be one. Justice as fairness might be yet another.

Rawls contributes an important component to this analysis by affirming rational selection of the initial principles (1971:17). The key to rational selection is that principles are selected and held, and they are pre-selected, not chosen in the moment of the analysis or situation. This distinction is important for ethical organizations and is related to the mission. However, Rawls assumes decision makers are equal, which is arguable in terms of the decisions needing to be made in health care and business, especially in health care. While all humans have foundational equalities for liberty and respect, the nature of the decisions required in health care rely upon expertise that implies an unequal dimension to the decisions needing to be made. Patients have different stages of illness and differential responses to them, based on age, disposition, or prior illnesses. The circumstances surrounding patients or the situations in which they become ill also vary.

In business organizations, leaders likewise by their positions assume assorted perspectives and often have more, or different, information than employees. But employees, too, may have relevant information about the reality of implementation of decisions. Each may have unequal levels of responsibility and accountability in his/her respective organizations. The type of information and position within these organizations occupied by various employees alters the nature of the approach in a system desiring justice. Thus it is important to agree upon foundational principles as Rawls suggests, but that does not also imply that all persons considering decisions are equal. In fact the very nature of decisions in both these systems with changing dimensions is why health care and business decisions are so challenging.

Another dimension Rawls (1971:20) introduces is the concept of 'reflective equilibrium.' This concept suggests ethical reflection with the emphasis on discernment for ethical decision making. Each decision requires some reflection upon its particular character and the potential implication of the outcomes. Where rules and strict adherence to duty may pale in the light of context or case, the reflective approach allows all parties to critically consider the current ethical situation and to do so balanced by the demands of all parties involved. It also implies use of analysis with attention to agreed-upon core values.

Each organization needs to frame its ethical decision making as a reflective process, an ethical analytical process upon concepts it holds consistent in the organization. As discussed in later chapters, organizations of excellence articulate key concepts and adhere to them. If we can agree that ethical reflection is paramount to the process, then the question is: which core concepts? The ones appearing most commonly are respect, integrity, fairness, even justice as fairness, and honesty. Trust also emerges but it is not a concept to be implemented. Rather, trust emerges as an important result of the implementation of these others; trust builds over time and emerges in the firm as one observes respect, honesty, fairness, and integrity.

Ethical discernment suggests a three-step approach, allowing for differences between health care and business systems. It appreciates the particulars of each firm, such as the type of business outcomes it offers, whether service (*e.g.*, long-term care) or product (*e.g.*, cars). Applying the ethical discernment considers the mission (1) of the firm as foundational, upon which a firm can explore the (2) situation or context adjusting for relevant parties to the current organization and the information they provide. Once these facets are understood, (3) key concepts are used to reflect or (to use Rawls' term) 'equilibrate' the situation in light of them: respect, honesty, integrity, and justice emerge as the central concepts upon which to reflect. This approach involves all aspects of any situation: the mission of the particular organization, consideration of the central parties or context involved in the specific case at a point in time,[3] balanced by core concepts important to the particular firm and its outcome. Among the core concepts for this work are respect and fairness, also understood as justice as fairness. Following is an outline of the salient steps.

Three-Step Model for Ethical Decision Making: Consider the

- Mission statement as a foundation for deliberation
- Situation for exploration in relevant context
- Core concepts for analysis relevant to context and mission

Organizational Ethics

Organizational ethics, although used increasingly in contemporary society, is rarely defined. It pertains, however, to exploration regarding the manner in which individuals ought to act in organizations. How should individuals behave as members of their work systems? Do we understand them to behave differently at work than in other roles or places, and if so, how and to what degree? If ethical relationships between and among individuals are construed as pertaining to the micro dimensions, then, in contrast, organizational ethics is construed to pertain to the macro dimensions. Melding the two concepts, organization and ethics, one finds that three or more persons collectively with a shared aim, are attentive to the 'ought' of their decisions, actions, and results. The individuals consider how they ought to behave within their systems and how those decisions or actions affect others. Thus organizational ethics is fundamentally concerned with ethical behavior, the *ought* of behavior among collectivities of individuals who share a common purpose.

The definition of organizational ethics brings us back to the purpose. Thus if one of our aims is expanding our knowledge about and understanding the measurement of ethics as a means to sustaining good conduct in health care and business settings, how do we go about this? What are the steps to attaining this end goal? It should be clear by now that to address organizational ethics is at once a combination of understanding organizations and ethics, but also a more complex phenomenon than merely adding the two together. Rather than an additive phenomenon, organizational ethics is an exponential phenomenon, as demonstrated in the following discussion.

Measuring and Conceptualizing Organizations

Measuring Organizations

The challenge of measuring ethics in organizations raises the question of how we understand organizations. Measurement relies upon conceptualization with valid assessment for several reasons. First, because decisions influence persons and their lives, especially in health care, it is critical to ensure that the information is of a high quality: valid and reliable. Secondly, results of decisions also incur monetary costs, so allocation of scarce resources in business and health care relies on good information. Thirdly, both previous reasons influence the mission of the organization. These lead to a focus on the implication of measurement in organizations with special attention to the caveats.

> A graduate student approached a professor, quite excited about his upcoming research project, one to be conducted as a group-learning venture in a course on organizational analysis. Briefly, he explained that he had arranged the data collection to include more than 200 subjects. At the inquiry of the professor the student also indicated that all of them worked in the same hospital, and he hoped to get a high response rate with the support of the hospital administration. The professor (since it was in the hallway) asked the student to make an appointment with her. At that time she noted, since the assessment target was organization, he had a sample of only one.

Unit of analysis The unit of analysis is critical to measurement and deserving of special consideration. In research, the measure of interest is the unit of analysis. The focus of the results, inferences, or conclusions drawn from information or data is the unit of analysis. Thus if the graduate student is interested in organizations, not the individuals who work in them, then the unit of analysis—target of concern—is the organization, regardless of how many employees work in it.[4] More to the point is the need to remain conceptually clear on the desired unit of analysis, since what occurs with groups may or may not be accurate for the individuals who comprise them. When a discussion of evaluation nimbly shifts from individuals or employees to corporations or organizations, it gives us pause; these shifts, back and forth, have significant measurement and conceptual implications. Organizational ethics is a complicated phenomenon.

Fallacies Researchers have acknowledged for some time that merely measuring an individual and extrapolating to the whole is problematic, potentially providing less than valid results. The reverse is also true. As with many complex phenomena, the issue, rather than additive, is an exponential one. Programming in which measures challenge evaluators are illustrated by the well-known Head Start and Comer

School Development Programs; both programs draw inferences about programs or classes based on individual measures (Cook, *et al.*, 1999).

The phenomenon of using groups to draw inferences *about* the individuals who comprise those groups, with unadjusted analysis, is referred to as the *ecological fallacy* (Selltiz, *et al.*, 1976:439). Basic to the ecological fallacy is a caveat about making assumptions regarding the way in which groups—classes, programs, departments, or organizations—behave and assuming the individuals for whom the inferences are drawn perform in the same manner, hence the fallacy of ecology or group. What occurs at group levels of analysis may not necessarily occur at individual levels of analysis. Group behavior may be different and inconsistent with the individuals' activities. Likewise, groups do not '... necessarily behave for the same reasons individuals do' (Selltiz, *et al.*, 1976:439).

In contrast, when assumptions are made *about* groups based on information obtained from individuals it is termed the *individualistic fallacy* (Selltiz, *et al.*, 1976:439-440; Rousseau and House, 1994:13-30). It is inappropriate to assume one can make accurate statements or inferences about groups based on observations about individuals comprising those groups; inferring groups' behavior from individuals without appropriate transformation is a second fallacy. As noted earlier, what occurs among individuals will not necessarily be true of the whole.

How do we discuss collectivities since, in almost all instances, we make inferences about groups based on information derived from individuals in order to discuss the groups? Several suggestions are offered to offset these problems. One step is clarity about the unit of analysis and obtaining very strong relationships linking the individual and the collectivity. A second step is being forthcoming about potential weaknesses in data analysis (Selltiz, *et al.*, 1979:438). Third, statistical methods can address both shifts in analysis.[5] It is therefore important to remain clear on the conceptual distinctions regarding the unit of analysis in order to draw accurate inferences based on those analyses, as the graduate student above learned. Since organizational ethics is grounded in discussion of ethics and organizations, the latter composed of individuals, these conceptual and methodological issues are foundational to accurate inferences about organizations and individual employees. This highlights the need for further consideration in organizational ethics of the conceptual framework on which we base the evolving ethics program and its analysis.

Conceptualizing Organizations

How, then, do we conceptualize the organization? More to the point, beyond definitions, what is the relationship between the corporation as a whole and the individuals who comprise it? To what, or whom, do we attribute ethical agency? If we are going to explore ethics and organizations and measurement of them, it is imperative that we clarify the conceptual distinctions germane to both, particularly since discussions about ethical environments raise the important issues of responsibility and accountability, and ethical and unethical behavior. Conceptual clarity is fundamental to valid measure. The debate coheres philosophically on whether one assumes the individual is the unit of analysis, and thereby fundamentally responsible for his/her own behavior, decisions, and interactions in the firm, or if in contrast the corporate body is the unit of analysis, thereby assuming the corporation is primarily responsible. Inherent to the development of a comprehensive ethical value system are the questions of responsibility, accountability, and consequences as a foundation for examining the ethics environment.

The debate about the relationship between corporate and individual stands in a long line of philosophers, beginning with Aristotle's reflections on community and individual. Discussion regarding accountability has important implications for applied ethics in organizations, and responsibility cohering on understanding of the relationship of the whole to the individual.[6] One way of framing the question is to ask whether one understands an organization to have moral or ethical responsibilities. What, if any, ethical agency does an organization have? Is this different than the responsibilities of the individuals? Although several arguments obtain,[7] we limit the discussion here to three possibilities; we might consider these three possibilities as representing loci of responsibility.

Employee as individual The first position assumes organizations are fundamentally comprised of individuals and it is *only individuals* who have responsibility in the organization. Advocates of this approach, sometimes referred to as the 'association' model, argue the organization is the sum of the individuals comprising the whole.[8] If one argues an individual employee within the firm is primary, from a measurement perspective he/she is the unit of analysis, or the target of the measure. Because corporations are comprised of their members as the various employees, this focus on the individual is a common approach. The whole can only be held accountable for actions as those acts can be linked to the individuals in the whole. Organization in this perspective is an 'artificial person' (Kitson and Campbell, 1996:99-100). The argument claims an organization *qua* system is not an entity beyond its individual members. Organizations are comprised of individuals, and while those individuals have ethical agency the system as a whole does not. This claim is not adding much to our prior knowledge, nor does it further our understanding about individual behavior within organizations or the ethical status of organizations.

Organizational responsibility, however, is diminished if one accepts the position that the individual—employee, physician, manager, practitioner, or salesperson—is responsible for ethical or unethical actions. More to the point is the implied assertion that it is *only* the individual employee who is responsible for and ethically accountable to actions taken while at work. Organizations which take this position also tend to assume that good persons will enter via hire, remain good, and exhibit good behavior as examined in more detail in Chapter Two. This argument plays down the importance of the corporate influence upon those individuals and dismisses corporate responsibility.

The claim regarding individual behavior is fraught with problems. Distinct from individuals, as noted earlier, we gather persons together collectively as systems because they perform functions individuals alone cannot. In that regard collectivities have properties in addition to those of the individuals comprising them. We make claims about corporations or hospitals, in terms of their specific dimensions that are different from those of individuals working alone. For example, we would not discuss the solidity or structures of individuals because that is not a property of individuals but of individuals *qua* collectivity. Likewise, we would not explore the anthropology of one person since it pertains to a tribe or identified group. If, however, these entities cannot be seen as other than the specific members, then it also allows one to argue the entity is not responsible for any actions taken as an organization. The collectivity has no ethical agency. The organization *qua* organization has no responsibility for decisions or actions taken by the individuals while at work on behalf of the system.

The argument for the individual poses additional difficulty. Examples are evident of wholes with different properties than compilation of the single units comprising them. If, for instance, we examine an impressionist painting done in the pointillist[9] method—composed of numerous dots—we can view and discuss the painting (as a whole). Thus painting *qua* painting is more than and qualitatively different than a million dots. This is not to deny the canvas contains a million dots; however, if purchased one (probably) would say, 'I bought a painting' not 'I bought one million dots.' Both the dots and the whole as painting have properties. Further, we can examine the various sub-parts within the painting: figures, background, and foreground that are neither dots nor painting but parts of the (overall) composition.[10] The example of a painting is selected not only because the author likes art, but because the impressionist painters, too, had a point: painting dots as collectivities differs depending on light, arrangement, and how the *dots are placed together.* Positioning the dots intentionally with contrasting hues, as one positions employees via different work groups in order to accomplish otherwise unaccomplished tasks, changes the perception of the individual dots; they take on the property of painting.

Similarly, organizations take on different properties when they contain collectivities of persons. Organizations have properties different than those of the individuals who comprise them. Numerous studies substantiate the presence of organizational culture, social systems, and system dynamics unique to the system as a whole in comparison to those of an individual; studies of group dynamics attest to the manner in which individuals behave while in groups,[11] which behaviors are not exhibited elsewhere or individually. Various individuals collected together around a work task and over time interact to form an entity with properties unique to the whole yet different from the individuals.[12] Individuals act differentially in different systems. Thus one position argues for the individual focus and responsibility, a claim that does not further our understanding about corporate responsibility or the ethical relationship and responsibilities between corporate and employee.

Organization as corporate whole The second and opposite position regards the organization as the relevant unit of analysis, in which only the whole is germane.

The claim of Emile Durkheim (1965) that each organization is *sui generis* and cannot be further sub-divided articulates this position. In contrast to the former claim, this approach, sometimes termed the 'autonomy' approach,[13] prioritizes the whole. If the whole prevails, then it is conceptually inaccurate to measure sub-units or individuals *qua* individuals within the organization. Measures and inferences about individuals working in the system would be irrelevant because the organization is the (only) unit of analysis.

The implication of this assertion is the whole cannot be broken into smaller parts, thereby prevailing over any divisions. Because only the organization *qua* organization exists, when individuals 'enter the office,' while they are performing their tasks, they are the organization. The well-known phrase 'organization man' is relevant to this point. The argument also denies the particularities of each individual actor, suggesting individual employees take on substantively different qualities. Likewise, this position assumes the decisions and acts by individuals on behalf of the organization are solely those of the system; individuals have no (or extremely limited) responsibility for actions while at work.

The central implication of the perspective regarding the whole is that individuals cannot be held accountable, if within firms only the corporation is responsible. To underscore the point, all decisions and acts of any and all individuals (while at work and on behalf of the system) are decisions of the organization.[14] The accountability lies with the firm as a whole rather than with the individuals who comprise the firm, denying the responsibility of the individual employee. In the Enron debacle the former CEO, Kenneth Lay, would not be held accountable for his individual actions since the organization is accountable. The question then is, who is (or is not) the organization, or how would one hold an organization accountable? Would all members of the firm be implicated? Would they all be accountable in a similar or equal way?

When the corporate prevails, it implies consensus about ethical-acceptable and *un*ethical-*un*acceptable behavior in the workplace. The model suggests not only a clear set of standards for the particular organization, but ideally each individual employee follows them. As any manager knows, this claim is an unrealistic assumption. The corporate behavior may represent higher or lower standards, or significantly different standards than those used generally in society or by any one individual. It is especially critical if the organizational standards are different (particularly if higher) than those of the personnel, the employees. In most workplaces, for example, it is deemed unacceptable to lie, steal, or disrespect persons. Taking action on observed unethical behavior is yet another issue. Thus many employees, unfortunately, may not agree on the appropriate action to take, although agreeing on the fact the behavior is unethical.

If one takes the position the whole prevails, then it leaves the larger question: what about the individuals in the firm? What are their individual responsibilities? Imbedded in the organizational 'whole' approach is a secondary concern for teaching employees about the values of the organization because it is important to have a consistent organizational approach among employees. In this approach (examined in more detail in Chapter Two) there is typically a program for in-service or continuing education including ethical decision making and compliant behavior. Emphasis in this model is on the actual behavior the health care and business employees exhibit within the organization and with their patients and customers. Courses and programs including ethics in the workplace normally have primary emphasis on the resolution of central situations emerging in the respective industry.

For the purposes of this discussion, allow it to suffice that although individuals are influenced by and also affect the whole, the individual as a single unit cannot be solely and wholly responsible nor can the corporate whole be responsible exclusive of its individual members. Both the whole and the individual have particular and unique responsibilities.[15] The issues have significant implications for organizational ethics and instilling of ethics in workers, especially as they pertain to measuring and establishing ethics within firms. They are considered under the following third position.

Conceptual rapprochement   As we examine the third position, a potential rapprochement, the question remains: Where does that leave us? Who, or what, is responsible for decisions made by employees? A major weakness in each prior conceptual claim is that both assume an underlying dichotomy as foundational to the approach. Implied is an either-or understanding of ethical responsibility and accountability regarding work. After all, responsibility is not a 'zero-sum' phenomenon in which there is limited responsibility in organizations. In contrast, suggested here is re-visioning to keep both in creative tension. Returning to the issue of how to understand organizations and their important relationships to the individuals who comprise them, it is neither foundationally prudent nor functionally realistic to assume an either-or posture. Neither does the dichotomous approach assist us in resolving ethically complex situations at work and assigning responsibility for their consequences.

The conceptual rapprochement recognizes the interactive dynamics of organizations as open systems thereby claiming that each party, the corporate and the individual, contributes to and has responsibility for actions taken within the organization. The expectations differ and the responsibilities also differ. Corporations are comprised of numerous individuals who, while each deserving of respect, have different tasks and thereby differing degrees of responsibility in the firm. Each individual who enters and works in a system contributes to the whole. Likewise, the whole influences and affects those individual members. Systems have organizational charts, policies and procedures, offices and departments, and other manifestations attesting to their corporate entity. There are also indicators of levels of decision making in a system such as supervisor and employee relationships, substantiated by human resource departments or labor unions. For these reasons corporations make decisions and take actions on decisions in ways similar to but not exactly those of any individual comprising the system. Policies and procedures of the corporation are guides to the decisions those individuals comprising the system make, both in terms of the range of the decisions and the limits of the decisions. These choices are unique to collective decisions, albeit made by individuals; they are *corporate decisions*.

Employees *qua* individuals work in systems, each employee having his/her own unique properties, and germane to this discussion, making decisions followed by actions with consequences. We can then argue decisions, actions, and their consequences represent analysis by individuals of what 'ought' to be done and are thereby ethical considerations. Individuals make ethical decisions and do so at work. However, when those individuals come together in the collectivity known as organization, their ethical decisions and the ensuing acts and consequences are different, unique to that collectivity. At this point of conceptualizing individuals in corporate endeavors, the decisions are *corporate-framed* ethical decisions. Corporate-framed ethical decisions result in corporate-framed ethical acts, responsibilities, and consequences. These decisions are different than those one might make individually because of the work environment and tasks and are unique to that particular organization. The dynamics of the system surround the individuals and their resulting decisions and influence the decisions made by individuals in those systems. Part of the surround—as it were—is the set of policies, procedures, standards, mission statements, ethical value statements, norms, culture, and other accoutrements of the particular firm; their presence in that firm is one part of the considered decision by the individual.

One needs to acknowledge thereby the whole and its unique and important dynamics that occur and evolve over time within an organization. Similar to the dynamics of small groups, dynamics replicated in operating rooms or project work teams within organizations, these organizational dynamics of the entity have strong influences upon their members. Terms such as organizational culture, group cohesion, climate in systems, and other similar concepts attempt to capture the significance of the dynamics within organizations. They are also substantiated by and foci of significant research (Cartwright and Zander, 1968). Thus in every organization there are dynamics unique to particular organizations as a whole. The complexity of act and responsibility occurring in organizations is, in large measure, due to the interactive influence of individual and whole and the resulting dynamics; dynamics also forming groups or smaller collectivities within the larger whole. Sage leaders recognize and acknowledge this dynamic phenomenon.

It is these dynamics that offer either positive or negative influences upon the organizational members. Why is it that in some organizations honesty prevails, whereas in others the culture supports troubling, even fraudulent, behavior? We turn to those in more detail in the following chapters. For our purposes it is necessary to understand the dynamics of the entity, the organization. Dynamics within the whole are therefore important, but interactions of the whole are not the only significant dynamics. Understanding the dynamics of the corporate whole is necessary but not sufficient, because the individuals comprising the whole create the dynamics.

Lest one conclude by suggesting a creative tension between whole and individual that neither is responsible, it is not the proposed conclusion. Rather, the conceptual rapprochement claims that each—the whole and the individual—has unique and special ethical responsibilities and accountabilities to the whole and to each other. Responsibilities of the organization and its leaders as ethical advocates are more fully explored in Chapter Eight. Furthermore, while significant attention in this book is donated to individuals, it should not imply the organization has less responsibility. The whole, too, has specific responsibility and accountability; both are responsible. As stated earlier, the phenomenon of examining individuals and their corporate work relationships and decisions is not one of addition; it is exponential, paralleling the argument Cartwright and Zander (1968) offer regarding group dynamics.

The conceptual rapprochement suggests acts (and consequences) individuals take while in the work setting are acts unique to the system, but not irrelevant to them as individuals. This should not imply the individuals become substantively different within the organization, but rather they—as individuals—behave within a unique context, one framed by the dynamics of that system including also the ethics frame. Just as the dots of a *pointillist* painting can be viewed individually, one-by-one, they can also be viewed as painting. At the macro level they take on properties different than and unique to the gathered dots; they become picture. Corporate leaders likewise need to recognize both the unique decisions and actions occurring within a system, and also their unique leadership responsibility in framing those acts for employees. One without the other will not produce an ethical environment, as both in their creative yet mutual tension need one another and contribute to one another. Ethics, as noted earlier, is not an additive phenomenon. Individuals cannot be merely measured, added, or subtracted, with an abstract or real average taken to provide an 'ethics mean' of an organization. Rather, because of the unique nature of the interactive dynamics occurring in the collectivities of individuals known as organizations, and because this is an exponential phenomenon it requires organizations to strive for each individual to remain ethical as a contributor to the ethical environment.

What are the particular responsibilities organizations and their leaders assume, ones examined in more detail in Chapter Eight? The corporation has responsibility for the *ethical frame* of the system. Ethical frames, differentiated from the ethical culture (or environment, ethos, ambience), are illustrated in mission statements, codes of ethics, value statements, policies and procedures for minimally acceptable behavior, special ethics meetings or committees that promulgate the ethics values; ethical frames are also needed for preferred behavior, behavior requiring monitoring and follow-up with explicit consequences. Systems that do not take steps to provide an ethical frame within their organizations provide ambivalent and questionable cultures for their employees. Firms have the right to expect their employees to engage in ethical behaviors, especially those that are (more) universal, such as honesty, promise keeping, or respect. But organizations, too, take on responsibility—as one form of leadership excellence—to provide their individual members with ethical guidance. Thus the corporation provides an 'ethics frame' supporting the ethical ethos of the system in which individual employees interact.

Concomitantly, individuals in those corporations, whether health care or business oriented, are responsible for enacting behavior representing the ethical frame; they implement the various policies and processes in the firm. The individual is then accountable for enacting the policies and procedures comprising the ethical frame. Individuals may also suggest revisions or policies and procedures to further enhance the ethical frame, expanding their (own individual) ethical responsibilities in the organization. These revisions may be based, in part, on critical analysis or reflection on the situation, current policies, or anticipated problems, thereby enacting a higher level of employee leadership in the firm. Particular individuals in the firm also assume a leadership role taking on the responsibility and accountability as ethical agents.

The conceptual rapprochement also claims the whole accepts responsibility for framing the endeavor in its corporate ethics including the varied employees within the corporate whole. Thus one responsibility of the organization, enacted by leaders as ethics advocates, is the 'framing' of the ethical expectations. Organizations are unique because they are open systems, yet the system cannot exist without the individual members. In a parallel analysis, while organizations have their own ethical mandates and expectations, each individual member contributes either positively or negatively to the organization's ethics; individuals have their own responsibility for actions within the whole. Because leaders desire organizations with ethical consistency, and employees prefer work in ethical cultures, attaining the ethical ethos requires attention to the whole and to the individual.

Thus the interactive and creative tension continues between the whole and the individual. Neither escapes responsibility and thus accountability for ethical—and unethical—action and behavior. Yet each has a unique set of responsibilities as each contributes to the enterprise known as organization. Individuals in organizations and their organizations assume responsibility, which is why assessing, developing, and sustaining are so important to attaining ethical environments. It is this unique interactive tension that makes organizations and therefore organizational ethics so challenging yet so creative and important.

Trans-National Organizations

Only briefly touched on here, the complex problem of trans-national organizations deserves its own manuscript. We mention it because relationships between the corporate whole and the individual are increasingly important as organizations become more international in scope (Elling, 1980; Donaldson, 2002). The special issue is the differentiation among aspects of the larger organization; the country-specific sub-units with different values, approaches, and ethics than those of the parent-national firm. While the majority of trans-national organizations are in the business world, the issues are also germane for intra-national but highly integrated care systems. Trans-national and intra-national organizations share common ethical challenges. To what does this refer?

If corporations are to accept their rightful responsibility for framing the expected ethics within their firms, the responsibility is even more complex for trans-national corporations, or highly integrated and intra-national systems. This is because the standards typically vary across national or state boundaries. In recent reports from Transparency International (*Helsingin Sanomat*, 2002:A1), a research group conducting research on international corporate fraud, the results reveal a wide range of expected behaviors among countries regarding fraud and corruption, especially bribery. Among those countries, Finland has been cited for several years as a county with the *least* corporate fraud compared to her sister global countries. For organizations spanning several countries it requires the top management to frame the core expectations of the corporation, since it is to this behavior individuals working in these firms need to adhere. The challenge, obviously, is when a subsidiary of the whole, representing a nation or specific culture, has a widely disparate understanding of acceptable ethics compared to the parent corporation and its values. The challenges continue for trans-national corporations.

Considerations and Stereotypes

Once the conceptual foundation for organizations is laid, it is possible to move forward for measurement of ethics. While the conceptual framework for organizations is foundational to understanding organizational ethics, the following aspects also need consideration when undertaking an ethics assessment. The discussion is not to suggest an exhaustive exploration, but rather to consider key issues potentially impeding the development of good measurement and its resulting ethical environment. These considerations are more conceptual in nature, rather than practical, yet may impinge upon the final outcome. In Chapter Five we turn to the practice of applying the ethical assessment. Here we explore three considerations as background: ethics as a discipline, organizational clarity, and client focus.

Ethics as a Discipline

A major consideration for the conduct of ethics assessment is the question of ethics itself. There is an assumption ethics cannot be assessed (Aguilar, 1994:70). Although the above statement emerges from a business context, there is a supposition that ethics is too 'soft' to be assessed, especially with empirical measures: ethics is a philosophically grounded endeavor and therefore has no evaluative basis. The use of ethics cases for teaching may contribute to this perception; however, cases are especially fruitful to development of critical thinking skills and assessing preferred solutions, even though they may be challenged for their reliability and validity. Advances in the study of ethics and in research regarding ethics demonstrate, indeed, ethics can be measured, although doing so is a challenge. Applied ethics offers the opportunity to measure the ethical views that people hold; their opinions and attitudes, or the perceptions of employees on sound measures. Likewise one may observe behavior, or ask employees to comment on designed cases within the framework of the organization's established norms. These are not the same as assuming to measure another employee's ethical position or morality. Thus applied ethics including biomedical ethics opens the door for a wide range of measures using robust approaches.

Organizational Clarity

The second challenge in measuring ethics is clarification of the target organization. Here the challenge is not so much to understand what an organization is, but rather how to identify and set a boundary for the relevant organization so it may be measured. This, too, is a conceptual matter. The issue is boundary to set parameters for measurement.

In the U.S., for example, the health system revisions introduce a highly integrated system. The significant change is the alteration from a relatively micro-oriented care system, to one in which macro dimensions of health service delivery are addressed. Fundamental to this change is an alteration in the reimbursement system. In contrast to the Nordic countries or the U.K., for example, the prior care system in the U.S. was a fee-for-service and retrospective system (Elling, 1980).

Integration also means that the boundary of the 'hospital' *per se* is less clear. For example, if Canadian HealthCare runs three hospitals and six clinics and nine nursing homes, from a management perspective the entire system—the integrated system wholly owned by Canadian HealthCare—is the health care system. In contrast, an evaluator may wish to assess only one clinic or hospital or nursing home rather than the entire system. Similar problems are posed for other nationally funded care systems, such as those found in the Nordic countries, Germany, or the U.K. Thus determining the boundary so an accurate assessment can be conducted is a major challenge in today's complex and integrated health care systems.

Due to costs, time, and energy, it is typical for a system to desire all facility aspects to be involved in the assessment. In order to retain quality, parity and consistency across integrated systems are critical. Assessments are one way to assure consistency of quality. Therefore one of the major challenges facing administrators in developing and sustaining ethical environments is the demarcation of the appropriate boundary to measure. Without clear parameters, the assessment has the potential to be inaccurate and less useful; it may influence the response rate. Conceptual clarity about the target organization, or even a sub-unit in an integrated system, is essential to accurate measures. Thus clarity about the parameter is a foundational step in eliciting quality responses, as well as attaining an appropriate response rate.

Client Focus

The third challenge pertains to the focus of the assessment to understand who or what is the client, paralleling the discussion earlier in this chapter on the unit of analysis. The concept, client focus, comes from program evaluation and refers to the manner in which the evaluator understands his/her relationship to the project; it regards who hired the evaluator. Discussion regarding the unit of analysis is quite relevant to the client focus. Furthermore, this concern of focus may appear simple on the surface but it has important implications for ethical conduct of the audit. While these ethical issues are important in any assessment, they are critical to evaluations conducted by an outside consultant (Argyris, 1993; Holloway, Lewis, and Mallory, 1995; Hultman and Gellerman, 2002:138).

If the organization is perceived as the client, then comments, assessments, opinions, and so forth about individuals are not germane to the exploration. With a focus on the entire system as the client, one would not be concerned about individuals in the system and likewise their promotion, retention, or dismissal. It is difficult to keep the focus on the macro issues and away from micro attention on individuals, albeit critical to the ethical process of a system-level evaluation. If the focus is on the individual as target the opposite obtains. Employees, then, need to be informed about the client focus and to understand the use of information obtained during an assessment. Normative, rather than defensive, values of the system need to be identified (Hultman and Gellerman, 2002:142). Fundamentally, however, retaining a clear and explicit focus on the agreed client *qua* target is essential to continuing quality assessment; it, too, coheres on a clear understanding regarding the client focus. The conceptual issues pertinent to measuring ethics raise a number of issues, one of which is how to instill ethics among employees, the topic of Chapter Two.

Notes

1   The original intention of Beauchamp and Childress is not understood as a set of principles *per se*, but rather guides for application and critical analysis in biomedical ethics. Nevertheless, the several principles are widely used in biomedical ethics and have become useful guides in medical curricula.
2   This conflates the way in which health care, too, is evolving in the direction of profit modalities; however, for the purposes here health care and business are fundamentally different in their initial aims.
3   For a more detailed discussion of models of decision making, refer to the bibliography.
4   Selltiz, *et al.* (1976:437) make the point that in addition to clarifying the unit of analysis, some characteristics are not interchangeable. For instance, while individuals have a pulse, groups of individuals as collectivities do not.
5   For a detailed discussion regarding statistical methods to address these analytical shifts see, for example, Cooke and Rousseau (1987).
6   While claims are made for either individual or corporate recognition and therefore responsibility, the more common claim is for individual responsibility.
7   For a more expansive discussion of these issues see also Kitson and Campbell (1996: 97-117), or Ruth Chadwick (Ed.), (1992), *Immanuel Kant: Critical assessments.*
8   This approach is supported, generally, by M. G. Velasquez (1983).
9   The method of impressionist painting known as *pointillist* was attributed to George Seurat, also known as post-impressionism. Composed of numerous small dots, usually

in primary colors, artists painted with the dots placed side-by-side to evoke illusion with light.

10 Conceptualizations of organizations need not be only foreground or background, or micro or macro in nature.

11 J. Richard Hackman's (1990) studies on cohesive work groups, or the work of Cartwright and Zander (Eds.), (1968) on group dynamics, are germane to this point and offer additional examination of behavior in groups.

12 It is important to recognize the distinction between individuals collected together informally, rather than those collected to perform work tasks and those in a continuing relationship over time, and (usually) consistently. The latter are relevant to this discussion and form more durable group dynamics, both negative and positive.

13 Peter French (1984) and Pat Werhane (1985) are several authors representing this approach, in which, for the latter, for example, organization is viewed as a second degree moral agent.

14 While we draw distinctions here regarding individual acts while at work on behalf of the organization, it raises the question about responsibility and understanding of acts done by corporate members, even on behalf of the firm, but not while at work. Extensions of this line of thinking explore acts done by corporate members while not at work but on behalf of the firm, such as a CEO at a Scout meeting or a football game. The question also presses the question of defined work. We limit our examination here but other authors explore the extended role of significant employees regarding ethical behavior.

15 For further exploration of collective responsibility, refer to Juha Räikkä (1997), 'On disassociating oneself from collective responsibility.'

References

Aguilar, F. (1994). *Managing corporate ethics*. Oxford, UK: Oxford University Press.

Argyris, C. (1953). *Executive leadership: An appraisal of a manager in action*. New York, NY: Harper and Brothers Publishers.

Argyris, C. (1993). *Knowledge for action: A guide to overcoming barriers to organizational change*. San Francisco, CA: Jossey-Bass Publishers.

Baier, K. (1992). Class Notes. Theories of Ethics, fall semester. University of Pittsburgh Graduate Program, Department of Philosophy. Pittsburgh, PA.

Beauchamp, T., and Childress, J. (1994). *Principles of biomedical ethics* (4th ed.). Oxford, UK: Oxford University Press.

Bourbonnais, R., and Mondor, M. (2001). Job strain and sickness absence among nurses in Province of Quebec. *American Journal of Industrial Medicine* 39:194-202.

Cartwright, D., and Zander, A. (Eds.). (1968). *Group dynamics: Research and theory* (3rd ed.). New York, NY: Harper and Row Publishers.

Chadwick, R. F. (Ed.) (1992). *Immanuel Kant: Critical assessments*. London, UK: Routledge Publishers.

Charns, M., and Schaefer, M. (1983). *Health care organizations: A model for management*. Englewood Cliffs, NJ: Prentice-Hall, Inc.

Cook, T. D., Habib, F-N., Phillips, M., Settersen, R., Shagle, S., and Degirmencioglu, S. (1999). Comer's School Development Program in Prince George's County, Maryland: A theory-based evaluation. *American Educational Research Journal* 36(3):543-597.

Donaldson, T. (2002, February). Presenter, Panel on Global Ethics. Association of Practical and Professional Ethics annual meeting, Cincinnati, Ohio.

Driscoll, D., and Hoffman, W. M. (2000). *Ethics matters: How to implement a values-driven management*. Waltham, MA: Center for Business Ethics.

Durkheim, E. (1965). *The rules of sociological method* (8th ed.). G. E. G. Catlin (Ed.). (Trans. by S. A. Solovay and J. H. Mueller). New York, NY: Free Press.

Elling, R. H. (1980). *Cross-national study of health systems: Concepts, methods, and data sources*. Detroit, MI: Gale Research Company Book Tower.

French, P. (1984). *Collective and corporate responsibility*. New York, NY: Columbia University Press.

Greengard, S. (1997). 50% of your employees are lying, cheating and stealing. *Workforce* 76:44-53.

Hall, R. T. (2000). *An introduction to healthcare organizational ethics*. Oxford, UK: Oxford University Press.

Helsingin Sanomat International Edition. (2002). Business and Finance Report. Finnish officials least corrupt once again. August 30:A1.

Hodge, B. J. (1988). *Organization Theory* (3rd ed.). Needham Heights, MA: Simon and Schuster Publishers.

Holloway, J., Lewis, J., and Mallory, G. (Eds.). (1995). *Performance, measurement, and evaluation*. London, UK: Sage Publications.

Hultman, K., and Gellerman, B. (2002). *Balancing individual and organizational values: Walking the tightrope to success*. San Francisco, CA: Jossey-Bass/Pfeiffer.

Kant, I. (1964). *Groundwork of the metaphysic of morals* (H.J. Paton Trans.). New York, NY: Harper and Row (Original work published in 1785).

Keyes, C., Hyson, S., and Lupo. K. (200). The positive organization: Leadership Legitimacy, employee well-being, and the bottom line. *The Psychologist-Manager Journal* 4(2): 143-153.

Kitson, A., and Campbell, R. (1996). *The ethical organization*. London, UK: Macmillan Press, Ltd.

Landeweerd, J. A., and Boumans, N. (1988). Work satisfaction, health, and stress: A study of Dutch nurses. *Work Stress* 2:17-26.

Levering, R. T. (2000). *A great place to work: What makes some so good (and most so bad)*. San Francisco, CA: Great Place to Work Institute, Inc.

Petterson, I-L., and Arnetz, B. B. (1997). Perceived relevance of psychosocial work site interventions for improved quality of health care work environment. *Nursing Science* 18:4-10.

Räikkä, J. (1997). On disassociating oneself from collective responsibility. *Social Theory and Practice* 23(1):93-108.

Rawls, J. (1971). *A theory of justice*. Cambridge, MA: Harvard University Press.

Reidenbach, R. E., and Robin, D. P. (1989). *Ethics and profits: A convergence of corporate America's economic and social responsibilities*. Englewood Cliffs, NJ: Prentice Hall.

Rousseau, D. M., and House, R. J. (1994). Meso organizational behavior: Avoiding three fundamental biases. In C. L. Cooper and D. M. Rousseau (Eds.), *Trends in organizational behavior* (Vol. 1, pp. 13-30). New York, NY: John Wiley and Sons, Ltd.

Selltiz, C., Wrightsman, L. S., and Cook, S. W. (1976). *Research methods in social relations* (3rd ed.). New York, NY: Holt, Rinehart and Winston.

Smith, A. (1995). *Adam Smith's wealth of nations: New interdisciplinary essays*. S. Copley and K. Sutherland (Eds.). New York, NY: St. Martin's Press.

Velasquez, M. G. (1983). Why corporations are not morally responsible for anything they do? *Business and Professional Ethics Journal Spring* 2:1-17.

von Bertalanffy, L. (1968). *General system theory*. New York, NY: George Brazillier Co.

Werhane, P. (1985). *Persons, rights, and corporations*. Englewood Cliffs, NJ: Prentice-Hall.

Woodstock, Theological Center. (1995). *Ethical considerations in the business aspects of health care*. Washington, DC: Georgetown University Press.

Chapter 2

Instilling Ethics in Employees

Introduction: The Importance of Employee Ethics

Organizations are comprised of various individuals employed in the firm, who collectively give shape and form to the organizations in which they work. Organizations attend to these individuals and collectivities of individuals to attain the organizational mission; through them, as employees, organizations address their goals. To achieve the mission of the organization, employers desire employees who enhance the productivity of the firm. One way leaders may enhance the productivity of firms is through ethics.

Leaders responsible for the organizational mission desire a cadre of employees who are ethical and demonstrate those ethics through their daily work for the firm. They want workers who represent the organization well and who present themselves and the firm fairly to the public and other individuals with whom they interact; organizations need employees who create a trustworthy relationship between the business and the customer or the provider and the patient. In organizations, it is typically the frontline employees who mediate between the organization and public. For the general public workers are the 'face' of the organization. For these reasons, it becomes imperative employers hire employees who behave ethically within the organization as well as in relationship to the firm's patients and customers since these interactions influence the firm's productivity.

Not only do wise employers want to hire ethical employees, they also want to retain those with high ethical standards. Leaders need and want workers who have a strong sense of value and share the work values of the organization with others. While those of us in ethics find it attractive to consider the motivation of employees, when considered on the whole, it is the actual and observable activities—the on-the-job behaviors—that are of concern for employers. Instilling ethics in employees is thus critical.

Similarly, employees desire to work in organizations that are ethical (McDaniel and Schoeps, 2003a) and value the employee (Hultman and Gellerman, 2000:166). Ethics enhances the willingness on the part of employees to remain on the job and to support the values and norms of the endeavor. Among those values are the ethics of the system. Ultimately, while employers and employees may desire a positive working ethos, the following questions remain: What difference does it make? What are the results of unethical atmospheres?

Statistics on the behavior of employees at work are revealing and translate directly into organizational financial outlay. Surveys report that 75 per cent of employees steal from their employers at least once, and between 33 and 75 per cent of employees engage in some type of sabotage, fraud, or vandalism in the workplace (Robinson and Greenberg, 1998:1). These numbers exclude reports of illicit alcohol, drug, or substance abuse on the job. Another seven per cent of employees report being threatened by physical violence at work. Harassment and other unethical behaviors often result in exorbitant liability claims. Cost is one reason why instilling ethics among employees is so important. Financial losses raise the central issue regarding the manner in which ethics may be instilled among employees.

Financial loss is not the only consideration for instilling ethics. Employees work better in situations where respect, fairness, and other aspects related to ethics are present. These ethical aspects influence the bottom line and affirm ethics as good business. Ethics also influences the overall quality of life for workers, extending beyond the job into social manifestations. Being in supportive situations enhances the health, welfare, and overall quality of work among employees. In contrast, harassment, unfair attitudes, and discrimination contribute to employee stress, resulting in additional layoffs that in turn reduce productivity. Ethics, illustrated as respect and justice at work, are important components contributing to the work ambience of employees. Ethics aids in retaining employees.

The Continuing Debate on Instilling Ethics

Organizational leaders agree that hire and retention of employees who are ethical, and demonstrate ethical behavior in their daily work life are important. Attaining the goal is another matter. One of the major challenges for any organization and its leadership is to develop an ethos within the organization instilling ethics among its employees. The desired result is employees who behave ethically as individuals and in groups. This statement is not to suggest employees are initially unethical or employees have inadequate ethics standards prior to accepting their employment in the organization. Rather, it is critical to the reputation, trust, and work ambience of the organization and continued relationships with customers that employees make ethical decisions and behave in a manner conveying trust, respect, and concern for consumers through actions serving as exemplars of ethical behaviors.

How do organizational leaders go about instilling ethics in their firms? What are the recognized approaches to obtaining ethical employees and keeping them on the job? These questions focus the conversation on two approaches frequently used by leaders. While each approach has merits, it can be debated whether one approach instills ethics in employees more readily, or sustains a higher level of integrity over time, than the other. Debate for the best approach continues, especially in light of an increased focus on corporate integrity. These questions are explored below.

Selection Method

One approach to instilling ethics in employees relies on selection to obtain desirable employees. Testing, personal interviews, and background checks supplemented by references, multiple interviews, fingerprinting, polygraphs, and other similar activities attest to the attention given the screening and selection of desirable employees. Selection also examines for absence of errant behaviors and testimony to integrity in the prior workplace. The selection approach relies on past experiences and assumes similar behaviors will continue in the future. It presumes hire of ethically good persons. Research in human resource management, organizational development, management and leadership theories, and studies on integrity in the workplace illustrate the importance of this approach (Hodson, 2001; Stodgill, 1974).

Personality assessment complements the selection of desired personnel for employment and is used extensively. As Ivan Robertson (1994:76-81) notes, the basis for the focus on personality assessments is the understanding on the part of human resource departments that job success is linked to personality. Thus assessing the personality of employees takes center stage in designing a good work force. Imbedded in the assessment of personality is the lingering question: Should one focus more on the external influences or the internal and personal ones? One of the challenges raised by research in this area is the ability to interrelate learning from situational influences with those revealed as important for selection based on personality processes. Additionally, a range of inventories is developed serving either as a criterion measure for assessment or as an important supplement to the overall assessment of persons for a job. A set of characteristics termed the 'big five' dominates the literature on personality assessment: extraversion, emotional stability, openness, agreeableness, and conscientiousness.

Two important aspects, however, are missing from consideration of personality assessments. Personnel administrators, first, may vary in terms of their intensity and priority placed on these characteristics, given certain jobs. Employees also change. The second and more central aspect for our conversation is ethics is missing from this list. Rarely is ethics a central concept in analyses of personnel development and positive work settings. The ability to be agreeable, for instance, which is one of the big five noted above, may be a deterrent factor if new employees have to 'bend' their ethical values to fit into an otherwise unethical setting. Examples are legion of negative cultural norms developed in industry, norms which are corrosive and undermine the overall goals of the organization. A recent case study from the food industry illustrates the nexus of the debate and emphasizes the point regarding fitting into the job context:

> In a firm specializing in production of food, reports from the managers revealed that employees were taking—stealing is more to the point—significant amounts of food. This was puzzling to the executive level of management as well as creating a deficit in profits. What was revealing, however, was the underlying attitude about the food products vis-a-vis the relationship between managers and front line staff, the delivery

persons. The drivers 'felt' they were not getting paid enough, surely not what the CEO and higher levels of management were, and therefore thought they were 'owed' some food as compensation. When stated explicitly they were stealing food that did not belong to them, the drivers acknowledged it was not right behavior. Nevertheless, neither did drivers perceive their actions as stealing. The actions were rationalized as acceptable behavior. The terms compensation and recompense came up in interviews with several drivers. Furthermore, there was a 'driver' culture—context—condoning the behavior and serving to reinforce removal of food at the front line. Several drivers mentioned redistribution of food.

Clearly, cohesion among the drivers above creates a 'we-they' mentality, representative of the overall relationship between the drivers and managers. The intra-group cohesion among drivers serves to reinforce the rationale for the proposed behavior, even in the face of acknowledging stealing is not 'right' action. Such climates are also reported in other industries. For example, early stories of soda bottles being stuffed into the gas lines of expensive cars by assembly line workers are common in the U.S. car industry. Instilling an ethical framework, therefore, means addressing the overall culture of the organization. Knowing what to do and doing the 'right thing' are not always supported in the work environment. Underlying issues may pervade the firm and require attention.

Organizations employing selection as the preferred means to instill ethics among employees assume hire of employees with explicit criteria for values, mores, and norms. The aim is persons who serve well in the setting. Good persons remain good and exhibit good behavior in a consistent manner. It plays down the importance of the contextual influence upon those employees. While prior actions are typically indicators of future behaviors, selection assumes prior actions are predictors of future behaviors.

What this approach does not adjust for, however, is the manner in which the climate, culture, or environment of the organization, including the many peers and work groups, will influence the new hire. It is essentially an *a*contextual approach. Reinhold Niebuhr (1932) and Linda Nash (1990) explore the challenges of group behavior. Niebuhr claims individuals in private behave better than in groups and, likewise, Nash finds group members behave in manners they would not otherwise consider, even immoral behaviors, as the drivers illustrate. Blake and his associates (1979) report the usual corporate ethos can negatively influence honest employees. Research also reveals the referent group is important and influential. As Badaracco (1992:71-72) notes, the context of the system influences managers and employees. The importance of the context—as the case above illustrates—cannot be ignored. While the selection approach favors hire of desirable employees, addressing the need to sustain those desirable behaviors is paramount for maintaining a cadre of employees who act ethically. The forces of one's surroundings are essential in the analysis of how to address ethical challenges. While hiring a good person is a first step, of continuing concern is the support to retain the sought-after values in workers. One important factor, then, in the process of instilling ethics in employees is being cognizant of the organizational environment, which turns our attention to the second primary approach to instilling ethics among employees.

Training Method

Once an employee is hired, concern shifts from selection to building and maintaining the level of integrity among employees, the second primary method for instilling ethics among personnel. This area of human resources has grown exponentially in the past several decades.[1] Select strategies develop the ethical stance of current employees. Examples of these strategies include provision of robust in-service ethics education, clinical ethics committees, on-site ethics support for employees, clinical ethics rounds, ethics discussions, or off-site ethics education including formal course work. Strategies include both formal and informal instruction. On-site, case-based education is often the pedagogy of choice. Employees need education regarding explicit expectations for behaviors, because organizations failing to clarify behaviors unwittingly encourage unethical ones (Velasquez, 1990:230). Increased attention to values of the organization, the manner in which work groups influence other members of a firm, and attention to training, are central components of personnel management, organizational development, and intra- and inter-group relationships on-site. They rely heavily on the reinforcement of desirable behaviors on the job.

The debate, however, raises the central question of whether it is possible to change the behaviors of individuals, *i.e.*, to actually teach ethics thereby enhancing ethical behavior. The question about ethics training is grounded in a similar debate about the teaching of ethics and is germane to the aim of instilling ethics among employees, with philosophical assumptions imbedded in both approaches. One question is whether instructors can teach ethics resulting in ethically enhanced individuals. Specifically, can instructors teach workers to be more ethical?

Substantial attention regarding this challenge emerges out of professional and business literature. Literature reviews reveal that instructors responsible for the education of physicians, dentists, and psychologists, are exploring ways to instill ethics in their students (Bebeau and Rest, 1985:225; Hébert, Meslin, and Dunn, 1992:144; Green, Miller, and Routh, 1995:234).[2] Medical faculties and business professors teach courses on professional ethics, using well-developed cases drawn from clinical practice and management files to demonstrate a more ethical manner of working with patients and customers. Business schools develop extensive files on ethics cases to impart critical ethical issues to students. These reports provide significant attention to research about the best way to teach ethics and analyze results of ethics teaching. They are fundamentally concerned with retaining an ethical stance among students.

International conferences also address this central question of whether ethics can be taught. During the early 1980s, an international conference on teaching of ethics was held at the Hastings Center in Hastings-on-Hudson, New York, the oldest center in the U.S. focusing on ethics. Gathered at this interdisciplinary conversation were key professors, researchers, and authors of works on ethics and teaching; the conference resulted in a concise report on teaching ethics (Callahan and Bok, 1980). Two lines of thought are presented in the report. The response to the question about teaching ethics, or for our purposes teaching employees ethics, implies adherence to one of two primary approaches for ethics training. A full exploration of the discussion is worthy of its own manuscript, but here the argument is briefly explored to highlight the key constituent features of two lines of thinking.

Ethical persons The Hastings Center's conference report highlights the prevalent question in conversations about instilling ethics among students and workers regarding the proposed purpose. An approach attractive to those in moral development is to enhance the ethics, also the morals, of individuals. Providing information about ethics may result in persons who are more ethical and desirable as potential employees. This argument, only briefly outlined here, proposes to attain as outcomes, employees who are more ethical in their nature.

For most of us working in ethics, the prospect of enhancing individuals from the standpoint of a more ethical human being is attractive, albeit challenging. Likewise is the need to assure patients and customers of ethical quality and excellence among an organization's employees. Training individuals or offering employees ethics education with the aim of making them better people, however, is an elusive goal. The lingering question addressed at the Hastings Center conference is whether the aim is realistic or attainable. Furthermore it is an objective fraught with problems, however desirable the outcome may be. If one were to undertake this goal, whether among corporate or health care workers, with the aim of creating more ethical persons, one would immediately encounter the challenges of outcome, time, and measure, briefly noted below.

Outcome, the first issue, raises the question of what behavior one desires to instill: the goal. Or, put another way, the ability to agree to the myriad outcomes of the changes sought is equally difficult. What exactly is a 'more moral human being?' How would one attain some agreement on such outcomes in today's diverse and complex society? Codes of professions and firms, and organizational mission statements can provide some guidance. Nevertheless, in typical organizations there are numerous and varied workers, all of whom may have different morals. These varying backgrounds beg the question of the differing religious or cultural dimensions represented in today's organizations. Even more pressing are the global or trans-national systems and their resulting diversity. Consensus on what characterizes an ethically or morally good person is elusive. The search to delineate final outcomes continues.

Most teaching of ethics, especially as it occurs in the educational domain, has a limited time frame; the second issue. This limitation may be less an issue in the health care and corporate world, but is not irrelevant. For instance, in the typical school of business or medicine ethics is taught in a one-semester time frame, hardly enough time to anticipate significant integrated change in ethically humane behavior. Thus the goal of enhancing persons ethically within a compressed time frame is a difficult if not an improbable task.

Likewise, the ability to measure the desired outcome, the third issue and one explored extensively in Chapter One, is needed. This point relates to one made here above regarding measuring outcomes. Measure relies on goal clarity.

Ambiguity undermines many a good ethics program and its measure. Even if agreement may be attained in one system, outcomes will vary across organizations. Employees need clarity for performing correctly and in consort with the expectations of the employer. Ability to document the desired ethical behavior or change in behavior also may be constrained by lack of good measures. Firms are developing their own measures and feedback mechanisms in order to provide feedback loops, obtain reports, and monitor behaviors of employees. Nevertheless, measuring enhanced morals proves problematic not only because such measures are difficult, but also because agreement on what outcome to measure complicates the challenge.

Critical thinking In contrast to enhancing individuals ethically, the Hastings Center's conference report suggests the primary goal of teaching ethics is to instill critical thinking skills among participants (Callahan and Bok, 1980), the second method explored for teaching ethics. The aim is increased knowledge about ethical theories and concepts, as well as schools of thought in the field. Although conversations from the conference are reported regarding change of behavior concomitant with what is typically referred to as creating more ethical persons, the focus is on analytical abilities. Implied is an important secondary aim: enhancing the ability to think about ethical issues so one might better address confounding societal situations.

The exploration of teaching ethics benefits from interdisciplinary work. Today many professional schools including medical and law schools, schools of business, and clinical internships in psychology require the teaching of professional ethics in their curricula. As these students emerge on the work scene and take responsible positions in organizations, they carry with them an understanding of ethics in the workplace as taught in these programs. If the courses and professors they encounter in their education accept the Hastings Report, these students learn to address complex and troubling ethical societal situations. Hire does not assume, however, these employees are better persons or the organization is hiring a 'more moral' employee than another.

Possible Agreement: A Coming Together

The difficulty with the former debate is that the two approaches of selection and training are treated as dichotomous: either-or.[3] One affirms either nature or nurture, or individual or corporate responsibility. Neither is a full account of the situation, however. There are too many contemporary stories of employees, apparently with high ethical standards, who emerge as 'whistleblowers' in the face of mounting peer or supervisory pressure, reporting the truth, attesting to their ethical standards.[4] Likewise, there are stories of seemingly honest individuals who for unknown reasons engage in scandalous behaviors. This manuscript presents the thesis that it is prudent to select desirable employees and then create an ethical environment in the workplace clearly conveying the preferred corporate values, so as to support the individuals in their continuing ethical behavior.

Most efficacious, therefore, is a program of selection *combined* with education for sustaining ethics in employees. Putting desirable employees to work in an ethically *un*desirable situation is tantamount to an outcome in which the employee leaves or engages in undesirable activity due to the surrounding situation. While employee departure is surely a loss for the organization, undesirable behavior becomes a loss for both employer and employee. Alteration in desirable behavior in order to retain one's employment is extremely stressful and is typically accompanied by lost productivity.

Having said all of the above, let's turn now to ways in which a rapprochement has merit. Surely employers, as well as employees, concur there are certain fundamental concepts representing ethical behaviors upon which most persons would agree. Individuals illustrating the behaviors—*e.g.*, fairness in treatment of employees by managers exhibiting justice, honesty on the job, keeping promises, or respect between and among employees—might be considered as 'better persons' or more moral individuals. The same parallels may be drawn for professionals— psychologists or social workers—in which relationships between provider and patient retain fiduciary dimensions built upon respect and honesty. The concepts illustrated in employee behavior and cited in Chapter One appear to have universal acceptance. Thus agreement could be reached about hiring of employees, combined with offering in-service programs during which critical analysis regarding fundamental ethical concepts is conveyed.

To emphasize the point about the Hastings Center aims and bring the conversation full circle for a potential rapprochement, this discussion suggests imparting information to employees might approximate enhancing ethics or instilling enhanced ethicality in employees. Indeed, providing information regarding ethics theories and concepts and teaching analytical approaches so employees discern ethical approaches to the many confounding and morally troubling situations they encounter on the job, heightens employees' sensitivity to ethical problems emerging at work. It enhances their abilities to analyze ethically challenging employment situations. Providing this information may arguably result in the enhancement of persons ethically.

If employees on the job more readily identify an ethical issue, are they not more ethically sensitive? Or when an ethical challenge emerges at work and workers deliberate to resolve the challenge, thereby also increasing their abilities to analyze the situation when it or one of similar nature emerges again, is this not improving employees ethically? Ethical information may also lead to actions reducing contentious relationships and unethical behaviors on the job. It surely decreases the influences of troubling and confounding ethical situations workers encounter in their daily work. Is this not a means of enhancing employees ethically?

Motivations, intentions, and underlying purposes are difficult to discern. Employees and managers necessarily rely upon employees' specific acts and observed behaviors. The interrelationship between motives—or purpose or intentions—and actual behaviors is another manuscript. In the work setting, managers rely primarily on the behaviors, actions, and observed work of employees. If these behaviors illustrate increased sensitivity to ethical issues, for instance, or ability to discuss ethical situations in a productive manner, would it not be possible to argue those employees are more ethical? Is ethics education, too, a way of enhancing employees?

If this fundamental approach can be supported, then the other approach is to attend to the context in which the employee is working. The concern is the ability to design a work setting in which desirable employees with ethical behaviors are not only retained but are also sustained in that work. Instilling ethics needs to be connected with assessing, developing, and sustaining an ethical environment. Strategies to address this challenge are explored in more detail in the second part of this book.

Fundamentally, ethical decisions and actions of employees and managers illustrate organizational ethics. While motivations are important, ethics at work is finally manifest in the behaviors we observe in others. Studies regarding the positive and negative influences of external forces in business reveal interesting behavioral results (Sethi and Sama, 1998:71). A highly competitive market, for example, encourages employees to act in less ethical ways rather than supporting ethical behaviors. Assessing the external ethos in which a firm is operating is therefore an important preventive component for instilling ethics in employees. If, as findings suggest, in highly competitive markets ethical behavior will be reduced, then CEOs and managers can anticipate in similar markets that increased monitoring and training will be required to retain ethical behaviors. The importance of recognizing extant behaviors and external influences enhances the ability to anticipate future potential behavior and address it in a proactive manner. Prevention of ethical problems is central to leadership excellence, explored in Chapter Eight.

Who or What is to Blame?

The relationship between the corporate and individual is a long-standing and vexing challenge as examined in Chapter One. Its centrality lies in the importance of decisions made by organizations as corporate bodies, their respective management, especially CEOs, and their employees, and the influence of those decisions on members internal and external to it including the various patients or customers of the organization. Furthermore, in professional organizations, of which hospitals, clinics, and outpatient services offer examples, the resulting decisions are often life-determinate if not critical. Likewise, in corporations managers and other designated personnel participate in decisions of varying types and degrees of importance. These decisions are central to processes and outcomes of organizational goals resulting in cars needing to run safely and well, in clothing needing to be of high quality and protective of humans, or food needing to provide safe and nutritious substance for consumption. Decisions in non-care systems are important and they, too, influence the lives of many human beings. Indeed, employees in health care and business entities want to know their work and decisions are important and have meaning for their positive effect on patients, products, and consumers; these are important ramifications of doing a job well.

The question about corporate and individual responsibility is vexing because leaders cannot make all decisions thereby delegating many decisions to others in the system. Decisions are made commensurate with one's expertise, education, skill, and level of responsibility. It is important that these decisions are carried out ethically and with accuracy. The challenge emerges when a decision or its resulting outcome fails, incurs an error, or is unethical. What happens when employees err? Who is at fault? The person? The system? Or both? The concern naturally arises when results do not go well, or as intended, rather than when acts are positive or result in the intended outcome. This focuses the nexus of the situation on accountability and correction, perhaps even retribution. The issue is how to assign blame and responsibility for unethical acts in the organization; who is responsible? The parallel question is whether the corporate entity has moral valiancy in the situation, or not? Do we assign blame, and if so to whom or what?[5]

Räikkä (1997) examined the relationship of collective responsibility in the context of ethnic, national, or cultural groups. Adapting the analyses to organizations and employees in the entity, we consider several key questions to focus the issue. The questions lead to the following: When an employee decision fails or an error occurs, if managers or other need to assign blame, can they do so? Thus we might ask the following questions about employees:

1. If there was an ethical problem, did all employees know it was unethical?
2. If an ethical problem, and all knew it was unethical, did all know about the case?
3. If there was an ethical concern, and all employees knew about it, did all employees disagree with it?
4. If 3, did all employees have an (equal) opportunity for access to oppose it?
5. If 4, did all employees have an (equal) opportunity to oppose it knowing it would make a difference, *i.e.*, not represent a useless act? For most employees would be the accompanying question regarding consequences: would opposing adversely affect them, their job, or their families?

If replies to all questions are affirmative, then one might, without assessing the respective weight of the decisions, argue all employees are responsible. Or if an employee knew and did not oppose an ethical problem, one might argue the employee was responsible. Conversely, if an employee was unaware of either the 'rule' or the problem, then it would be more difficult to argue the employee was responsible. Problems posed in large and multi-layered firms suggest the probability that unethical acts might occur and not all employees would know. Realistically, with most unethical activities there is an attempt to hide the acts as illustrated by fraud, harassment, or stealing. Thus it would seem improbable that all employees would be responsible, as rarely would all know about the situation in order to object. The more probable case is that a few employees know about a situation and 'look the other way,' thereby serving as an example of complacency. Such action presses the concern for the system's role in the case, continuing the thesis that both corporate and individual have responsibility.

Examination when employees err also raises the pressing question of the responsibility of the CEO, top management, and others of high-level decision making in the same organization. Issues for them might be posed in this manner:

1. If there is an ethical concern, did leaders previously inform all employees about the identity of that ethical concern?
2. If employees are informed, and all recognize the problem, were all employees informed of the actual issue?
3. If all employees are informed, and the unethical case occurs, has the organization informed all employees on how to respond when it is identified?
4. If 3, has the organization provided all employees with (confidential) access to situations in which they may discuss the identified problem or access to a service (*e.g.*, employee hot-line) to oppose the concern?
5. If 4, will the organization address the concern so employees know their efforts are worthwhile and not futile? The last question also poses the following possible questions: How will the organization inform employees, given its possible confidential nature? What will be the result?

The above questions pose issues for employees in organizations as well as leaders in the same organization. The latter question-set suggests responsibilities leaders have in relationship to their employees. Thus, if any one of the questions in set two is answered in the negative, then the organization is probably remiss in its responsibilities to the employees. The last question is especially important as a form of reinforcement and consistency in the system, letting employees know their efforts for ethical behavior are supported.

The common understanding is that if employees know about or are aware of an unethical or immoral act, then they are held responsible for acting. These are the considered special circumstances surrounding the unethical or immoral act. This is particularly accurate when an organization informs employees of unacceptable acts, and proper routes to address the act, and provides access to avenues redressing the situation. Even more impressive is an organization completing the above and following through on the consequences of the act, either terminating an employee as Truett Cathy illustrates in Chapter Eight, or otherwise letting employees know of the outcomes.

There are arguments that every member of a group is held responsible for actions taken by the group. In large and integrated multi-layered firms, such as health care services, this seems implausible. It may even dissuade employees from behaving appropriately if they think they will be blamed for every act in a firm when they perceive themselves to be acting ethically. Rather, it is more fruitful to explore the role of the members and managers. Theologians and moral philosophers agree with this. Reinhold Niebuhr (1932), for instance, in discussing relationships of love, pointed out the problem of shifting from understanding individuals in relationships to assuming the corporate as a recipient of moral blame or concepts applied to it. Arguing all individuals are responsible does not aid us in understanding ethical behaviors among collectivities.

What many of these discussions avoid is the relative *weight* of decisions made in collectivities. Designated leaders have more weight of both action and responsibility for decisions they make. Likewise, there is a differential power in the relationship and among decisions made. This makes for a very complex assessment of decisions. The major point is that when management and other key decision makers enact a decision it is perceived as different than a non-leader or non-management decision. Employees know this.

If employees have no opportunity to disagree with an unethical act, then one questions the validity of an argument for corporate responsibility of all employees. Surely there is always one individual employee who knows about it–in addition to the one committing the act—and disagrees with an unethical act. The question in corporations is whether the disagreeing individual employee knew about the unethical act prior to the act occurring. Did he/she have an opportunity to resist it?

The discussion also raises several critical points for leaders in organizations and their responsibility and accountability for acts they perform and for those of their employees. The first is the responsibility to provide an 'ethical frame,' a set of guides or parameters for employees. Recognizing not all cases and their consequences can be predicted, or even anticipated, leaders, can, however, anticipate many of them as illustrated by a compliance program. Leaders know that harassment on the job is a possibility, as is theft, inappropriate use of company property and job time, and so on. Strong value statements clarifying the expectations in the particular firm are necessary.

Second, while it is important to offer guides, leaders need to ensure that employees are provided with information aiding them in *identifying* the ethical problem as well as what to do when employees observe it occurring, the point of question one in the set above. While there is consensus on many acts, such as killing, lying, or stealing, among collectivities, other acts have variation in context. We shall not explore those further. The issue is the leaders' responsibility to articulate a set of norms that is expected in the particular organization in which the employee is working. 'At Quality Company we always report our hours honestly,' and 'The person enacting an error at Good Care Hospital reports the error as soon as it is realized,' are both illustrations of system norms.

Third, leaders also need to ensure that employees have access to avenues to redress the situation or at minimum to express their opposition, inform the appropriate leaders in the firm. Fourth, leaders have a responsibility to delegate authority to others in the organization to act on information that is received and, fifth, to let employees know action is being taken on the situation. This is not to suggest the consequences need public display or announcement. However, employees involved in the initial reporting need to know their actions are worthwhile; employees need reinforcement of ethical actions and sanctions for unethical ones. Researchers know behaviors lacking follow-up or consequence are rendered meaningless.

Lastly, leaders need to comport to the behavior themselves. This is the point of serving as an exemplar. Leaders who expect their employees to behave other than they are inexperienced or naive. Or perhaps they have gotten by with unethical behaviors in the past, thereby serving as a reinforcement. Leaders of excellence ensure the values and norms of the organization are permeated throughout the organization, and are not just a conforming glaze. The reason ethical consistency is so critical is that ethical consistency implies the values are woven throughout the organization and not uneven or enacted in only certain places, typically those near to the CEO or compliance or risk management office. Hospitals do not need to be concerned about a Joint Commission review when ethical consistency is the norm in their system; likewise, corporations with clear values monitored daily need not fear a new compliance initiative in the firm.

A number of authors have raised questions about the moral agency of the collectivity. It would be pertinent to argue that a system without the ethical guides outlined above could be claimed to lack moral agency. On the other hand, an ethics advocate that takes care and responsibility to ensure the above seems to meet the expectations for ethical agency as a collectivity. Organizations as systems have policies, procedures, and 'chains of command'; and when they are ethically operational they as enacted by their leaders have met the responsibility. Where many organizations fail is in lack of follow-up and consistency throughout the firm. Lack of ethical advocacy among CEOs appears to be a global concern as well.

The point to be stressed here is that leaders—CEOs, top management, and other managers, clinical directors, department chairs—have a specific responsibility within their organizations as ethical advocates in their provision of an ethical frame. The parallel responsibility is that of the individual employee who works in that organization to enact and follow the ethical frame they provide. Indeed, one might even go so far as to suggest that employees at certain levels of responsibility might ask for policies and procedures when such are not forthcoming, thereby expanding their roles as ethical agents to include advocacy for support of self and coworkers. Female employees have been reported to ask for harassment training among peers, or health care workers have requested in-service educational programs addressing medication practices. This mid-range set of ethical acts by employees, implements what Rawls earlier was cited to suggest, ethical equilibration. They are also examples of high-level responsibility among employees and serve as a form of ethical agency. If these sets of decisions and acts can be conceptualized as management setting the ethical frame and employees implementing the ethical frame, it sets a standard for expectations thereby also noting that each has responsibilities that complement and supplement each other as members of these decisions-sets, but that do not exactly replicate each other.

Returning to the question of the moral agency of a corporation, each collectivity has moral ethical responsibilities as outlined above and takes on responsibility as an ethical system. Corporations may be held accountable for (some) acts performed by the employees including CEOs and top management. Since it is impossible to anticipate all cases and to provide all guides, when, for instance, clearly identified ethical norms are breeched by a manager, the manager is individually responsible. When an employee, in another instance, acts unethically but the corporation has not provided any guidance—an ethical frame— for it, questions then return to the lack of ethical valence on the part of the corporation.

The lingering challenge is the wide range of cases occurring unanticipated in a collectivity that managers might argue an employee 'should have known was unethical,' but for which the employee claims ignorance. In these cases and without the behaviors being included in the ethical frame, it would be more difficult to argue with strong validity the employee is solely responsible and the collectivity has no responsibility. In a dense ethical culture it is more difficult for an employee to argue he/she had 'no idea' this was a problem or that 'everyone else is doing it,' so why should I not do it.

Considering Related Issues

Other issues related to instilling ethics emerge in the work setting, four of which are briefly explored below: empowerment, workplace deviance, reporting errors and whistleblowing, and contextualization. They, too, are linked to ethics and the work of employees.

Empowerment

Related to training for more ethical behavior is the phenomenon of empowerment. Why is empowerment of concern? The primary aim of empowerment strategies is to enhance the employees' work (Walsh, *et al.*, 1998:103). Another aim is enhancing the competency and confidence of employees in their interpersonal relations. Empowerment may also serve as a means to enhance competence and therefore less reliance of workers on negative peer pressure—or other adverse aspects of work life—unsupportive of ethical behaviors. Empowerment, for example, may enhance the ability of female workers to avert harassment on the job, to instill confidence in minority workers to deflect negative comments by other employees, or to learn constructive behaviors for all employees—male and female—decreasing negative and unethical behaviors in their work. When the opposite of empowerment occurs, evidenced in low self-esteem, depression, or feelings of powerlessness, the ability to make competent decisions is threatened, reducing employees' ability to critically analyze ethical problems they face on the job. Ultimately, decreased empowerment also leads to reduced work competency and productivity on the job.

Research on social capital (Blake, *et al.*, 1976) and cohesive work groups (Hackman, 1990) emphasizes the importance of networks and social groupings as dimensions of peer relationships at work. Positive relationships instill trust and respect and build upon a model of beneficence instructive to ethical environments. The fact that individual employees are treated as valuable for themselves, rather than 'merely' as employees, supports the Kantian (1964) perspective that individuals are to be respected and treated as ends unto themselves. Mutuality and reciprocity are concomitant both to empowerment of individuals and to ethical relationships. The underlying assumption is empowered employees have the strength of conviction and confidence to assert themselves in times of conflict or ethically troubling situations. The thesis behind empowerment relies upon an unspoken assumption that empowered employees also know how to think about and respond to troubling ethical situations. As many leaders know, the latter is not always an accurate assumption. Thus while empowerment is laudable, it may not address the pressing issue of critical thinking leading to resolution of *ethically* challenging situations occurring in the work setting.

Empowerment leaves unanswered the question of how to develop individuals with the desired *ethical* attitudes, behaviors, and critical thinking skills. How would one develop an educational program instilling empowerment with an eye to enhancing ethical behaviors? Suggestions include role modeling, leadership training, constructive reward systems, job enrichment, better development and use of mutual relationships at work, and development of a participative climate at work (Walsh, *et al.*, 1998:109). Combining ethics cases with empowerment strategies may be instructive. Another potentially fruitful strategy is assertiveness training, combining assertiveness with ethics education in the workplace.[6]

Workplace Deviance

Although we have explored what happens when employees err, we introduce the concept of workplace deviance because some researchers claim deviance is a special consideration in employee behavior. Conversations about instilling ethics in employees pertain to workplace deviance as a form of unethical behavior on the job. The initial and global challenge, however, is a more precise definition of deviance (Robinson and Greenberg, 1998:3). Is unethical behavior deviance, or is deviance always unethical? Reports highlight numerous and varied approaches to deviance. Deviance includes, for instance, minor forms of antisocial behaviors illustrated by employees who do not want to work in groups or participate in social activities at work. These activities would typically not be considered unethical behaviors. However, deviance also includes actual violence and aggression on the job, as well as forms of non-compliant behaviors influencing abilities of workers and teams to complete a task: slowdowns, 'time theft,' and other activities recognized among a wide range of industries.

Attempts to further understand deviance at work lead researchers to categorize damage caused by deviance. Harm or damage is divided into potential and actual harm caused by the behavior. Harm is, indeed, malfeasant behavior raising ethical concerns for employees. One illustration of harm is counterproductive behavior at work, and is an ethical problem for employees and the organization. Such behavior can also result in significant financial outlay for the corporation. For these reasons, actual harmful behaviors are further sub-divided into those with consequences causing minor harm and significant harm either to employees or organizations. Researchers also attempt to clarify deviant employee behavior by exploring the intention and focus of the act. Another line of research explores whether the behavior is perpetrated by inside or outside agents.

In addition to the actual harm and its resulting deleterious effects, there is also concern for the etiology of the behavior. Motivations and causes become important. Research on the causes of workplace deviance reveals antecedents in three categories: individual or personal factors, social and interpersonal factors, and organizational factors (Robinson and Greenberg, 1998:14-16). Personality type and demographic aspects, social pressure and unfair interpersonal treatment, and organizational style and reward factors on the job illustrate the three respective categories. While deviance is variously defined, deviant behaviors at work are fundamentally unacceptable behaviors. From an ethical perspective, and depending on the theoretical approach, malfeasance and lack of beneficent behavior on the job, lack of respect and fairness, are all behaviors at work suggesting deviant behaviors examined in research among organizations are considered unethical behaviors.

Reviews about the categories and causes of deviant behavior only reinforce its complex and multi-faceted nature. A critique of the current conceptualization of workplace deviance is that it tends to ignore the situational determinants and how they change over time (Robinson and Greenberg, 1998). The multi-dimensional nature of deviance implies assessments addressing the individual and organization result in more ethical behavior on the job and a clearer understanding of workplace deviance. It supports the thesis in this chapter that a combined effort on selection and training is efficacious. Continued development on the job including both personnel and organizational changes is an important complement to programs addressing workplace deviance. Training and development programs attending to ethical decision-making and forms of ethical interaction relevant to a specific workplace offer a greater likelihood of success.

Regardless of these nuances, harmful behaviors are unethical and need to be addressed. As Carol Bayley (2002) reports in assessing error among employees in health care, a 'missed error'—an erroneous act resulting from deviance but without harmful consequences—has the potential for later becoming an actual and harmful error. Similarly, employees who exhibit high potential for deviance need to be addressed as a preventive measure and for the protection of coworkers. Indeed ignoring such behavior raises ethical questions for the organization and its management. Employers therefore need to consider deviant work behaviors within the realm of ethical-unethical behaviors.

Reporting Errors and Whistleblowing

Naturally if CEOs, managers, and employers are investing in the process of instilling ethics among their employees, they are also concerned with eradicating behavior that is *un*ethical. This concern moves the discussion beyond the issues of deviance and compliance explored in Chapter Three. For this conversation, it segues directly into the issue of errors, corporate grievance procedures, and options employees have to report problematic and unethical behaviors at work, including acts of whistleblowing. What options are there for employees who observe unethical activities not condoned at work? What are the challenges for reporting errors at work? Instilling ethics implies that employees observing unethical behavior will not look the other way. But will they?

Reporting unethical behavior is necessary in organizations wanting to develop and sustain an ethical atmosphere. In any firm of more than a few persons, unethical behavior is probable. Such, alas, is the nature of human beings. Like it or not, employees differ in their behavior. When they begin to demonstrate unacceptable behaviors, the behaviors need to be reported. Indeed, organizations typically have written lists of reportable behaviors and procedures for reporting. One may even raise the ethical question about *not* reporting unacceptable behaviors at work, especially those behaviors with potential for harm to employees or organizations. Reporting one's coworkers for unacceptable behavior, however, is quite difficult for most employees.

Unethical behavior also raises the question of whistleblowing, differentiated from reporting of errors or unethical behavior generally. Behaviors leading to whistleblowing may include fraud, financial theft, or hiding product error that could lead to damage—even death—among consumers. Whistleblowers inform on another or make public the discovery of corruption or wrongdoing (Random House, 1999:1960). Due to the public nature of the involvement, it takes reporting to a different level. Typically one or few individuals perceive the corporation, its managers, or key leaders as behaving in an unethical manner. In contrast to the internal reporting of unethical behaviors already discussed, with whistleblowing the internal mechanisms fail and the reporting employee takes risks to employment, and potentially to personal safety, in order to report the activity. Some consider whistleblowing a sign of organizational failure since whistleblowers report activity to the public, having previously reported it internally without adequate response. The recent law by Sarbanes-Oxley (2002) addresses this concern providing protection to employees who serve as whistleblowers in organizations. The metaphor of David and Goliath comes to mind, because a single or a few employees address the corporation. *Time* (2002) Magazine's front cover of 'Persons of the Year' portrayed three females who were whistleblowers.

Although general reporting of inappropriate behaviors and whistleblowing are different, they both raise the question of what to report and to whom to report. Reporting also presses the central issue of the ethical responsibility for acting on observed *un*ethical behaviors. Employees have expressed fear of retaliation from both supervisors and coworkers when behaviors are reported (McDaniel and Schoeps, 2003a). The more serious the effect on the reported employee, the more difficult it becomes for workers to report their coworkers. In-service training programs need to include conversations about reporting coworkers with clear explanations of procedures and processes. Role-plays of potential situations are effective for these situations. For these reasons, a major consideration to address in the training programs is the responsibility of the supervisor or person to whom the behavior is originally signaled. Providing clear mandates supported by training ensures that unethical behavior reported to supervisors by their subordinates is appropriately addressed to avert future whistleblowing.

Not only do employees cite a fear of retaliation from coworkers, but they also fear their reports will not be handled in a professional manner. Ignoring reports of unacceptable behaviors or dismissing their concerns are concomitant aspects of employees working in less than ethical situations. If employees perceive their supervisors are unsupportive of their ethical concerns, they report lack of support as a problematic employment situation (McDaniel, Schoeps, and Lincourt, 2001). Employees who are concerned with ethical behavior want to know when they are faced with complex and confounding ethical situations their supervisors will advise them in the face of these challenges. Perceptions regarding supervisors who are less than supportive, even dismissive of their ethical concerns, parallel reports of a less ethical workplace by employees. Turnover is also high. These findings, too, hold across various types of personnel and organizational settings: large and small, business and health care.

International and U.S. results are similar. Finnish health care workers are interested in ethical problems arising at work and their ability to access structures in the work setting allowing them to engage in resolution of emerging problems (McDaniel and Schoeps, 2003b). Workers reporting a perception of a relatively low ethical environment also report lack of access to ethics discussions. It is not surprising in the health care industry in the U.S. then, that the Joint Commission on Accreditation of Healthcare Organizations (JCAHO) has expanded its list of standards. Accreditation now requires an ethics committee—an institutional structure—allowing employees to submit cases and garner conversations about ethically complex and troubling situations at work. Hospitals, clinics, and other health care facilities desiring JCAHO accreditation have committees accessible to all providers of health care, providing employees across disciplines and levels in the institution inclusion in conversations about ethics. Patients and their families are also able to address ethical situations emerging for themselves and their loved ones. Ethics committees and recent laws to protect whistleblowers offer employees avenues to redress ethical issues in organizations. Regulated mandates clarify the role of the organization in relationship to the employee, explored in the next chapter.

Contextualization

Instilling ethics in corporate and health care professionals also means addressing a common assumption about one's work, that of context. Contextualization is receiving increasing attention in health care and business settings and is an important consideration for ethical problem solving.[7] We have already explored the importance of considering the context in ethical analysis in Chapter One. The context is important because it particularizes ethical analysis for employees and organizations. Exclusive reliance upon the context to make decisions, however, may prove problematic in some organizations. Iwao Taka highlights several of the disadvantages of relying heavily on the context, using the Japanese car industry as an example (1998:331). If contextualization is understood as determining one's actions based primarily on the social context, then peer groups, work groups, and other sub-groupings within an organization are critical to assess for their ethical valence in order to instill ethics. Consistency and fairness representing justice in the workplace may be difficult to establish when relying only on context as a background for ethical decisions.

While context is important, total reliance upon the individual adjudication of context or contextualization of decisions, especially those with ethical dimensions, may prove problematic and lessen the ethical ambience desired by CEOs. Therefore, as explored in more detail in Part Two, the use of established core values, clear communication, mission statements, ethics codes, and other company statements clarifying and affirming the values of the specific organization are critical to instilling ethics among employees. As will be examined in more detail in Chapter Eight, these core principles frame the organizational ethic for employees. Communication and clarity about organizational norms and values are central in developing an understanding of the organizational context. Reasons noted above thereby indicate why core values and ethical concepts in a particular context are important to the organization. This segues to the discussion in Chapter Three on ethics and compliance.

Notes

1 Readers may want to explore further research in the field of moral development. A special issue of the *Journal of Moral Development* 2003 31(3), has several articles on the topic.
2 Research studies are available on the influences of ethics teaching. Refer also to Bebeau (1985) or Hébert (1992).
3 The author expresses appreciation to Bruce Jennings of the Hastings Center for his reference to more recent publications regarding ways to address the dichotomy, received after this writing; the material is corroborated by the position of this chapter.
4 *Time* Magazine's 'Persons of the Year' for 2002 reports on three whistleblowers.
5 The author expresses appreciation to Nicholas Fotion for critical comments on this section of the chapter.
6 While authors draw distinctions between empowerment and assertiveness training, for the purposes of this brief discussion they are treated synonymously.
7 A significant and important similar approach is situational ethics, articulated by the late Joseph Fletcher.

References

Badaracco, J. L., Jr. (2002). *Leading quietly: An unorthodox guide to doing the right thing.* Boston, MA: Harvard Business School Press.

Bayley, C. (2002, October 26). Addressing Errors. Presentation at American Society of Bioethics and Humanities. Chicago, IL.

Bebeau, M., Rest, J., and Yamoor, C. (1985). Measuring dental students' ethical sensitivity. *The Journal of Dental Education 49*:225.

Blake, D. H., Frederick, W. C., and Myers, M. S. (1976). *Social auditing: Evaluating the impact of corporate programs.* New York, NY: Praeger Publishers.

Callahan, D., and Bok, S., (Eds.). (1980). *Teaching of ethics in higher education.* New York, NY: Plenum Press.

Green, B., Milet, P., and Routh, C. (1995). Teaching ethics in psychiatry: A one-day workshop for clinical students. *Journal of Medical Ethics 21*:234.

Hackman, J. R. (Ed.). (1990). *Groups that work (and those that don't).* Oxford, UK: Jossey-Bass Publishers.

Hébert, P. C., Meslin, E. M., and Dunn, E. V. (1992). Measuring the ethical sensitivity of medical students: A study at the University of Toronto. *Journal of Medical Ethics 18*:142-147.

Hodson, R. (2001). *Dignity at work.* Cambridge, UK: Cambridge University Press.

Hultman, K., and Gellerman, B. (2002). *Balancing individual and organizational values: Walking the tightrope to success.* San Francisco, CA: Jossey-Bass/Pfeiffer.

Kant, I. (1964). *Groundwork of the metaphysic of morals* (H. J. Paton, Trans.). New York, NY: Harper and Row (Original work published 1785).

McDaniel, C., and Schoeps, N. (2003a). Ethics in Corporations: Employee Position and Organizational Ethics. In process.

McDaniel, C., and Schoeps, N. (2003b). Physician perceptions of ethical environments: Study of Finnish health care providers. In process.

McDaniel, C., Schoeps, N., and Lincourt, J. (2001). Organizational ethics: Perceptions of employees by gender. *Journal of Business Ethics 33*:245-256.

Nash, L. (1990). *Good intentions aside: A manager's guide to resolving ethical problems.* Harvard Business School. Boston, MA: Harvard University Press.

Niebuhr, R. (1932). *Moral man and immoral society: A study in ethics and politics.* New York, NY: Scribner's Sons.

Räikkä, J. (1997). On disassociating oneself from collective responsibility. *Social Theory and Practice 23*(1):93-108.

Random House Webster's college dictionary (2nd ed.). (1999). New York, NY: Random House, 1487.

Robertson, I. T. (1994). Personality and personnel selection. In C. L. Cooper and D. M. Rousseau (Eds.), *Trends in organizational behavior* (Vol. 1, pp. 75-89). New York, NY: John Wiley and Sons, Ltd.

Robinson, S. L., and Greenberg, J. (1998). Employees behaving badly: Dimensions, determinants and dilemmas in the study of workplace deviance. In C. L. Cooper and D. M. Rousseau (Eds.), *Trends in organizational behavior* (Vol. 5, pp. 1-30). New York, NY: John Wiley and Sons, Ltd.

Sarbanes-Oxley Act. (2002, January 23). Pubic Law No. 107-204, 116 Stat. 745. Regarding reform legislation covering governance of public corporations, including protection of whistleblowers. See: U.S. Government, 107th Congress.

Sethi, S. P., and Sama, L. M. (1998). The competitive context of ethical decision making in business. In B. N. Kumar and H. Steinmann (Eds.), *Ethics in international management* (pp. 65-86). Berlin, GR: Walter de Gruyter Publishers.

Stodgill, R. (1974). *Handbook of leadership: A survey of theory and research.* New York, NY: Free Press.

Taka, I. (1998). 'Contextualism' in business and ethical issues in Japan. In B. N. Kumar and H. Steinmann (Eds.), *Ethics in international management*. Berlin, GR: Walter de Gruyter Publishers.

Time Magazine. (2002, December 30). Persons of the Year, The Whistleblowers. Cover story by R. Locayo and A. Ripley, p. 30.

Velasquez, M. (1990). Corporate ethics: Losing it, having it, getting it. In P. Madsen and J. Shafritz (Eds.), *Essentials of business ethics* (pp. 228-243). New York, NY: Meridian Publishers.

Walsh, K., Bartunek, J. M., and Lacey, C. (1998). A relational approach to empowerment. In C. L. Cooper and D. M. Rousseau (Eds.), *Trends in organizational behavior* (Vol. 5, pp. 103-126). New York, NY: John Wiley and Sons, Ltd.

Chapter 3

Ethics and Compliance: Distinguishing Features

Introduction

Federal regulations complemented by recent developments in the United States reveal a number of changes in corporate and health care firms. These adjustments result in several sweeping mandates comprising a federal compliance program. Concern on the part of the U.S. Department of Health and Human Services (HHS) for waste, fraud, and abuse date an initial set of regulations, now called compliance, to 1981 (Khushf, 2001:165). In 1984, the U.S. Congress developed the Sentencing Commission to enhance uniformity for those guilty of violating federal laws (HCCA, 2002). This was followed in 1991 by the Federal Sentencing Guidelines, developed by the U.S. Sentencing Commission (U.S., 1993), resulting in the first set of regulations regarding organizational compliance. Guidelines also mandate good corporate citizenship, thereby outlining a structure of punishment. Thus the later part of the 20st century observes the emergence of the compliance field in the U.S.

Dramatic additional changes in the U.S. in the later part of the 20th century illustrate problems in reimbursement, cost control, quality, and access, especially in health care, but within organizations more generally (Lavelle, 2002:58). Results of these changes have increased attention to compliance within facilities. Compliance officers have emerged as persons who consult with CEOs and other leaders in their respective firms to sustain agreement with federal guidelines. Other countries are reportedly following suit, with similar developments emerging in Australia, Canada, and the U.K. (Heller, 2001:xi; Fisk, 1979:160).

Significant changes also emerge from corporate scandals. Contemporary debacles illustrated by the German company Bayer and the U.S. firms of Enron, WorldCom, and Tyco, to name a few, result in an unprecedented focus on compliance. Today, corporations throughout the U.S. respond to regulatory concerns. Compliance programs and officers react to the basic challenge of how to retain appropriate norms of conduct, and, even more relevant to this work, how to demonstrate a desirable level of organizational ethics within the target company. The question is germane to health care and business organizations, as well as educational ones, and, even more recently, to religious institutions. How then, do leaders know a desired degree of appropriate behavior is occurring in their firms?

More to the point, what is compliance, and what is its relationship to ethics? If one has a compliant organization, is it therefore ethical?

Why is compliance a concern? As explored in the last chapter, instilling ethical behavior among employees is a high priority for organizations. Current attention to deviance on the job raises concerns about aberrant behaviors and monetary losses, shifting the dialogue to issues of compliance. Deviant and unethical behaviors detract from positive workplace atmospheres. Studies noted in the previous chapter pertaining to deviance reinforce its complex and multifaceted nature (Robinson and Greenberg, 1998:14-16). Approaches need to address the employee and the work environment to result in more ethical behaviors on the job, redressing a major conceptual weakness with a dichotomous approach.

Another reason to explore compliance is an apparent trend in some organizational domains illustrated by U.S. health care in which ethics is being subsumed under compliance.[1] Rather than developing programs for compliance and ethics as two separate programs, there is an inclination toward emphasizing compliance with ethics integrated into compliance or subsumed under compliance. We will now explore these trends and their resulting implications. Emphases in firms on financial stability and regulations lead directly to an exploration of the distinctions between ethics and compliance. Since ethics is explored in Chapter One, the discussion, below, turns to compliance.

Compliance

What is compliance? Is it the same as ethics, and, if so, in what way? As defined by the Health Care Compliance Association, compliance is meeting the expectations of others (HCCA, 2002). To elaborate on this definition, compliance is meeting expectations of the U.S. regulatory bodies outlined in the Federal Sentencing Guidelines developed by the Sentencing Commission. To be in compliance, therefore, is to be in agreement with specified guides relevant to organizations.

Essentially, compliance is the ability of an organization to adhere to and exhibit behaviors indicating awareness of and agreement with federal regulations. In health care facilities, it also means the system is attentive to the U.S. regulations required by agencies such as the Joint Commission on Accreditation for Healthcare Organizations (JCAHO). The JCAHO regulations and agreement with compliance standards result in accreditation—or continuing accreditation—for health care systems accepting and using federal funds. Given the vast numbers of hospitals in the U.S. accepting reimbursement for Medicare and Medicaid, for instance, accreditation is significant. Compliance also includes other features outlined in the seven elements forming a good compliance program, noted below, adapted from the HCCA web page (HCCA Web page, 2002):

1. Personnel in top management responsible for overseeing compliance.
2. Standards and procedures on compliance adhered to by personnel.

3. Limited discretionary authority for any individual who the organization knows—or should know—has a propensity for illegal activities.
4. Communication of standards and procedures to all employees and agents with checks that they are understood.
5. Implementation of monitoring systems; publicizing systems for employees to report violations of standards, as well as criminal conduct, without fear of retribution.
6. Standards consistently enforced with appropriate disciplinary mechanisms.
7. Taking all reasonable steps to respond appropriately to offenses and prevent further similar occurrences.[2]

Compliance with federal regulations extends to the hire and dismissal of personnel, attention to diversity in the workplace, and hire of persons with disability. A compliance program identifies individuals who provide oversight for attaining agreement of an organization with the stated regulations. The 1991 U.S. Sentencing Guidelines note compliance personnel 'have been assigned overall responsibility to oversee compliance with standards and procedures' (U.S. Sentencing Guidelines Manual, 1993: % 8A1.2). Additionally, the primary purpose of a system-wide program of compliance is to detect and prevent wrongdoing (Murphy, 2001:19). Compliance officers and their programs play an important role in the unlawful environment, as well as in civil litigation; authority to enact standards is clearly needed by these individuals.

Agreement with regulations is critical to organizations. It is important for employees to know they are working in a compliant system, and that they are treated in concordance with acceptable procedures for hire, retention, and dismissal; evaluations, for example, should be fair, impartial, and consistent across the organization. Likewise, persons with physical challenges want to be assured that they will have access to facilities essential to their job functions. Indeed, no employee desires work in a known non-compliant firm.

Given the recent concerns for cost containment, one method of addressing compliance has been the joining of institutional ethics programs with compliance services. Recent developments in the U.S., substantiated by statistics on ethics committees, reveal a trend toward the melding of ethics programs with compliance offices (ASBH, 2002). This is best illustrated with revisions in ethics committees. In several cases the department on compliance subsumes the ethics committee and its functions, thereby integrating the responsibilities of the two and blurring the distinctions between them. In these situations compliance offices take precedence over ethics programming. While it is surely understandable that corporations, both in health care as well as in business, want to streamline job functions and responsibilities, there are clear distinctions between ethics and compliance. To meld the two programs together blurs the boundaries between them, especially when the results are less than coequal. It also assumes they are not distinct entities each with a unique set of purposes, functions, responsibilities, and accountabilities in their respective domains. The underlying assumptions pertaining to integration of the two is problematic for organizations desiring to create an organizational ethic.

Having said the above, the debate continues over the degree to which an ethics program and a compliance initiative replicate one another and where distinctions, if any, should be drawn. There are critical differences, however, between the purposes and functions of compliance and ethics programs. Thus for the purposes of this discussion, compliance and ethics are more dissimilar than similar. As currently understood, it would be unwise to subsume ethics under compliance programming as the current trend suggests. Some of the distinguishing aspects are (more) conceptual in nature whereas others are (more) functional. The conceptual and functions dimensions are discussed below, with exploration of their implications following.

Distinguishing Ethics and Compliance

Purpose

The primary purposes of compliance are regulatory and financial with significant functional distinctions. There is disagreement about these purposes because, originally, among several incentives, the compliance initiatives sought parity, quality, access, and reduced waste across organizations (Khushf, 2001:162).[3] Today, however, the primary incentive for regulations leading to the sentencing guidelines is fundamentally monetary in nature. Financial stability, of course, is a realistic concern of any facility. Continued reimbursement, a laudatory concern, is a key incentive for hospitals seeking initial or continued accreditation. Hospitals, nursing homes, or clinics that comply continue to receive federal funding. Compliant corporations likewise avoid significant fines for noncompliant behavior, extending activities to risk management and averting forms of liability. Thus compliance serves functionally to assure continued financial stability and monetary reimbursement of organizations.

Ethics, in contrast, may aid in these aspects of organizational development. Indeed, ethics is arguably good business, whether for health care or business institutions. However, the primary aim of ethics is not related to finances. It pertains primarily to interactions between and among human beings, whether those interactions influence finances or not. Ethics, while surely suggesting behaviors (though not in a regulatory manner), allows individuals to discern, analyze, and critically examine what one *ought* to do in specific situations; it is primarily reflective in nature. While there are undoubtedly secondary dimensions of finances that emerge, the point here regarding purpose is that ethics is not primarily concerned with the regulatory and financial aspects of the target organization, whereas compliance always has these concerns. Thus ethics and compliance differ in their primary purposes.

Scope

The second distinguishing feature pertains to scope. While compliance and ethics have related aims and overlapping features, compliance is not the same as ethics because ethics is broader in scope than compliance. As noted in Chapter One, ethics addresses how one ought to behave in relationships with other persons (Beauchamp and Childress, 1994). It concerns itself with the values and ambience for behaviors exhibiting justice, respect, or beneficence on the job, for example. According to authors working in the field of compliance, as currently defined and articulated, compliance is too narrow to fulfill 'the promise' of work in organizational ethics (Khushf, 2001:157). While compliance like ethics sets a standard for behavior, compliance, in contrast, sets the *minimum* standard.

Compliance also is narrowly focused on the agreement with norms and expectations pertaining to a specific set of behaviors rather than on more broadly construed foci on the behaviors of persons in relationships generally. There is, indeed, little regulation of etiquette, manners, respect, or consideration among and between employees and their employers; these behaviors, however, enact the 'oughts' of ethics. Where compliance enforces behaviors, ethics denotes behaviors one ought to embrace. Ethics thereby is a broader concept than compliance (Hall, 2000:219). As an example of this difference between ethics and compliance, respect for persons is an ethical norm germane to any individual, not just to health care; it is also not federally mandated in the Sentencing Guidelines. Although the compliance initiative emerges out of a need for an ethics of organizations, the two concepts, ethics and compliance, remain distinct, both in terms of conceptualization as well as function. Ethics is guided by what one 'ought to do' and thereby has no limit on its behavior; it does not pertain to a minimum set of behaviors, thereby denoting a difference between the two concepts pertaining to their scope.

Etiology

The etiology of compliance and ethics differs conceptually and functionally; the third distinction. From the conceptual viewpoint, compliance is concerned with expectations emerging from federal regulations, whereas ethics emerges from concern for interactions between and among persons, from concern for what 'ought' to be done. Alternatively stated, compliance relies upon a fundamental power basis (Khushf, 2001:157) that is rarely a concern for ethics. While 'oughts' suggest preferred behaviors, compliance suggests behaviors about which one has little, if any, choice. Regulations are stronger than oughts, and ethics is not regulatory programming; compliance connotes regulations, rules, or mandates. Compliance with regulations is required.

Not only is the etiology different conceptually, but the two concepts also have different functional sources. Compliance arises externally and its etiology is typically another regulatory body, whereas ethics is internal and influences the values and thinking of persons; it is rarely imposed by an external entity or regulatory body. Ethics committees in hospitals, for instance, are advisory in nature, and internal to the system. Compliance expectations originate from the federal government with emphasis on quality and control. No one will argue with the important need for quality leading to increased control and improvement, especially as it pertains to health care services. Likewise, the search for standards and parity across organizations is laudatory. Nevertheless, while regulations attempt to enhance the quality of services, they may miss important nuances of care or service in certain domains or for particular populations primarily because they are external to the organization. Their attention to rule and quality in a universal domain may thereby mitigate implementation of the particular. Therefore, concerns for compliance and ethics emerge both conceptually and functionally from different etiologies.

Discretionary Actions

Discretionary action defines a fourth difference between compliance and ethics and highlights a central concern in health care. The professional relationship between the provider, typically a physician, and the recipients of services, the various patients, as articulated in the 20th century, has a fiduciary responsibility; altruism is inherent to this relationship (May, 2001; Pellegrino, 1979; Parsons, 1964). Primary is the best interests of the patient emanating from the fiduciary concern and altruistic nature of the relationship; contractual arrangements are incompatible with the altruistic relationships between physicians and patients, for instance.[4] Furthermore, the discretionary judgment regarding care for the patient lies mainly with the expertise, sound judgment, and skills of the patient's provider. These characteristics are foundational to being called a professional and form the basis of discretionary judgments. Ethics with its emphasis on critical analysis supports discretionary decisions and judgments. Compliance, in contrast, has limited, if any, allowance for such discretionary judgment.

In the provider-patient relationship, a relationship about which much of the concern for ethics and compliance emerges, due to the high degree of decision making required in the physician-patient relationship, offering of care to patients is conceptualized as significantly different from the rigid adherence to rules. The ethical relationship between physician and patient denotes concern for the person, a concern often determined by and acted upon by the provider. Through its adherence to federal regulations, compliance delimits discretionary decisions and resulting behaviors. Compliance potentially delimits the range of individual judgment and thereby risks constraining discretionary decisions providers make. Discretionary decisions also have a down side: the processes and outcomes take more time and are potentially ambiguous, respectively. The following medical case highlights discretionary judgment:

> A physician meets with a patient following work-ups with the aim of ruling out cancer; however, the tests reveal cancer of the GI tract. There are no federal regulations telling the physician what to say; nevertheless, the professional ethics inherent in the

physician–patient relationship suggests that in contemporary society physicians do not lie to patients but rather tell them the truth. Even more important is the physician's assessment of how much detail to offer and how to position the treatment plan and prognosis for the specific patient. Would the physician tell the whole story at once or perhaps relay it over several days? Would the doctor suggest another appointment in which a patient's family member could join them? The answers reflect 'judgment calls' and the discretionary decisions competent physicians make in relationship to patients. Such decisions are the daily stuff of good medicine. What is being implied here is not that physicians convey an untruth or withhold information. Rather what is being suggested is an assessment of how best to convey information to a patient so the patient may absorb it, comprehend it, and move forward with a relevant and realistic plan. Regulation is not the issue. Sensitive and ethical relationships with patients are the norms in this situation in order to attain the optimum outcome for patients.

The delimiting nature of compliance is also germane to decisions made in various business or industrial settings. In today's competitive markets, CEOs and managers seek workers who think creatively and who apply critical thinking to their work. Does a compliance-oriented organization encourage these behaviors? Compliance results in a markedly different conceptualization of the relationship between employees in business or members of project teams in industry. If an organization encourages conformance it may also reduce the level of creativity and innovation sought in a productive and forward-looking system. Employees find it difficult to both conform and 'think outside of the box' without encouragement. Thus the fourth difference lies in the level of discretion compliance and ethics encourage, with ethics providing more emphasis on critical thinking and discretionary decisions than compliance.

Means and Ends

The fifth and last distinction between ethics and compliance pertains to ethical relationships among persons: compliance potentially serves as a means to an end and in that regard raises issues regarding the foundational understanding of humans, especially as the understanding pertains to respect. Ethical interactions explicated by Kant (1964) avoid placing persons in the web of means to the ends, treating others with the same respect we would want. This categorical imperative excludes treating persons as other than ends unto themselves. Ethical settings illustrating this foundational mandate find ways to express concern for persons' dignity and show respect for employees throughout the system, rather than treating persons as means to other ends, especially ones exploiting employees. In an ethical organization, employees are treated as persons with respect and rights because they are important and contribute to the organization; the principles within the firm support these fundamental rights. Employees who work for others in hire situations may approximate means, but with compliance this relationship is explicit; with ethical relationships persons are potentially less likely to be relegated to means as ends.

In contrast to ethics, when viewed from the perspective of the compliance programming with its emphasis on financial and regulatory dimensions, compliance serves as a means to an end: complying is a means of retaining financial incentives and external control via federal regulations. Because compliance seeks to instill adherence to a pre-set framework of rules and regulations, the guides thereby become the means to the desired end of control. When persons collaborate in meeting these rules and regulations, they, too, get caught in the snare of means to an end. Thus a central differentiation is means and ends in which compliance emphasizes the means whereas—in a Kantian framework—ethics places emphasis on persons as the end, whether health care providers or business persons.

Summary

In summary, the examination of the distinctions between ethics and compliance reveal that compliance and ethics are more dissimilar than similar and the differences are substantive. Compliance has a different purpose than ethics and is focused on a (more) narrow domain whereas ethics is broader in purpose, conceptualization, and functional scope. Etiologically, compliance is external; ethics is internal. Likewise, compliance limits analysis germane to a specific type of organization and its industry, and ethics is expansive. Compliance assumes a monitoring posture with guidelines or regulations; it is based on a specific set of rules or regulations and allows little if any discretionary decision-making. The other, ethics, requires in-depth analysis and thinking about theories and concepts in light of situations and their application to concerns. Compliance is more set, firm, and clear whereas ethics is more flexible but also takes more time and is potentially more ambiguous.

Affirmatively, compliance aids in establishing parity across organizations and in meeting minimum federal standards. Bringing outlying organizations into compliance around employment standards and employee behaviors is important, even necessary. One does not typically think of regulating ethics *per se* in organizations however deeply management might desire justice, respect, and honesty in the firm. Nevertheless, ethics offers a potentially broader scope and depth. Fundamentally, compliance due to its regulations and requirements is necessary but not sufficient for attaining an ethical organization. Thus the two concepts, compliance and ethics, are more different than similar, raising important implications for organizations, the topic of the next discussion.

Implications for Organizations

What are the implications for organizations when compliance and ethics programs are integrated? What is gained and lost? What about providers and patients, or supervisors and employees? On the one hand, leaders and managers might argue the integration of ethics and compliance programs is a step toward increased efficiency and better use of scarce resources, such as personnel. Indeed, there are similar concerns and issues emerging for departments on compliance and programs regarding ethics. On the other hand, however, the purposes of the two programs are quite dissimilar. Subsuming or melding ethics with compliance programming ignores the distinctions and thereby their primary functions. Six implications for organizations catch our attention.

Punitive Environment

Compliance may lead to an atmosphere in which employees adhere primarily because those employees have concern for *non*compliance, even fear for the results of noncompliance. Emphasis upon compliance may result in a more punitive than supportive environment. Ethics does not emphasize a system of retribution or fear but rather of what one ought to do in relationship with other persons. Although compliance programs desire to both prevent and detect, many activities heretofore focus more on the detection—the error or inappropriate behavior—rather than prevention of problematic behaviors before they occur.

Regulations, upon which compliance is based, commonly emerge in response to a situation, a concern, or a former problem. Compliance regulates interactions germane to individuals within a target organization. Rather than relatively proactive, the initiatives are more reactive in nature. They act as a response agent in detecting error as opposed to preventing error. The guides, however, do not articulate the type and form of responsibility the organization has in relationship to the individual. Ethical approaches, in contrast, tend to be proactive, suggesting what one ought to do when one encounters a certain situation. While persons reflect upon prior situations, an ethical framework allows one to articulate a posture in relationship to persons prior to a challenge emerging. Ethics, with attention to what one ought to do, provides guides for appropriate behavior adaptable to a wide range of situations, implying a more proactive and positive ethos within the organization and one less punitive in nature. By assuming a primary reactive posture in response to regulations, rather than using ethics to develop positive and creative approaches, melding of compliance and ethics into one office, implies the organization may lose important innovative, creative, and anticipatory thinking about its work, and relationships between and among its employees. Since compliance is concerned primarily with the detection rather than the prevention of errors, the first significant result of a subordination of ethics to compliance is likely to be a trend to a potentially more reactive and punitive ethos in the firm.

Critical Thinking and Professional Judgment

Ethics, unlike compliance, emphasizes analytical and critical thinking skills. The purpose of ethics teaching is to expand knowledge of ethical theories, concepts, and history, as well as to enhance employees' abilities to think critically about these in relationship to behaviors discussed in Chapter Two (Callahan and Bok,

1980). Also encouraged in critical thinking is the ability of the employees (learners) to address important societal issues. Ethics enhances the ability, for instance, of employees to think critically and creatively about the many complex and troubling moral issues emerging in their daily employment; it aids them in identifying ethics issues when they emerge at work. Critical reflection is not prioritized in a compliance program, which, rather, serves to enact rules and regulations. While compliance programs and their personnel are not necessarily rigid, flexibility for negotiation and critical analysis is limited; negotiation and contextual analysis are minimized within compliance. This latter point, raising the issue of professional autonomy and discretionary judgment, is critical for professionals and is the second negative implication.

Furthermore, compliance, and its associated defensive atmosphere, may not support an organizational climate consonant with professional work. In highly professionalized organizations such as hospitals or clinics, counseling services, legal practices, or higher-level computer businesses, for example, the minimum standard offered by compliance and the limited range of decision making it encourages could pose constraints. This may also accurately describe other types of businesses in which the employees take great pride in their work and their relationships to customers. Employees of these organizations—like others who seek progressive atmospheres—desire a constructive and creative work setting supporting their work and education. Employees prefer settings in which critical analysis is expected, appreciated, and rewarded, as will be discussed in Chapter Four. Health care professionals, likewise, prefer employment sites in which education for discretionary decisions is supported, a critical issue under managed care (Dubler and Marcus, 1994; Pellegrino, 1979). Paramount, naturally, are the professional responsibility and accountability commensurate with professional discretion, freedom, and creative thinking. The *quid pro quo* between discretionary activity and responsibility is also fundamental to professional work. Nevertheless, integrating ethics into compliance suggests that employees and thereby their organizations may lose the benefit of analysis when the emphasis is on rules, regulations, and adherence without reflection. Professionals and professional organizations are especially constrained in such settings with both losing the benefits of critical analysis and reflective thinking applied to their mutual concerns. In these systems health care patients and business customers may also lose.

Review, Revision, and Power

The third difficulty in reducing ethics to compliance emerges from a critical perspective with implications for organizational functions. Compliance programs and their officers are, by definition, addressing a set of externally imposed expectations (Heller, *et al.*, 2001). From an organizational perspective, however, there is no means developed for critical analysis or review of these externally imposed expectations. Because accountability lies outside of the specific system it results in a significant amount of inaccessible power located in the compliance officer and program (Khushf, 2001: 157-188). Furthermore, power embedded in the compliance office is potentially a form of unchecked implementation with insistence on regulatory compliance without recourse for review. Should ethics be reduced to compliance, organizations would lose the potential for critical reflection and negotiation.

The current system of compliance prescribed by federal sources lacks a built-in system of review and revision, thereby constituting a potentially unchecked external source of institutional power. Ethics analysis rather is built on reflection and conversation. Since ethics committees, as one ethics example, potentially serve as a means to rebalance power by providing a common language for conversation and by engaging interdisciplinary and cross-professional dialogue, there is greater opportunity for representative involvement in conversations germane to the work setting (McDaniel, 1998b; 1999). With ethics, the foci of these conversations may include the regulations, guides, and other manifestations of the compliance program; compliance itself does not provide for such conversations, thereby implying a very limited potential for review and redress of external power. Thus the distinction between ethics and compliance regarding review, revision, and power implies less capacity for review and revision for compliance than for ethics, while acknowledging that compliance has more power than ethics in organizations.

Ethicality

The fourth way of articulating an organizational implication is to examine necessary and sufficient conditions. Organizations may be compliant without necessarily being ethical. That is, to be ethical it may be necessary to be compliant, but not sufficient. To treat persons without discriminating in their hire or dismissal is to attend to their employment in impartial ways, for instance; impartiality is grounded in the need to adhere to regulations, thereby resulting in a compliant system. Compliance with regulations is important. Impartiality understood as justice is also grounded in ethics. However, respect is foundational to ethics moving to another level of ethical behavior and implying that while a system may be compliant in its hiring practices, nevertheless, it may not achieve the most ethically desirable employee ambience. Respect, as an ethical concept, is integrated throughout the system but is not regulated by either rules or regulations.

Furthermore, although it seems unlikely, it may be possible that an employee is acting in an ethical manner and yet not in compliance. What come to mind are examples of error reporting or whistleblowing on the part of ethically concerned individuals. Even though whistleblowing may be expected from regulatory agencies, in some situations going around the 'chain of command' in organizations may be ethical but deemed noncompliant. Since leaders of organizations desire employees who think creatively and thoughtfully about the various ethically challenging situations facing health care and business today, it may result in tension between compliance and best outcomes.

Allow the point above to be pursued further using a health care example. From an ethical standpoint, one might argue the compliance regulations are *un*ethical.

This may seem bold, but consider the possibility. Let's propose, for instance, a patient enters into a relationship with a physician based on the established societal understanding of fiduciary relationships, including the community standards of good care used in assessing appropriate medical care. Allowing patients, however, to assume that the fundamental discretionary care evident in the former pre-managed care fiduciary relationship prevails, may be unethical. Compliance and managed care limit the discretionary judgment and the ensuing action and treatment by physicians through financial regulations. It would, therefore, from an ethical perspective, behoove providers to detail the limits and set out their (significant) constraints and implications for patients. Constraint is a fundamental issue for many physicians and is addressed in the literature under the issue of physician control (Dubler and Marcus, 1994). Since the primacy financial consideration has been argued to undermine the ethical as well as the scientific domain of modern medicine (Khushf, 2001:162), not to make those limits explicit may be deemed *un*ethical, as it creates a false impression regarding current fiduciary relationships.

The conflict between ethics and compliance surrounding professional relationships articulated above is germane to other professionals such as psychologists, human resource managers, and perhaps to a slightly lesser degree, managers in business, for instance. It would be potentially disadvantageous to health care providers and the care relationship, or to a sales person in business and the sales transaction, to denote explicitly the constraints above, thereby also potentially having adverse effects upon the system itself. Thus it is doubtful whether providers or sales personnel would do so. Furthermore, such revelations would probably go unsupported by their administrators and managers. The result, ethically and practically, is to place health care providers and employees in awkward situations. Are these awkward situations also unethical?

To bring this point full circle, is it not possible compliance is, at times, unethical? That is, to comply in the face of certain situations counters discretionary decisions and raises the question of ethical analysis surrounding it. Adhering to regulations and guidelines emanating from external sources and for financial ends has the potential for compromising the significant relationship(s) between the providers of health care and their service recipients. The same may be true for employees and customers. To put a pointedly different spin on the result, melding ethics and compliance may become a form of *ethical iatrogenesis*. While this result is surely not the intention, it nevertheless could arguably be a significant ethical breach of norms and undermine the ability of management to create an organizational ethic.

Education

The education of professionals in health care and business is not sustained by the current trend of melding compliance and ethics, raising the fifth implication for examination. Physicians, for instance, continue to be educated under the Hippocratic Oath relying on the formation of a relationship as viewed from the conception in ethics, rather than the paradigm of compliance.[5] Likewise, schools of business or engineering, for example, seek students who can analyze and arrive at solutions, are ethical and enhance the productivity and work of the corporation. Employers generally prefer not only ethical workers but ones who are innovative thinkers. While these distinctions have important philosophical implications, they also have significant functional implications for health services and business transactions.

Education is also relevant to preparation for compliance. Although the situation varies by organization, an officer typically exemplifies the compliance program; the office is (often vested in) the compliance officer. Currently, however, there is limited education for compliance officers (or programs) primarily because compliance is relatively new. Although the office affects the entire system, it represents a position for which there is uneven and limited educational preparation to support the role. While Heller (2001) and others are concerned for a more professional approach to the domain of compliance—one surely applauded here—at the current time compliance implies one or few individuals with uneven education assume significant power and influence within the organization. In contrast, an institutional ethics committee typically has wide representation from within the facility. While these individuals, too, have been criticized for their lack of training and expertise for ethics committee membership (Agich and Youngner, 1991), the counterbalance of community members, patients and their families, plus professionals, allows members to approximate representation of the concerns across the care system. Ethics committees have a mix of members including many who are highly educated (McDaniel, 1999) and/or who have been formally educated in ethics, such as pastors or theologians. Thus the melding of ethics into compliance implies less educationally prepared offices for deliberating important decisions occurring in organizations, especially concerns of an ethical nature.

Integrated Programs

The last and sixth implication for organizations suggests priorities in today's health care and business organizations are typically tilted toward compliance rather than ethics. Organizational integration normally subsumes the ethics program—the institutional ethics program, institutional review board, or ethics rounds—under the compliance program; because they are mandated, regulations prevail. What this means is that compliance holds sway over ethics, mainly due to constrained finances and personnel. Fewer and fewer health care facilities have resources of personnel and finances to afford both compliance and ethics programs; albeit, this begs the issue that in most instances ethics committees are conducted at work on salary. Compliance officers typically have paid positions with concomitant titles, offices, and staff, however minimum the last may be.

With melded or integrated programs the emphasis shifts away from critical reflection and analysis with discussion to adherence of regulations. When compliance subsumes ethics, the organizational ethic becomes less a matter of analytical thinking and decision-making and evolves instead into adherence to pre-set regulations. Because ethics structures offer a *significantly different* and wider representation for the organization than typical compliance programming does, the distinctions explored earlier are lost or diminished if ethics is subsumed under compliance programs.

With integration of ethics *into* compliance, the eventual result appears to be an increased emphasis on compliance with less emphasis on ethics. An anticipated and ultimate result is lessened attention to an ethical ambience with its concomitant emphasis on critical thinking and thereby less critical and creative reflection on ethically challenging behaviors within the system. A related result is that the organizations thereby accept a *base* approach to behaviors in the organization because compliance establishes a minimum standard. Are CEOs and top management desirous of minimum standards in their organizations? It needs to be reiterated that few, if any, contemporary organizations want only the minimum as implied under compliance.

For the reasons noted earlier, the melding of ethics and compliance, even for efficiency of resources, may result in more loss than gain, on balance, than warranted by the situation. Melding ethics programming into compliance offices may be a short-term gain with a long-term loss. Lest the reader conclude this discussion implies compliance is negative or poor, although required, that would not be an accurate discernment. Rather, while compliance provides important strengths to health care and business organizations, the argument is against integration of ethics with compliance losing the distinct qualities of both, but especially of ethics. Caution should be the byword for subsuming ethics and its programming under contemporary compliance programs, especially in the health care domain. Likewise, a compliance *and* ethics initiative would enhance and strengthen health care and business systems.

Suggestions for the Future

Given these implications and the increasing need for critical reflection upon ethical situations and their probable outcomes, the discussion now turns to possible suggestions for the future. The organizational implication of subsuming ethics under compliance would be that ethics would have less influence and power—even voice—in the discussion of the many ethically troubling situations arising in organizations. Ethics programs, however, need a separate voice, ones by which the programs and their activities may complement and inform regulatory bodies, with compliance offices continuing their work.

Thus if compliance is a set of guides for minimally acceptable actions and the etiology is regulatory, federal, and external to organizations, perhaps the logical evolution is to develop the compliance program and address the minimum as foundational aspects. No one will argue health care institutions need standards for quality care and service. Likewise, interactions between employees and customers need standards. Nevertheless, building upon the compliance standard one could move to ethics, allowing ethics to reflect critically upon *both* the ethically challenging situations emerging in the organization, and, the compliance activities and behaviors. Justice, fairness, honesty, and keeping of fiduciary relationships come to mind as core ingredients. These concepts, however, emerge from a long-standing tradition of care and interpersonal relationships with attention to ethics. Once these behaviors are in place, the organizational activities and behaviors once affirmed as ethical concepts and standards may then move to the next level of policies or procedures, then regulation or guideline, although they originally emerge from ethics. Thus the circle of compliance, ethics, and compliance is complete. Minimum standards shift from compliance, moving to ethics; the ethical analysis may then be followed by compliance standards.

Unfortunately many organizations in contemporary society begin with regulations rather than with ethics. Indeed, both ethics and compliance are needed. Ethics and compliance programs need each other and need to remain separate realms of functions so they may benefit from the objective and distinct perspective each brings to the conversation. Compliance, with its regulations, guidelines, and standards enforced by federal mandates, can contribute to the parity and quality desired of all organizations around the issues of employment hire, dismissal, and evaluation. Ethics can provide reflection on these and other critical moral issues, as well as an opportunity to reflect upon compliance using critical analysis so foundational to ethics.

Research results also suggest retaining distinctions between compliance and ethics programs. Compliance, by its nature, focuses on conforming behaviors among employees in an organization. For this reason, Ricky Griffin and his associates (1998:66-67) note research on compliance tends to focus on concepts of cohesiveness, cooperation, communication patterns, and other work group attributes. The aim appears to be improved functions within the organization. Rather dysfunctional behaviors are defined as behaviors having negative consequences for the individual, groups of individuals, or for the organization.

Another aspect research highlights also supports differentiation between the two programs. Given changes in situation, intent, or outcome, behaviors may or may not be dysfunctional (Robinson and Greenberg, 1998). Discussion on employees' behaviors includes motivations, going beyond the scope of compliance but of interest for ethics. Indeed, it might be ethical to raise concerns—and therefore unethical not to—emanating from compliance regulations as noted earlier regarding the provider-patient relationship. If, however, the ethics program were integrated into the compliance office, the opportunity for critical analysis by ethics about compliance would be lost. Reflection *on* compliance by ethics would be highly improbable, albeit desirable.

Thus the benefit of having both an ethics structure and a compliance office extends beyond patients and providers to a wider range of employee behaviors. Representation across organizations by an institutionalized structure regarding ethics concerns is a desirable feature in health care and business organizations. Rather than melding organizational ethics into one program under compliance, it would be prudent to consider the distinct contributions and advantages of both functioning well. In business and corporate firms, consideration might be given to parallel structures similar to those employed in health care giving access to employees for conversations about their ethical concerns.

Regardless of the line of inquiry, there is a continuing search for ways in which employee behavior is encouraged to remain within desirable limits. Behavior deemed dysfunctional by organizations is to be discouraged if not outright prevented among employers and employees. Employees, too, prefer to work in organizations compliant with and attentive to legal and ethical concerns. Subsuming ethics under compliance or merely addressing regulations erases significant distinguishing contributions to the ethos of today's health care and business concerns, contributions enhancing the quality outcomes for society. The current trend of subsuming ethics under compliance has the potential for losing the important creative contributions ethics provides in the organization, ones enhancing organizational ethics. Since compliance is necessary in today's organizations but not sufficient for organizational ethics, retaining two separate entities is central. Distinguishing ethics and compliance and encouraging both affords the opportunity for critical reflection on ethics *and* compliance, and has the advantage of two programs to enhance organizational ethics. The result is an employment site desired by employees in health care and business. Preferable workplaces lead, naturally, to the discussion topic of the following chapter, what employees desire.

Notes

1 The information provided is based on reports and conversations, acknowledging statistics on the issue are difficult to acquire.
2 Appreciation is extended to Ray Snell, President, HCCA, for permission to cite the seven criteria of a compliance program, August 2003.
3 The author expresses appreciation to George Khushf for drawing attention to this work, cited.
4 The author is indebted to Mary Rorty for comments on altruism and fiduciary relationships.
5 For a fuller discussion of the topic, see, for example, William May (2001).

References

Agich, G., and Youngner, S. (1991). For experts only: Access to hospital ethics committees. *Hastings Center Report 21*:17-25.
American Society for Bioethics and Humanities (ASBH). (2002). Annual meeting, Group on organizational ethics and compliance: Report. October 22-26. Baltimore, MD.
Beauchamp, T., and Childress, J. (1994). *Principles of biomedical ethics* (4th ed.). Oxford, UK: Oxford University Press.
Callahan, D., and Bok, S. (Eds.). (1980). *Ethics teaching in higher education*. New York, NY: Plenum Press.
Dubler, N., and Marcus, L. J. (1994). *Mediating bioethical disputes*. New York, NY: United Hospital Fund.

Fisk, G. (1979). Issues, priorities and sanctions for enforcing social responsibilities in European business firms. In G. Fisk and P. E. Korsvold (Eds.), *Social responsibility in business: Scandinavian viewpoints* (pp. 158-169). Lund, Sweden: Studentlitteratur.

Griffin, R. W., Kelly, A. O., and Collins, J. (1998). Dysfunctional work behaviors in organizations. In C. L. Cooper and D. M. Rousseau (Eds.), *Trends in organizational behavior* (Vol. 5, pp. 65-82). New York, NY: John Wiley and Sons, Ltd.

Hall, R. T. (2000). *An introduction to healthcare organizational ethics*. Oxford, UK: Oxford University Press.

Health Care Compliance Association (HCCA). (2002). *Corporate compliance for the health care professional*. Retrieved August 4, from: http://www.hcca-info.org/html/compliance.html.

Heller, J. C. (2001). Preface. In J. C. Heller, J. E. Murphy, and M. E. Meaney (Eds.), *Guide to professional development in compliance* (pp. xi-xii). Gaithersburg, MD: Aspen Publishers, Inc.

Kant, I. (1964). *Groundwork of the metaphysic of morals* (H. J. Paton, Trans.). New York, NY: Harper and Row (Original work published 1785).

Khushf, G. (2001). Organizational ethics and compliance. In J. C. Heller, J. E. Murphy, and M. E. Meaney (Eds.), *Guide to professional development in compliance* (pp. 157-188). Gaithersburg, MD: Aspen Publishers, Inc.

Lavelle, L. (2002, October 7). The best's worst boards: Special report. How the corporate scandals are sparking a revolution in government. *Business Week (European ed.)*. New York: NY: McGraw-Hill, p. 58.

May, W. F. (2001). *Beleaguered rulers: The public obligation of the professional*. Louisville, KY: Westminster John Knox Press.

McDaniel, C. (1998b). Hospital ethics committees and nurses' participation. *Journal of Nursing Administration 28*(9):47-51.

McDaniel, C. (1999). Clergy contributions to healthcare ethics committees. *HEC Forum 11*(2):140-154.

McDaniel, C., Schoeps, N., and Lincourt, J. (2001). Organizational ethics: Perceptions of employees by gender. *Journal of business ethics 33(3):*245-256.

Murphy, J. E. (2001). The compliance officer: Delimiting the domain. In J. C. Heller, J. E. Murphy, and M. E. Meaney (Eds.), *Guide to professional development in compliance* (pp. 19-35). Gaithersburg, MD: Aspen Publishes, Inc.

Parsons, T. (1964). *Social structure and personality*. New York, NY: Free Press of Glencoe.

Pellegrino, E. (1979*). Humanism and the physician*. Knoxville, TN: University of Tennessee Press.

Robinson, S. L., and Greenberg, J. (1998). Employees behaving badly: Dimensions, determinants and dilemmas in the study of workplace deviance. In C. L. Cooper and D. M. Rousseau, (Eds.), *Trends in organizational behavior* (Vol. 5, pp. 1-30). New York, NY: John Wiley and Sons, Ltd.

United States Sentencing Guidelines Manual (1993). %8A1.2. Amendments as of November 1, 2002. http://www.ussc.gov/GUIDELIN.HTML.

Chapter Four

What Employees Desire

Introduction

For years, employers have asked the question: What is it that employees desire in the workplace? Another way to focus the issue is to ask what will keep good employees at work, and working well. As we saw in earlier chapters, working well also implies working ethically. Although a substantial body of literature addresses the general question of what makes a workplace a desirable one, a precise answer continues to elude both researchers and leaders. When individual employees locate great places in which to work, however, those settings become known among employees as desirable organizations for work (*Fortune*, 2002). Companies such as Synovus in Columbus, Georgia, or Nokia in Finland are among sought-after places to work.

Determining desirable places to work and identifying the specific characteristics of places providing desirable situations offer leaders the opportunity to build on those characteristics. Leaders in organizations can alter features to enhance positive or diminish negative aspects affecting employees. Signal features could be replicated in other work sites to make those locations more desirable. Employee training can be developed to enhance traits creating more desirable employment sites. Indeed, there are cogent reasons for identifying desirable workplaces as well as the particular aspects contributing to their desirability. One reason, explored more fully in this chapter, is the ability to attract and retain employees thereby enhancing the overall productivity of the organization. Desirable places for work positively influence employees, and they by their numbers and interactions influence their communities and thus society at large.

Considerations in Employee Desires

In Chapter Two we explored briefly the question of why ethics is important to employees and organizations; essentially, why ethics is good business for organizations. In this section, relying upon the earlier discussion, we turn to what it is employees desire in good places of work. Building from the more general approach to the question, this chapter explores specific characteristics of desirable workplaces, with special attention to those relating to ethics.

Employees' work preferences develop in contexts and pertain to their particular job situations. Several are explored here. Related to employees' desires is the opportunity for employees' maximum possible expression of personality while at the same time meeting demands of the system for productivity at the highest optimum level. According to Argyris (1964:130), integration of the individual with the organization needs to occur in order to achieve this aim. Research regarding the integration and balance of personality and organization indicates the manner in which this is accomplished to be challenging (Schein, 1992:196). Attaining a realistic balance is one of the fundamental challenges to employees in organizations, and is especially vexing to leaders and employers since it influences the meaning of work among employees and affects their productivity.

Finding meaning in their work and understanding the relationship between employees' contributions and their organizations are significant to employees. Kant's (1964) assertion that humans are to be viewed as ends, thereby avoiding treating humans as means, provides a standard for interactions between and among persons.[1] Respect prevails in such work situations. Rather, when human beings are treated as merely means to ends, however altruistic those ends may be deemed, the relationship has the potential for exploiting persons, an undesirable outcome. Employees who perceive their work to be unsatisfactory, who find limited meaning in their work, or who work in undesirable situations are more likely to perceive themselves as being regarded as *merely* means to an end. They typically also experience limited integration with the organization. Balance between means and ends is critical because it influences perceptions of work. A constructive balance is enhanced by attention to meaning, justice, and quality work environments. It offers the potential for integrating the employees with work, as Argyris (1964; 1962) reports.

Employees differ, however, in terms of their preferences for desirable work and they vary along developmental lines: a younger employee has different needs from a soon-to-be-retired employee. Preferences are also culturally informed. Some individuals prefer a more differentiated life with clear demarcation between family and work; Canada, the U.K. and U.S. are examples of countries in which this attitude prevails (Schein, 1992:126). In contrast, Mexican and South American employees represent cultures preferring less differentiation between family and work. These fundamental cultural differences inform employees' work preferences.

Questions about whether employees' desires are met are also contingent upon the current labor market, since supply and demand influence perceptions of good jobs. In a tight job market there is less concern for what employees desire because there are fewer jobs thus giving employers the upper edge. When the job market is tight financial security takes precedence, changing views about what constitutes a desirable job. On the other hand, in a tight labor marker when desirable employees are in short supply, there is an increasing emphasis on recruitment, employment packages, and retention of valued employees. This balance—between supply and demand, or labor and position—influences the perception of what makes a job a desirable one, as well as the willingness of employees to remain in less than desirable places. The search for desirable workplaces continues; however, few studies approach the question from the standpoint of ethics as a contributor to the quality of work. It is to this conversation that we now turn.

Ethics, the Missing Component

Fruitful results can be elicited by approaching the question regarding features employees desire in work by asking, what has been ignored? The response, in part, is ethics. Regardless of a long-standing analysis of work, ethics is rarely the central concept of concern for assessing or determining desirable workplaces. For our purposes in organizational ethics, one significant feature of work life relatively unexamined but desired by employees is ethics at work. While this is a conversation of expansive possibilities, the focus here is on research exploring the relationship of ethics to work settings, and those in health care and business.[2]

We examine work sites that employees perceive to be ethical so we can identify contributing factors to those settings, and explore potential relevance to other work settings. The features of ethics employees cite most often are examined in more detail because they offer insight into what constitutes a quality place for employees to engage in work. Many indicators of quality workplaces, good places to work, or desirable sites for employees are ethical ones. When an ethical environment is perceived employees also cite it as a highly desirable workplace. Thus another way to transition into the conversation pertaining to ethics and work is to ask, what components of desirable workplaces are linked to ethics?

Ethics and Work Retention

Employees desire quality work environments that are ethical environments as evidenced in their high retention (and low turnover) in those places. While employees desire job security, employers desire to retain workers who work well; retention is an indicator of desirable workplaces. Work sites in health care and business in which employees state they 'love their jobs' are perceived as ethical and employees want to remain (McDaniel, 1998c; McDaniel and Schoeps, 2003a). Work retention in these ethical sites is high. Ethical environments, overall, prove to be ones in which employees desire to work; they remain in such settings for a longer period of time than employees reporting a less desirable ethical ethos. Employees enjoy their jobs; they are, in other words, satisfied with their jobs and committed to the work setting. When the question is posed about what employees desire with an eye on ethics, it is clear positive ethical environments are highly desirable and enhance retention.

In contrast, among those employees whose low opinion of the ethics of the work environment is low (what one might be tempted to call an unethical or less ethically positive site), the retention rates are low (McDaniel and Schoeps, 2003a; McDaniel, 1998c). According to follow-up interviews with those employees who perceive poor work ethics, many of those employees are planning to leave. While some merely discuss leaving, others have a firm plan and many are actively searching for other positions. These findings obtain across levels of employment position as well. It does not take an astute leader to recognize in such situations employees are also less committed to the current work and are, overall, potentially less productive. This begs the question of the atmosphere they in turn create in their own work units. When employees are actively leaving and make their imminent departure known to other workers, it contributes to an adverse employment situation. Cohesion is reduced and productivity thereby lessened (Hackman, 1990), since it is relatively well known that disgruntled or departing employees detract from the work morale. Employees who perceive their workplace as ethical thereby are more likely to remain than those in less positive situations.

Ethics and Structures

Employees also indicate it is important to them and their work quality to have an opportunity to discuss the many troubling and challenging ethical situations emerging in their work (McDaniel, 1995; McDaniel and Schoeps, 2003b). Essentially, employees desire formal means to explore ethically challenging situations. Equally important, however, is an ongoing—continuing—place for such conversations to occur. Health care systems provide an example that might be informative to business. Employees in health care desire an institutionalized structure for conversations regarding ethics. They desire an ethics committee, but also rounds for clinical discussions and team gatherings addressing ethically complex issues emerging at work. The purpose of the formal structures is to ensure conversation. An *ad hoc* conversation, an infrequent meeting, or a sporadic arrangement is not adequate. Employees seek structures representing a systematic and continuing opportunity for conversation.

While the initial findings above occur in health care, employees in business settings share the desire (McDaniel, Schoeps, and Lincourt, 2001; McDaniel and Schoeps, 2003a); workers in corporations desire similar structures. In a study of one large company, employees who rated the ethics of their company highly also desired an opportunity for conversations regarding ethics. Employees commented, 'I wish we had one,' or, 'why don't we have such a committee?' It is important to point out the focus and thus the functions of a hospital ethics committee might be different than a business ethics committee. For instance, in most hospital ethics committee a primary concern is relationships between providers and patients, although other relationships and functions such as education and policy formation are considered. While business systems have the customer as the corollary, it is not the same relationship in business as in health care with patients. Likewise, businesses may offer a compliance committee with similar functions. Nevertheless, business ethics structures might take the form of a regularly scheduled team meeting or a departmental conversation. Regardless of its form, the ethics structures offer access to employees for the troubling ethical concerns arising at work.

Since hospital regulations, including the Joint Commission (1994:10) standards for ethics mandate access to ethics committees, formal and institutionalized committees tend to be more prevalent in health care than in business. The idea of an ethics structure, however, is highly attractive to employees in business, albeit elusive for many of them. The Conference Board (1992:8) reports only ten per cent of its U.S. business members have an ethics committee. Such committees are less common among its European members.

Why is a formalized ethics structure important? Reviews of research on employee engagement, well-being, and quality of work life, reveal cognitive involvement of employees is important; cognitive aspects are in turn related to positive outcomes of work (Harter, Schmidt, and Keyes, 2003). These findings corroborate earlier studies regarding the integration of personality and organization and the importance of self-esteem. Ethics structures offer a means of attaining cognitive involvement in the work site, especially for workers in the health care setting. Conversations in ethics committees regarding ethically complex and challenging situations at work provide involvement for employees. Ethics discussions, ethics rounds, or team meetings focused on ethics, would indeed, offer employees one avenue to this sought-after dimension of their work life. Ethics structures provide avenues of influence and involvement for workers in their daily work life and the integration of the person with organizational needs that Argyris (1964) reported.

Ethics and Access

Another characteristic employees find desirable in work settings they deem ethical is *access* to deliberations in which ethical concerns are explored. This phenomenon is termed ethics access, differentiating it from ethics structures. While it might seem straightforward that structures for discussion and exploration of ethical concerns would provide access, access is not necessarily forthcoming. Thus the third aspect employees desire at work is access to structured avenues of deliberation. An expression 'sitting at the table' is germane to and captures the central point of the concerns, as the following case highlights:

> Susan Sanchez and Mark Romero were conducting follow-up interviews to a survey regarding institutional ethics committees among urban hospitals. During an interview with physicians at a large 500-bed hospital, several doctors reported the hospital had an ethics committee. The physicians were pleased with the committee. The two interviewers, however, pointed out the limited information about the committee and little, if any, system-wide information regarding its calendar, where it met, and how to access it for submission of ethics concerns occurring within the hospital. Two physicians present stated they were 'OK with the arrangement' and were 'hopeful other employees would not find out about it' because it would probably mean a 'lot more conversations about ethics at work.' The physicians made it clear they were not eager for more discussion; such conversations, they noted, would probably 'alter their treatments.' Not all physicians shared this view. Although it had been in existence for several years, social workers, respiratory therapists, and registered nurses, for example, were, essentially, unaware of the committee. Family members had never

used the committee, assumedly, because they did not know of its presence. Thus for an ethics structure to be valid it needs facility-wide access.

Findings among several studies in different employment situations in which workers desire an opportunity to deliberate about ethical issues, are consistent with the classic seminal Hawthorne study of production line workers conducted by Frederick Roethlisberger and William J. Dickson (1939). Workers in the Hawthorne study appreciated the interactions represented by comradeship, attention, and conversations with the supervisors and researchers more than features of work life such as length of breaks. These interactions are also important to contemporary workers. In particular, today's employees seek an opportunity to talk about their ethical concerns regarding the work they are performing with their coworkers.[3] Employees want deliberations about the most ethically feasible solutions to the many troubling and challenging moral situations they face.

What employees seek are ways to exert influence regarding ethical issues arising at work about which they are conflicted. Complex and confounding ethical issues emerging in daily life are troubling for employees; they seek a way to explore them and to engage in dialogue with their coworkers. Employees most desire ways to examine issues within the work context to arrive at probable solutions. Involvement in decisions is central to employees' ongoing interests and commitments to the work (Baumeister and Leary, 1995); employees desire inclusion. Involvement or inclusion also represents respect. This is not to suggest employees desire consensus on ethical problems; rather, they want an opportunity to examine problems and explore the several ways in which perplexing ethics concerns may be resolved.

Empirical analyses of contributions offered by hospital ethics committee may shed some light on the topic of influence. Studies reveal that most members contribute consistently to committee deliberations, even though some occupations have higher proportional membership and verbal contributions than others (McDaniel, 1998b; 1999). Clergy, physicians, and social workers all participate as members of ethics committees, and registered nurses, who report under-representation on committees (Agich and Youngner, 1991), are well-represented and modestly active members. Ethics committees represent this context of opportunity, an opportunity for influence upon the ethical concerns workers address in their daily tasks, with its balance of power that is important to these employees.

Typical ethics committees have representation from across the facility. While the committees may have disproportionate membership from several occupations (Agich and Youngner, 1991:17-25), there is a mandate for thoughtful and respectful conversations. Examination of ethics committees highlights the need for feedback of an ethical nature at both top management and care provider or employee level. Ethics committees, whether in health care or business settings, provide an opportunity for employee involvement and influence about work they deem important. These findings are related to perceptions employment situations are fair and respect prevails among employees.

Desire for access is stronger for employees in health care than in business sites (McDaniel, 1998c; McDaniel and Schoeps, 2003a). Nevertheless, employees in both health care and business desire access to a formal means of conversation regarding ethically troubling situations influencing them and their work. A theme emerging from these employees is the ability to have a voice in their work or to have some semblance of influence regarding morally complex issues. Influence may indicate respect of employees and trust in their opinions. These findings parallel those noted above regarding cognitive involvement, sense of care, and concern among colleagues occurring in ethics committees. Ethics committees offer members a way to influence their work setting; through it they, in turn, may develop policies or procedures used in clinical care settings or business arenas. Ethics committees illustrate a means of gaining entry into discussions in which influence may be exerted and change of former decisions might emerge. A voice in work illustrating involvement or cognitive domains appear to be predominant concerns for workers.

Ethics and Supervisor Support

Supervisors supporting employees in their work are also desirable and linked to perceptions of an ethical ethos (McDaniel and Schoeps, 2003a). Employees want the person to whom they must report—the supervisor, boss, or manager—to be willing to listen to concerns they have at work regarding ethically difficult situations. This finding parallels studies of desirable places to work, in which workers report the need for a supervisor with whom they can disagree (Levering, 2000). Managers who pay attention to employees' concerns enhance the employees' sense of interest and positively influence their outcomes (Freidrickson, 1998).

Not only is it important to have a supervisor supportive of one's work, it is also desirable for the supervisor to sustain employees when there are ethical problems on the job (McDaniel and Schoeps, 2003a). Almost every employee in today's work world encounters some ethical conflict in the work setting. Ethical challenges, unfortunately, are ubiquitous and anticipated. When they do occur, workers want to know there is a person on-site who supports them. Support in this context, however, does not necessarily imply agreement but rather a supervisor who listens and allows employees to explore the ethical issue. Willingness to listen, offer advice, and provide relevant information regarding possible solutions and policies and procedures is desired. What is not desired is a boss who dismisses an ethical issue, does not listen, or ignores the ethical concerns and feelings of the employee. While supportive coworkers and peers at work are important, central to a worker's perception of the ethical climate in the workplace is a supervisor in a position of authority who attends to the worker regarding his/her ethical concerns.

Preference for supervisory support, however, differs by gender. Males express themselves as less in need of supervisory support than females (McDaniel, Schoeps, and Lincourt, 2001), and females are significantly more concerned than their male counterparts. These differences remain across education and position level in employment. Upon further examination of such findings, one finds considerably more males than females employed in managerial positions. Differential employment by gender may provide a certain comfort zone in which males are more protected from ethical concerns and, likewise, would in most instances, also have another male as a supervisor. Reduction of the disparity between males and females in management could lessen concern on the part of males regarding ethical concerns on the job. Variation in employment by gender also introduces the ethical concerns for respect and justice at work. The findings highlight differences in perception of ethics at work among diverse employee groups and point to the importance for providing education regarding ethics at work.

Ethics, Policies, and Procedures

In addition to the aspects noted above, employees who perceive themselves to be working in ethical supportive situations also desire work settings in which those various procedures and policies are available and applied in fair manner among employees (McDaniel and Schoeps, 2003a). Justice as fairness is desirable. This preference is substantiated by desire for respect and integrity among employees (Hodson, 2001). Likewise, researchers reveal positive employment situations are related to how consistently and openly decisions are made (Cohen, 1986). Organizational policies and procedures may also represent what other researchers have termed 'expectations' of clarity on the job (Harter, Schmidt, and Keyes, 2003).

Rather, when standards in the work setting are implemented in uneven ways, employees perceive the work setting to be less than ethical (McDaniel and Schoeps, 2003a). Sites from which employees would prefer to leave are also those sites in which they have observed supervisors treating their coworkers or themselves with bias, experienced or observed unfair employment practices, or observed supervisors creating ways of 'working around' standards for fair employment practices on the job; justice is lacking. These findings and experiences are similar in business and health care; however, in health care the addition of uneven patient care assignments is added to the growing list of ethical concerns. Well-implemented procedures go beyond mere means to ends, because they also result in behavior signaling the underlying ethical obligations for work (Robinson and Greenberg, 1998:176). If we observe how policies and procedures are applied in the work site we understand extant ethics at work. Thus workers look to the use of polices and procedures as indicators of the organizational—or unit, clinic, departmental—ethics. Ethics at work, translated into justice as fairness, and impartial application of extant policies and procedures at work, is highly desirable among today's employees.

While most employees realize that not all situations or employees are exactly alike, overall, they desire work settings in which workers are treated fairly, as found in the discussion of diversity below. Even though employees recognize differences among themselves, workers want implementation of requirements to be applied in an even and just manner. Justice at work is a foundational concern for most employees, revealed in their concern for the manner in which is it exhibited by the use of policies and procedures by their bosses, various supervisors, and administrators in their work sites.

Ethics and Guidance

Employees also report that when ethical problems emerge they desire someone who is willing to guide them. Beyond support, employees want guidance on ethically confounding interactions and situations occurring in their work. Need for guidance is even more pressing when workers must report a coworker. The ability to report a fellow worker in the face of an ethical situation is consistent with perception of support from the supervisor in reporting the coworker. Indeed, linked to backing from supervisors is the parallel concern for reporting coworkers without receiving retaliation from them or others in the work site (McDaniel and Schoeps, 2003a). Reporting fellow workers is one of the most difficult situations employees face due to the fear of retaliation from and disruption among coworkers. It is even more complicated by the need to report their *un*ethical behavior. For this and other reasons, employees also desire coworkers who are ethical and share their values. Employees desire a supervisor who supports them in their ethical pursuits, and a work environment in which guidance is forthcoming regarding ethically complex situations in the work. We turn to the important role of the ethics advocate in the last, eighth, chapter.

Ethics and Communication

Employees express directly the need for open and honest communication about situations occurring at work they deem unethical, or pertain to ethics (McDaniel and Schoeps, 2003a) They want open communication and they want honest interactions. Many of the components above are linked to quality communication. The manner in which supervisors work with employees, implementation of policies and procedures, and engaging in discussions of ethically challenging situations are all connected to communication. Communication is the underlying ingredient of their implementation.

It would seem straightforward for employees to find positive communication desirable, but its obverse is what is evident. Employees in situations they perceive to be *less* than ethical cite lack of communication, inability to garner feedback or information they desire, and lack of candid conversations about problems they observe in the work cite. Ignoring ethical issues, looking the other way, or being overtly dishonest are all examples of behaviors reported in places of work where employees think it is less than ethical. In these places they are also dissatisfied with the work environs and are seeking other opportunities for work. Communication is a central feature in ethical environments and informs many other aspects of quality workplaces for employees.

Related Features

Features explored above in this chapter are those employees desire, as revealed in research regarding ethics. There are other components of good workplaces unexplored in relationship to ethics but noted in other studies as important to employees and contributing to a positive work site; they have projected links to ethics in the workplace. Three—diversity, trust, and dignity—are briefly explored below.

Diversity

Diversity is increasing in the global workplace. As society—whether in Africa, Europe, or the U.S.—has become more diverse, employers respond to increasing diversity. Expanding numbers of diversity programs around the globe illustrate this response. Diversity, however, is not limited to cultural or ethnic-racial issues; it implies a value for and general appreciation of differences. Valuing diversity among employees allows a company to recognize the importance of each person as a resource to the firm, thus conveying respect for persons. Foundational to a work site in which diversity is appreciated is one in which each individual is appreciated for his/her unique contributions to the endeavor. Implied is that employees are working in a safe environment without fear of retaliation, where dialogue may occur across numerous lines to facilitate productive outcomes. Such organizations also report creativity, a synergy in which expression of ideas for the betterment of the work product is also evident (Brown, 1998). Creativity and energy are heightened.

Valuing all employees, their work, and their decisions is also a way to instill ethics within the firm. Studies show there is an enhanced sense of value and ethics (Brown, 1998:245) in organizations where a wide and diverse range of employees are hired and work together. Diversity is linked to ethics. Appreciating diversity means creating an environment in which difference is valued and respect for persons and fairness prevails. Understanding diversity extends beyond management of employees to appreciation coworkers have for one another; workers want to work in settings where there is trust and they gain meaning in work. Trust and meaning at work are also ramifications of employee diversity at work. Studies regarding diversity bring the conversation full circle: acceptance of persons for whom they are, with different ideas or backgrounds, relates to their sense of justice and respect in the work setting; respect prevails and is evident in the workplace. Acceptance of diversity also creates a culture of ethics, supporting the Kantian (1964) imperative: employees are appreciated for him/herself while enhancing the sense of respect among them.

Trust

Trust is cited as a core ingredient in the workplace, influencing the relationships between employees and employers. A Canadian workforce study reveals organizational performance is enhanced by work life quality and improved relationships among employees; trust is an important dimension reported in those relationships (Lowe and Schellenberg, 2001). Assessments by the Great Places to Work Institute corroborate those findings, revealing trust is an essential component among good places to work (Levering, 2000). In great workplaces, working relationships are built on trust rather than aggressive self-interest or non-sharing forms of relationships. As Robert Levering points out, the types of relationships facilitating positive work trust are often contrary to relationships in the general marketplace. He especially notes those developed in highly capitalistic cultures, corroborating the work of Prakash Sethi and Linda Sama (1998): highly competitive work situations may *detract* from an ethical workplace.

A dimension of employee trust is the perception that supervisors consider individual employees in their interpersonal relationships, corroborating earlier findings that employees desire supervisors supportive of their ethical concerns and willing to listen to feedback on the job. A continuing theme in literature on the workplace is the understanding among employees that their employment setting is of good quality, linking satisfaction of the job, work performance, and job commitment to employment (Lowe, 2000; Lowe and Schellenberg, 2001). Studies of high-performance work systems (Applebaum, *et al.*, 2000; Shortell, *et al.*, 1991; 1994) reveal that productivity is linked with good environments for work, among which trust is a key ingredient.

Trust is difficult to define and may be elusive to measurement. Trust is also the result of interactions over time; trust is not built in a day but rather emerges from the many interactions and conversations in which employers and employees engage over the duration of their work. Like retention, trust is an indicator of a good place to work for employees. Trust is also a value of which employees want their employers and organizations to be worthy. One of the ways in which trust can be built, is through conversations regarding ethically challenging situations emerging at work. Ethics committees and other similar structures for ethics enhance employee interactions and thereby enhance trust, extending to employees' trust in the organization. Such interactions around ethical issues may exhibit promise keeping, autonomy, and integrity. Trust also emerges from features of interpersonal interactions revealing principles evident in ethical relationships. Features which aid in building trust—justice as fairness, honesty, and respect—are foundational to ethics. Trust is thereby closely related to ethics in the organization and may be enhanced by deliberations regarding ethical concerns at work.

Dignity

Working with dignity connects with ethics through its synonym, self-respect. However, in contrast to a macro or organizational approach, self-respect or respect identified with dignity typically focuses on the micro or inter-personal relationships. Here, we want to explore the manner in which dignity influences the work environment and is linked with organizational ethics. Though studies of dignity do not directly employ ethics as a concept, we examine dignity as it relates to ethics.

Respect, which is a foundational ethical concept, needs to be exhibited throughout the employment system. Dignity as a dimension of respect is a long-sought and desirable component of work pervading much of workers' lives. Few workers, if any, desire a position without its related feature of dignity at work. As Hodson (2001) points out, workers seek dignity in their work lives: 'Working with dignity is a foundation for a fully realized life (xiii).' Or as also claimed, 'Dignity is essential for a life well lived, ...' (22). Through time and across the globe, workers in various settings seek workplaces where they experience dignity allowing them to feel good about their work, to contribute to their coworkers' relationships, and to encourage them in their productivity. Dignity is a measure of self-respect and respect is a fundamental ethical component. Respect is identified in the Kantian (1964) imperative of treating persons as ends rather than as means, and is thereby important in the work setting. Examination of dignity finds relationships with coworkers, employee involvement, autonomy, and good management enhances and safeguards dignity. In contrast, abuse at work, overwork, mismanagement, and lack of involvement all constrain dignity in work. As Hodson (2001) claims, and as supported in this work, the majority of workers want dignity and the majority of workers desire an ethical place in which to work, respectively. The two constructs of dignity and respect complement one another and are exhibited in desirable and ethical workplaces.

Conclusion

Research regarding positive ethical environments reveals where employees perceive the environment as ethical, there is strong retention corroborated by employees who enjoy their work; they report having a supervisor supporting them in their work, as well as access to and structures for conversations about ethically troubling concerns. These behaviors allow workers to experience involvement and influence regarding their work and ethical decisions affecting employment. Employees desire ethical policies and procedures implemented in a just and consistent manner. Similarly, employees seek sites providing them with ethical guidance and exhibiting open and honest communication. Examination of research on related dimensions of ethical work reveal that meaning and quality in work, diversity, trust, and dignity are also desirable work features. These last features are suggested to link with ethics through related studies, thereby influencing employees, their organizations and communities, in positive ways.

Without pressing the parallels too far, if diversity is appreciated and affirmed at work then the culture is reported as positive and workers feel respected; diversity is thereby linked to ethics (Brown, 1998:248-9). In workplaces where supervisors support their employees, one also anticipates a perception of trust; honesty prevails. Likewise, when employees have access to structures so they may address and potentially resolve ethically challenging work situations, there is an enhanced sense of control and ability to manage conflicts; attitudes toward employees are not dismissive. These aspects of the work setting also occur among employees in well-led and managed health care units and are settings in which employees perceive themselves to be more productive (Shortell, *et. al.*, 1991). Granted, studies do not link all of these various features in one comprehensive research project; however, the elements of an ethically positive work situation appear to be present in related examinations of productive working environments. Findings from research projects suggest that among features in the employment situation, one essential feature of a desirable and productive workplace is ethics.

Assessing quality work continues, implying a multidisciplinary and holistic approach is fruitful for further research. Managers and other leaders in systems can alter the work setting thereby improving the work sites of employees. Consideration also needs to recognize the fast-paced and ever-changing work environment of contemporary organizations. These realities influence the ability to garner time and resources for ethics deliberations at work. Of necessity, decision makers also need to respond to pressures occurring both internally and externally in organizations. Macro concerns to leaders representing features external to organizations are highlighted in a Canadian study of employees: they include political pressures to eliminate deficits and cut costs, labor supply and demand imbalance, and population-workforce ageing (Koehoorn, *et al.*, 2002:4). These factors, too, influence the organization and the choices leaders make. Indeed, leaders in business and health care organizations can alter the workplace for employees, thereby developing and enhancing features employees seek. These features enhance the ethical environment and add to perceptions among employees that they work in an ethical and desirable context. Ethics at work and employees' desires follows in our next discussion. If we ask what is the current status and measure for ethics, examined in Chapter One, what are the relevant issues, examined in Chapter Two and Three, and what are the components decision makers can alter also reflecting desirable workplaces, examined here in Chapter Four, then we are positioned to begin the process of creating (more) ethical environments. How we proceed toward ethics, strategies used to address ethics, application of ethics, and the central leadership roles are the foci of the second part of this work.

Notes

1   We recognize employees working for hire are in situations serving as means to ends, including also their end of financial stability. However, in keeping with the Kantian imperative, we strive for employment situations in which the means are balanced with the ends and respect and other ethical concerns are evidenced in the workplace.

2   Research is reported in summary manner for the reader. Details of statistical analyses, methodology, and procedures may be found in referenced studies.

3   For a fuller discussion of work groups and needs, see: Clayton Alderfer (1972:45).

References

Agich, G., and Youngner, S. (1991). For experts only: Access to hospital ethics committees. *Hastings Center Report 21*:17-25.

Alderfer, C. P. (1972). *Existence, relatedness, and growth: Human needs and organizational settings.* New York, NY: The Free Press.

Applebaum, E., Baily, T., Berg, M., and Kalleberg, A. (2000). *Manufacturing advantage: Why high-performance work systems pay off.* Ithaca, NY: Cornell University Press.

Argyris, C. (1964). *Integrating the individual and the organization.* New York, NY: John Wiley and Sons, Inc.

Argyris, C. (1962). *Interpersonal competence and organizational effectiveness.* Homewood, IL: Dorsey Press.

Baumeister, R., and Leary, M. (1995). The need to belong: Desire for interpersonal attachments as a fundamental human motivation. *Psychological Bulletin 117*(3):497 ff.

Brown, M. T. (1998). Concepts and experience of the 'Valuing Diversity and Ethics' workshops at Levi Strauss and Company. In B. N. Kumar and H. Steinmann (Eds.), *Ethics in international management* (pp. 243-257). Berlin, GR: Walter de Gruyter.

Cohen, R. I. (1986). *Justice: Views from the social sciences.* New York, NY: Plenum Press.

Conference Board. (1994). *Business ethics: Generating trust in the 1990s and beyond* (Report #1057-94-CH; S. J. Garone, Ed.). New York, NY: Author.

Conference Board. (1992). *Corporate ethics: Developing new standards for accountability.* New York, NY: Author, p. 8.

Fortune Magazine (2002). Listing of best companies in U.S. *Fortune 154(2):*111.

Hackman, J. R. (Ed.). (1990). *Groups that work (and those that don't).* San Francisco, CA: Jossey-Bass Publishers.

Harter, J. K., Schmidt, F. L., and Keyes, C. L. M. (2003). Well-being in the workplace and its relationship to business outcomes: A review of the Gallup Studies. In C. L. M. Keyes and J. Haidt (Eds.), *Flourishing.* Washington, DC: American Psychological Association.

Hodson, R. (2001). *Dignity at work.* Cambridge, UK: Cambridge University Press.

Joint Commission on Accreditation of Healthcare Organizations. (1994). *Accreditation Manual.* Oakbrook Terrace, IL: Author.

Kant, I. (1964). *Groundwork of the metaphysic of morals* (H. J. Paton, Trans.). New York, NY: Harper and Row (Original work published 1785).

Koehoorn, M., Lowe, G. S., Rondeau, K. V., Schellenberg, G., and Wagar, T. H. (2002). Creating high-quality health workplaces. *Canadian Policy Research Networks' Discussion Paper No.*W/14. Ottawa, CA: Canadian Policy Research Networks.

Levering, R. T. (2000). *A great place to work: What makes some employers so good (and some so bad).* San Francisco, CA: Great Place to Work Institute, Inc.

Lowe, G. (2000). *The quality of work: A people-centered agenda.* Toronto, CA: Oxford University Press.

Lowe, G., and Schellenberg, G. (2001). *What's a good job? The importance of employment relationships.* Canadian Policy Research Network (CPRN) Study W-05. Ottawa, CA: Canadian Policy Research Networks.

McDaniel, C. (1995). Organizational culture, ethics work satisfaction. *Journal of Nursing Administration 23*(11):15-21.

McDaniel, C. (1998b). Hospital ethics committees and nurses' participation. *Journal of Nursing Administration 28*(9):47-51.

McDaniel, C. (1998c). Ethical environment: Reports of practicing nurses. *Nursing Clinics of North America 33*(2):363-373.

McDaniel, C. (1999). Clergy contributions to healthcare ethics committees. *HEC Forum* 11(2):140-154.

McDaniel, C., and Schoeps, N. (2003a). Ethics in corporations: Employee position and organizational ethics. In process.

McDaniel, C., and Schoeps, N. (2003b). Physician perception of ethical environments: Study of Finnish health care providers. In process.

McDaniel, C., Schoeps, N., and Lincourt, J. (2001). Organizational ethics: Perceptions of employees by gender. *Journal of Business Ethics* 33(3):245-256.

Robinson, S. L., and Greenberg, J. (1998). Employees behaving badly: Dimensions, determinants and dilemmas in the study of workplace deviance. In C. L. Cooper and D. M. Rousseau (Eds.), *Trends in organizational behavior* (Vol. 5, pp. 1-30). New York, NY: John Wiley and Sons, Ltd.

Roethlisberger, F., and Dickson, W. J. (1939). *Management and the worker*. Cambridge, MA: Harvard University Press.

Schein, E. H. (1992). *Organizational culture and leadership*. San Francisco, CA: Jossey-Bass Publishers.

Sethi, S., and Sama, L. M. (1998). The competitive context of ethical decision-making in business. In B. N. Kumar and H. Steinmann (Eds.), *Ethics in international management* (pp. 65-84). Berlin, GR: Walter de Gruyter Publishers.

Shortell, S., Zimmerman, J. Rousseau, D. M., Gilles, R., Wagner, D., Draper, E., Knaus, W., and Duffy, J. (1994). The performance of intensive care units: Does good management make a difference? *Medical Care* 32(5):508-525.

Shortell, S., Rousseau, D., Gillies, R., Devers, K., and Simons, T. (1991). Organizational assessment in ICUs. *Medical Care* 29(8):709-720.

PART II
APPLYING
ORGANIZATIONAL ETHICS

Chapter Five

Assessing for Ethical Environments

Introduction

In this second part of the book, emphasis shifts from theoretical explorations to application of ethics, turning our attention to the implementation of steps to achieve the ethical organization. The following three chapters focus on the three-part process of moving the organization toward an ethical environment: assessing, developing, and sustaining. Chapter Five gives special attention to analysis, with strategies and methods to achieve organizational ethics.

Why are we conducting an evaluation? What is the purpose? What would CEOs expect to achieve through an ethics evaluation? Why focus attention on appraisal of the organization, especially when resources are typically constrained? We have established in Part One the importance of an ethical organization, and we have explored conceptual issues relevant to achieving this aim. The conceptual issues explored in the first part on organizational ethics address the questions of what to measure and relevant issues to consider regarding measurement, relationships between individual and corporate regarding ethics, instilling ethics among employees, and, ethically, what employees desire. We examined organizations as corporate entities with particular responsibilities for ethics and employees as individuals with unique responsibilities for their ethical roles in their employment situations. What we have not explored are the practical dimensions to achieve the ethical organization; we have not, yet, discussed the application of ethics. Without the first and essential step of evaluation, other steps remain ambiguous.

Evaluations serve several purposes. An assessment forms the basis for future decisions and highlights what this author terms the *ethics path*. Other steps follow and build upon it, also focusing appropriate next steps resulting in an ethical organization. The evaluation provides a decision base and further establishes the importance of evaluation to create ethical organizations. Quality evaluation describes the extant situation and provides information for further analyses or actions. It provides leaders with information about positive and negative aspects of the corporation pertaining to ethics. In addition to a description, it indicates areas in the firm requiring attention and those features already serving positively in the organization; the latter serve as exemplars for the former. All organizations contain some ethical activities; thus, evaluations also indicate activities achieved and those yet to be achieved.

If CEOs desire to create an atmosphere in which more ethical behavior is supported among their employees, and if the initiative implies use of financial and personnel resources, it is safe to assume CEOs want to know if intended changes work. Questions typically raised by CEOs might include the following: How are we doing in our firm? Did the ethics program positively influence employees and their behavior? Is the ethics program worth the effort? On the other hand, questions should not be asked or raised unless top management is willing to follow though and address the results of the assessment. To come full circle regarding the importance of evaluation, if top management is *un*interested in such outcomes, a wise ethics director questions management's investment and thereby the legitimacy of the ethics program. Creating an ethics ethos relies on evaluative information to make rational decisions and answer questions about goal attainment.

Altering an organization to become more ethical also implies a plan. It involves rational and intentional work. This chapter suggests an organization desiring to instill ethics in its setting is, indeed, embarking on a *program* of organizational ethics. Therefore, in addition to exploring the potential for assessing the ethical environment, it also implies evaluation of an ethics program, the second type of evaluation explored in this chapter. The questions remaining, then, are the central considerations for ethics evaluation and how and what to assess.

Another point relevant to this chapter is the distinction drawn between audit and program evaluation. Given the earlier assertion that audit, appraisement, assessment, or evaluation would be treated synonymously, of those terms, audit potentially has a more specific connotation. It may reference a one-time, stand-alone assessment in contrast to a continuous appraisal often connoted by the term evaluation. While the use remains, it is important to draw a distinction between audit as one-time evaluation and program evaluation. Further elucidation of these distinctions will be drawn below, but to avoid any confusion the point of distinction is noted.

The discussion on ethics assessing begins with expansion of an underlying assumption of this book, the need for evaluation in ethics demonstrating ethicality. Building upon the points raised in Part One, we move now to explore several considerations for conducting an ethical evaluation for ethics, whether for an ethics audit or for a program evaluation.

Ethical Considerations in Ethics Evaluations

Since the aim of assessment is to enhance the work of ethics, assessment of any ethics endeavor needs to illustrate ethics by its processes and methods; we begin with considerations for the assessment process. Ethical processes are relevant to initial assessment and program evaluation and should be complementary to the assessment culture of the organization.[1] The ethics evaluation serves as an illustration or reference for ethics, an *ethics referent*, reflecting ethical processes and procedures; the ethics evaluation becomes a model of ethics in the organization. Because ethics evaluation needs to demonstrate ethics, it is important to explore several issues pertinent to conducting an ethical assessment, but especially critical for the assessment of an ethics program. Rather than suggest these considerations are *un*important to evaluations generally, we suggest the considerations have particular centrality in conversations about ethics. Attending to them enhances the assessment quality from the perspective of process and outcome. Four considerations catch our attention as we explore ways to retain ethical processes in the ethical evaluations: utilization, confidentiality, participation, and effectiveness. A case serves to capture several of these concepts.

Margaret Petersen was hired as a consultant to aid in the development of a hospital's ethics code, a task assigned by the hospital administrator. A survey provided a baseline audit to identify needed areas for in-service education and clinical rounds for physicians and nurses. A written agreement included, among other items, confidentiality for individuals whereas clinical units could be identified for follow-up or intervention. Following the data analysis, one in which several clinical units received low ratings by employees, Margaret received a visit; the visitor wanted to know '…who are these [low-rated] clinical directors as we need to deal with them.' Margaret refused politely to reveal their identities referring to the central aim.

Utilization

The first consideration in assessment pertains to utilization of the information obtained: the intended use.[2] Utilization coheres on the purpose of the specific type of evaluation. The primary use is typically for organizational improvement. If employees provide candid assessments, they want to know what will be done with evaluation results (Kraut, 1996:5), that data are used appropriately. Will respondents, for example, be demoted or fired if results are not positive? What would a negative outcome imply or signify for them? A major concern is that employees will not experience retaliation from coworkers or supervisors. Retaliation is seldom identified in settings with a constructive ethical ethos. Thus clarity about use is essential for a quality evaluation.

Utilization also influences the resulting information quality and takes on different meanings for employees. Developing an ethics code as the case above proposes is not the same as demoting or firing a clinical care director. Likewise, use for program revision is significantly different from promotion or termination of employees. Utilization also links to the issue of client focus examined in Chapter One. If personnel know the results will be used to enhance care—or improve business practices—rather than to affect their employment or punish them, then a higher degree of cooperation is possible (Harrison, 1994:123; Shirom and Harrison, 1995). Utilization normally is for internal service to the organization and typically for organizational improvement. Seldom is an evaluation used for comparison among employees or similar organizations.

Furthermore, utilization of the information needs to be made explicit to employees prior to requesting their participation. Once made, the mandate cannot be ethically changed as the consultant, Margaret, reiterates. It is possible resulting data may suggest an additional *un*anticipated use within organizations; however, any change must be conveyed to the employees with clear explanations. An evaluator, either external or internal to the firm, who breaches this procedure, runs the risk of adversely affecting the participation rate and validity of *future* assessments within the firm. It is therefore essential that intended and stated use of the assessment be conveyed to and retained for employees.

Confidentiality

Second among the central issues is confidentiality of which two dimensions are relevant to our discussion. The first dimension of confidentiality is protection of employees and their rights. Employees asked to participate in an assessment need to know the parameters surrounding the nature of their participation. These issues involve confidentiality. Evaluators need to remember the distinction between confidential and anonymous data. Confidential data may be traced to respondents, but evaluators, keeping confidences, do not reveal any link between respondents and respondents' replies. Anonymous data lacking any personal identifiers, on the other hand, *cannot* be traced to respondents.[3] Development of a process in which employee participants know the material is handled in a manner protecting their rights is an essential first step. Confidentiality exemplifies an ethical ethos and reflects the consistency important to ethical conduct of an evaluation. Also conveyed are the respect and fairness sought in ethical organizations.

Whether the assessment is a baseline evaluation or a program evaluation, standards exist for assessments with employees. The Joint Commission for Educational Evaluation (1994) designed evaluative standards following upon the General Accounting Office's (Comptroller General) 1988 U.S. standards. Both sets provide standards for assessors. A director of ethics who conducts an evaluation comes under these guidelines. Central to these guides is the mandate that any assessment must protect employees' rights to privacy and confidentiality. Even though the employing site may claim rights to information and expect full participation among employees, the parameters surrounding the nature of collected information need to be articulated for any employee participant. If an evaluator wishes to cite a comment or anecdote of a particular employee, written permission is needed, just as with research and informed consent. Depending on the sensitivity of the requested data, the informed consent is tailored to the evaluation to protect employees. Assessment within an organization begins with a clear understanding of the national and site-specific requirements for protection of employees, including confidentiality.

In addition to employee protection, the second dimension surrounding confidentiality among respondents is attaining adequate response rates and ensuring quality results. Addressing confidentiality enhances the information quality. What one does not want are returned data or inaccurate employee comments. There are reports of employees who provide inaccurate data or partial information when completing questionnaires or participating in interviews to protect themselves and their jobs. To be useful, data need to be accurate depictions of the actual situations and employee behaviors; less-than-candid assessments compromise results. Such assessments thus lack validity and will not aid decision makers in moving forward on the ethical challenges facing the organization. These assessments are in many ways less helpful than not obtaining information at all. It cannot be stressed enough that an atmosphere in which employees know the data are treated confidentially is essential to quality evaluation processes and outcomes.

An important question regarding confidentiality and employee rights concerns who will see the responses and thereby potentially influence employees' positions. This question is one of several concerns employees have and connects back to utilization. If an employee is candid about his/her supervisor, will the supervisor see the results? If not, who will? Where are the data stored, how are they retrieved, and by whom? If there are misgivings among employees about divulgement, retaliation, or other adverse uses of their information, as explored in Chapter One regarding client focus, the quality of the results may be compromised. For these reasons, it requires evaluators to design a method regarding confidentiality in which employees are protected or allowed to limit participation. Attendant to the assessment method is conveying information to employees about the procedures for confidentiality. As the above case with Margaret illustrates, stated procedures also need to be consistent throughout the evaluation process.

Participation

The third dimension for assessment concerns employee participation. Can employees refuse to participate? Is full employee participation essential to a quality assessment? Employees have rights within their employing firm; therefore, participation needs to be carefully considered prior to initiating the appraisement. Participation is directly linked to the use and confidentiality just explored; it also relates to the tone or culture in the organization regarding appraisement. Imperative to explore is the influence upon employees' jobs if they wish to limit involvement or not participate. If employees have a high degree of trust in the organization, it is anticipated voluntary participation will be forthcoming. When an employer requires employees to participate, however, the participation mandate needs to be balanced with potential gain and loss. Will the replies be as reliable as when employees participate voluntarily?

Participation always presents benefits and risks to be balanced. A typical benefit of *required* participation is ensuring an adequate response rate to obtain a full representation of all the issues germane to the evaluation, for instance, attitudes or opinions about ethics at work. If participation is required, one assumes the assessment occurs on work time and on-site. Given layoffs, turnovers, and gaps in personnel, it is tempting to have employees participate in off-work time. Employees want to know they are not means to an end but are instead valued as part of the endeavor, ends in themselves (Hultman and Gellerman, 2002:166). Employees desire respect. Giving employees time to participate in work-related functions demonstrates such respect and is consistent with the desired work atmosphere. Providing employees time to engage in evaluation on the job demonstrates the development of an ethos valuing assessment as an integral part of quality services as explored more fully in Chapter Seven under feedback loop. Continuing evaluation facilitates an advancing quality organization. Involvement in evaluation is part of the professional ambience leaders create in the work site, developing a culture of evaluation in which it is expected employees participate and participate well. On-site completion also allows evaluation administrators to control the time allotted for completion and may ensure a higher completion rate overall.

Participation that is required also incurs risks. An additional consideration for type of participation, either required or voluntary, is the quality of the results. Validity may be adversely affected if employees are required to reply. Invalid results may emanate from data collected while employees are off-work and disgruntled or angry about the requirement to participate in the survey. Due to fear of retaliation or negative attitudes emanating from required participation, employees may limit their responses or alter them as a form of protection or retaliation. The response rate may be high while the data are potentially less valid and thereby less useful. Unfortunately, employers will not know if compulsory replies are accurate reflections of the employees' 'true' perceptions, opinions, or attitudes and may make decisions on these less-than-accurate data. While it is always possible employees engaging in any assessment will alter their responses, they appear to do so *less* frequently in voluntary and well-designed situations. Leaders in health care and business, where critical decisions regarding patient care and business transactions follow from the results, cannot afford to allow workers to participate in required but off-time assessment or in assessments that in other ways might compromise the results when the outcomes are related to critical health care and business considerations.

Participation that is *voluntary* also has benefits and risks. The common benefit of voluntary participation is the assumption that employees participate with greater commitment and higher quality than with required participation. Volunteer response allows employees to control involvement in the evaluation in relationship to their level of comfort and investment. In contrast, the risk of an all-volunteer participation is employees may not participate thereby potentially rendering a low response rate. Equally important for consideration is that responses from volunteer participation may be less representative in comparison to a required but randomly selected survey attaining even representation of the variables of interest among employees. Balance between these two risks is critical since a high response rate of poor quality data is not fruitful either. There are pros and cons to each—required and voluntary—participation method. However, ethically it is essential to clarify with employees the issues posed prior to initiating participation.

One way to determine the participation method is to examine the substance of the questions. Highly sensitive questions lend themselves to a voluntary method whereas less sensitive ones may render good results even if required. Sensitive questions include items regarding religion, political opinions, sexual behavior or preference, opinions about supervisors or coworkers, and other similar items. Ethics is also considered a sensitive subject, especially when it involves *un*ethical or problematic behaviors of coworkers. In contrast, if the questions (merely) ask employees to rate their opinions regarding the format of an ethics seminar or level of satisfaction with in-service instruction, these questions clearly render less sensitive information and are minimally influenced by required responses.

Another ethical consideration with required use is retaining employees' identifiers to confirm their participation. Retaining identifiers further complicates the ethics evaluation. For these reasons, this author suggests that voluntary forms of participation—in most instances—are preferable to required procedures. Recognizing most researchers use voluntary participation in order to meet high standards for informed consent, employers need to balance carefully the information to be obtained and its proposed use prior to selecting the method of participation.

Employment situations have an additional and important consideration researchers may not. Employers and employees continue working relationships, involving all levels of positions: between supervisors and subordinates, and among continuing employees. The manner in which the evaluation is conducted, and the substance of the questions, contributes to the ethical ambience of these work relationships in organizations. Continuation of working relationships is a critical consideration for evaluation pertaining to questions and issues addressed, and the manner in which data are gathered.

Effectiveness

In addition to consideration of ethical parameters is the fourth dimension of effectiveness. Effective assessment is critical to determining the appropriate methods and design. It is germane to both baseline and program evaluations for ethics. Indeed, effectiveness is relevant to ethics as one may want to argue implementing a program evaluation that is ineffective or lacks feasibility is an *un*ethical use of valuable resources in today's organizations; personnel, time, and finances represent continuing scarce resources in business and health care.

Prior to setting up the initial assessment, considerations of effectiveness are worth attention to aid in enhancing the evaluation success. The following questions, adapted from Wholey, *et al.* (1994:15-39), enhance the possibility that top managers achieve their desired outcomes. These questions also apply to ensuing ethics assessments or evaluations of ethics programs, and are based on the aim of the evaluation. If any one of the points below is answered in the negative, then the assessor needs to consider a revision of the procedures. Can the evaluations

- answer the core question(s)?
- influence future decisions?
- conclude by a decision-appropriate time?
- offer results significant to justify assessment?

The importance of the evaluation and responses to the items above regarding effectiveness are determined by the anticipated ethics *outcome*. Outcome here implies a perceived need to enhance the organization's aims. If the desired outcome(s) of the ethics assessment cannot be linked to the mission of the organization, even indirectly, the ethics director needs to establish relevance prior to undertaking the appraisement. Value of the ethics assessment is consistent with the credibility and usefulness of the outcomes, and they rely in large measure upon the validity of the results. The more valid and thereby more useful data are for making decisions, the more value the ethics evaluation holds. Evaluation significance is integrally interrelated with the outcomes of assessment and their link to the organizational mission. They also link back to utilization, confidentiality, and participation of the respondent employees.

Another way to ask questions about the results is to ask whether the outcome justifies the effort, a modified form of benefit assessment and raising the question of significance. Significance, however, is one issue many ethics program managers ignore; because ethics is important, they assume the ethics work is significant. Questions of significance imply an assessment balancing the intended outcomes with the proposed costs affecting the effectiveness. In health care and business, a program to instill ethics is assumed to be of significance since care of patients and business transactions with customers imply respect, honesty and other ethical dimensions; however, balancing outcomes and costs are still important to the effectiveness of the assessment.

Because many health care organizations and businesses currently do not have a program in place that develops and sustains ethics in the setting, this is an opportune time to suggest that a quality ethics program design should be accompanied by an evaluation plan, including effectiveness. If, however, the persons setting up the assessment cannot design a program of ethics evaluation with clear outcomes, one questions effectiveness and feasibility of the endeavor. To make this point another way, an ethics program being initiated should have explicit outcomes; if the outcomes cannot be articulated and thereby measured, one may—from the beginning—raise a question about the program and its feasibility. Any ethics program should (be able to) be measured with some form of evaluation integrated into the outcome process, representing formative and summative dimensions of the program.

The following discussion begins with distinctions between ethics audits and program evaluations and their goals and quality. Examination of evaluation designs, personnel, data collection and analysis, along with considerations for ethical evaluations, combines audits and program evaluations since they are similar and pertain to both. We turn now to a discussion of audits and program evaluations and their conceptualization.

Conceptualizing the Evaluation

Conceptualization of ethics evaluation is important to its success. We differentiate between an audit and program evaluation. The distinction, to some extent, relies on the manner in which each is conceptualized. Realistically, one may use an audit as the first step for a program evaluation, or an audit may supplement the program assessment; an audit may also be used singly without further assessment. However, because of the nature of the audit compared to program evaluation and the manner in which both are conceptualized, they are differentiated.

To reiterate the purpose stated initially, the objective of an ethics assessment is to make decisions, to capture a picture of the organization, and to determine an appropriate focus for change. CEOs desire organizations to illustrate consistency throughout, which an assessment reveals. To accomplish this aim there are few single evaluation strategies resulting in a comprehensive ethics depiction, thereby suggesting evaluation designs may employ several approaches combined to gain a full profile of the current ethics situation. For that reason, we discuss several areas to consider in designing the evaluation so the evaluator obtains a full depiction of ethics within the entire firm. We begin the discussion with two central forms of evaluation, the audit, treated conceptually here as a one-time or stand-alone event, and program evaluation.

Ethics Audits

What is an audit? The term audit comes from the Latin word *audiere* meaning to hear or check, as in a formal checking of the finances; it typically refers to a financial audit. However, more recent application of the term audit has expanded to include a social audit (Blake, Frederick, and Myers, 1976), a compliance audit, and an ethics audit. An ethics audit implies a check or a review of ethics in an organization. While an audit connotes a one-time or stand-alone assessment this is not concomitant to an audit, whether for ethics or other domains.

Goal and use of ethics audits The typical purpose of an ethics audit is to determine the status of the target organization regarding its ethics, with the primary purpose being to improve the organization. The audit provides a 'check' on the organization's ethics. An audit reveals weaknesses and strengths, describes the current status of organizational ethics, or denotes indicators for future steps; it profiles the organization's ethics. It links to decisions. An ethics audit is commonly thought of as a comprehensive approach to the organization. Synovus in Columbus, Georgia, for instance, uses sequential evaluation which they conceptualize as a 'Three-sixty Assessment,' referring to the three hundred sixty degrees in a circle. The implication is a comprehensive assessment of their entire endeavor.

In addition, the audit conducted as a one-time comprehensive survey provides critical information to set priorities. It not only suggests the ethics path but also aids in highlighting priorities among several different routes to achieve the ethics objectives. Audits may also highlight discrepancies between real and desired behaviors. If the firm wants to instill ethics among employees as explored in Chapter Two, an audit indicates areas in which to initiate the plan or suggest strategies for achieving the goal. How extensive is the value reach in a firm? How do employees perceive ethics in their work settings? The common analogy is the financial or social audit conducted one time, once a year, or in tandem with a significant change or anticipated regulation in the organization. The Joint Commission on Accreditation of Healthcare Organizations in the U.S. has an assessment similar to an audit resulting in accreditation for health care systems. Federal Sentencing Guides conduct audits to check on the degree of compliance within a corporation.

Quality ethics audits   To serve the intended purposes of the ethics audit, those investing in the process want quality outcomes; the results need to be good. What are the criteria for a high quality audit of ethics? How would CEOs know if they had good audits? What are the indicators of an audit of excellence? Quality is not necessarily based on size or comprehensiveness of the audit; it pertains to goals of the assessment and results obtained in relationship to the goals. The following list offers examples of indicators of quality audits, but tailored to each situation and organization. Minimally, audits exhibit the following qualities:

- Relevance
- Replies to criterion question(s)
- Quality information obtained
- Ethical processes
- Being cost effective (the audit balances cost with information obtained)

In addition, it is important to obtain an understanding of the discrepancies between the desired and actual behaviors of employees, and between ethical policies and their implementation. Since an ethics audit aids in fact-finding or discerning actual ethical and unethical behaviors occurring in the organization, revealing discrepancies is another possible use.

Ethics Program Evaluation

In contrast to an ethics audit, ethics *program evaluation* refers to systematic assessment of the ethics initiative. A program is 'a set of resources and activities directed toward one or more common goals' (Newcomer, Hatry, and Wholey, 1994:3). The resources and activities are specific to each organization but focused on designated objectives. Such a program typically also has an identified administrator.

An ethics program comprises resources, both formal and informal, aimed at enhancing the organizational ethics, including those identified under the definition of program. Theoretically, all features and resources under the rubric of the ethics program link to the program aim and are therefore relevant to the evaluation of the program. Again, depending on conceptualization, an ethics audit may be one part of the program evaluation. For an ethics program, this resource-set may include the ethics director and other personnel, an ethics mission statement, brochures and the dissemination of information on ethics, actual ethics events such as lectures, in-service events, ethics rounds, ethics committees, participation of employees in ethics events, and evaluation of the work. Program evaluation assesses (all) formal dimensions of the ethics initiative. Ironically and ethically, an ethics appraisement should also assess the evaluation of ethics.

Since the focus thus far has been on development of an ethical organization, it would not be prudent to assume a formally developed ethics *program*. Likewise, it is important to recognize in some institutions there may be an ethics program whose administrator has not conducted foundational audits of the organization; both situations are probable. For these reasons, we focus now on the specific aspects of program evaluation.

If we understand what a program is, then the remaining question concerns what program evaluation is. Blaine Worthen and James Sanders (1973:129) state it is the 'process of delineating, obtaining, and providing useful information for assessing decision alternatives.' Another definition used by Kathryn E. Newcomer and her associates (1994:3) states a program evaluation is the '... systematic assessment of program results...' Where feasible, a program evaluation also systematically appraises whether the program causes the outcomes. Clearly, in this latter definition, the outcomes are essential to quality program evaluation. Likewise, the assessment is systematic.

Goals of program evaluation Goals are essential and integral to evaluations. Two types of goals are relevant to this discussion: goals of the *ethics program* and goals of the *evaluation*. Both are important to consider and differentiate as one begins ethics program evaluation, and are critical for effective evaluation. If the goal of the ethics program is to enhance employees' abilities in ethical analysis or improve employees' sensitivities for identifying ethical situations emerging at work, then the evaluation assesses how well the ethics program meets the goals in order to enhance the continuing performance of the ethics program. Is the ethics program successful in enhancing ethics abilities or improving sensitivities to ethical issues among employees, and if so, to what degree?

Essential for effective program evaluation is the second concern of determining desired evaluation (outcome) goals and attaining agreement regarding them. The major goal of program evaluation is to improve performance (Newcomer, Hatry, and Wholey, 1994:2). Agreed upon outcomes of the program are necessary for a quality assessment. Unless the director of the ethics program and the CEO, top managers and/or others who may initiate the program evaluation come to a modicum of agreement, the assessment may be futile. If the CEO has differing goals from the ethics program director, these divergent goals pose problematic disagreement on what constitutes program success. We explored the inherent challenges to the goal of 'enhancing persons ethically' in Chapter Two and the difficulty in meeting aims. Not only do divergent goals pose problems, an ethics program with divergent goals has greater potential for failure from the outset. Indeed, one might argue it is *un*ethical to assess employees on matters for which they are not prepared or on information not imparted to them. The point is agreement within the firm regarding the desired outcomes is necessary prior to designing the ethics program evaluation. Regardless of the ethics program goal, the aim of the program assessment is systematic appraisal of the program outcomes, and determination of the degree to which the ethics program creates those intended results.

Quality ethics program evaluation If an assessment provides the foundation upon which to build other steps, what does a quality program assessment involve? What are the essential components? The following are considered essential for quality program assessment, including attention to the criterion for systematic assessment:

- Goals for the outcome including proposed use and agreement
- Complete list of ethics program components
- Resources for implementation
- Systematic means of assessment (qualitative [*e.g.*, observations] or quantitative [*e.g.*, instruments])
- Clarity of real and potential conflicts of interest
- Key personnel to be involved
- Definition of the client focus and accountability
- Identification of the current culture for ethics, assessment, and change

The following case makes the point that the best of design plans may be problematic if the parts (above) are not planned into the product.

> The management team of a one-hundred-year-old family-owned concern hired Kari Karolainen. The wood and pulp mill company, situated in the middle of Finland, prided itself as an ethically run business, documented, in part, by a high retention rate among employees. Many employees had been with the company for their entire working life. The company's ethics code was also long-standing and a matter of company pride.
>
> When Karolainen arrived at the company, the leader of the management team asked to see him. Would he implement a new program of ethics, including a mode to determine pay raises and hire and release procedures? The manager added that, although few firings occurred in the firm, the team wanted to be proactive. The firm had also recently purchased two nearby mills, so parity was another issue to address.
>
> Eager to do a good job, Karolainen spent several days in his office drawing up plans and policies; he presented these to the management team. The team also included mid- and low-positioned personnel in the firm for some—but not all—discussions. He presented several approaches with accompanying policies to implement the desired ethics plan. The central authority for the decisions resided with the management leader.
>
> After this initial presentation, there was limited conversation; the team decided to table it to another meeting for a fuller discussion, scheduled for the following week. Prior to the meeting Karolainen was apprised of consternation about the new plan. It

became apparent the proposal did not have support of the team; in fact, most opposed it. Several mid-level managers disagreed with the goals. During the discussion, he tried to assess what the underlying issues were, as well as which parts, if any, of the plan were acceptable. In sum, the ethics plan did not meet with the approval of the management team and personnel representatives. The team was reluctant to embark on a new program, but the major objection was the designation of one person with authority to hire and fire. This Finnish-owned company operated as a community. The long-standing corporate culture suggested consensus on significant decisions. Many employees were concerned about the ethical parameters and longest-hired personnel. Had Karolainen conducted a more through assessment of the management team, culture, and feasibility of the new proposal, he would have recognized the family-type and community-oriented culture suggested a different mode for decisions.

Evaluation Personnel

This section discusses personnel for both ethics audits and program evaluations, primarily as similar areas of expertise are desired for both. Furthermore, it would be unlikely that an individual had expertise in one evaluation type with no experience or expertise in the other.

Persons who are hired to conduct the appraisal need to meet two primary criteria: expertise and experience. The theoretical issues explored in part one may serve as a quality guide for expertise in ethics evaluation. Evaluators need to have expertise coupled with experience in the conduct of a system-wide evaluation and knowledgeable about ethics. If an evaluator has extensive expertise in (program) evaluation but not in ethics, this disparity may pose a problem in deciding on the outcomes and assessment methods for an ethics program, including also the manner in which ethics is measured. Likewise, if persons with background in ethics are involved in the assessment, they may not have the expertise in evaluating programs; expertise in ethics *per se* does not guarantee expertise in evaluation, especially quantitative methodology. Therefore, a combination of personnel may be desirable. An oversight team can guide the assessment, a team on which experts in ethics, evaluation, and other relevant domains are represented. For that reason, personnel who direct the program and implement the assessment need to be in constant communication with one another, including other related departments such as risk management or human resource. The potential for slippage on this aspect of the assessment is enormous, resulting in either an invalid outcome or misuse of scarce resources and wasted financial outlay.

Obtaining expertise in evaluation *and* ethics may pose a challenge thereby suggesting a team of evaluators. However, top management needs persons who can conduct audits resulting in data addressing the central questions and retaining quality. While exceptions may be made contingent upon both the impetus for the audit and the particular individual, significant consideration needs to be given to personnel who conduct the ethics audit. The answer to the question aids in guiding decisions about who conducts the appraisal.

What personnel are needed and are appropriate to the program evaluation? Can company insiders find the inherent problems and risks? Driscoll and Hoffman

(2000:46) claim they probably cannot. The questions are, in part, contingent upon purposes of the evaluation. The answer to the questions may be influenced by two additional questions: (1) when in the life of the ethics program is the assessment occurring, and (2) what is the primary purpose? To address the former point, if the assessment under discussion represents the first time an ethics program has been evaluated, or if it is part of a formal and summative review, then serious consideration needs to be given to outside personnel conducting the review in order to avoid perceived or real conflicts of interest.

Likewise, if the purpose includes the possibility for major revisions, including termination or repositioning of personnel central to the program, an outside person is preferable. It would be impossible to avoid a conflict of interest in a program evaluation in which the key players—the director, manager, or others centrally associated with it—are privy to the assessment and also under employment review or program revision. It is possible the ethics personnel can aid in the formation of the assessment including allowing access to critical information. Personnel involved in the program would, however, have difficulty conducting an objective review if their positions—or the program in which they are invested—are vulnerable to the outcome(s). Therefore, in setting up the evaluation and determining the purpose, these two issues, timing and purpose, guide decisions about evaluators. One only needs to reflect on the global attention to Enron and Arthur Andersen to see the saliency of the point.

On the other hand, if the program assessment is one part of continuous reviews that program managers of excellence implement and data can be obtained in a manner protecting the confidentially of individuals, then an insider may be prudent. An illustration is continuing evaluation with feedback loops explored in Chapter Seven. Termed formative assessment, such reviews illustrate continuing assessment used for quality improvement. Obtaining information to retain excellence in a program, for decisions regarding revision, or for 'fine-tuning' of a program, is not just important; it is the responsibility of good managers. Contingent upon the purpose, however, decisions can be made on whether to employ an outside evaluator or use extant personnel. As an alternative, it may be wise to use a combination of both external and internal evaluators. The criterion question is whether quality data can be obtained to meet the purposes of the desired assessment. If positions or finances are to be determined by the results, the importance of planning well and planning in advance for the ethics program assessment cannot be stressed enough.

Designs for Ethics Evaluations

Designing evaluation for ethics assessment or an ethics program evaluation includes a number of choices and strategies. For the purposes of this discussion, we begin with potential design questions for ethics *assessments*, discussed under the respective headings below. The discussion is followed by designs for ethics *program evaluations* to encourage managers to address the various challenges often present in ethics programming. We begin, however, by distinguishing research from ethics assessment and program evaluation.

Research and Evaluation

As we consider various designs for ethics assessment and program evaluation, a question naturally arises about research. What is the difference between (what is conceptualized) as research and program evaluation? Is evaluation research? Is there a significant difference? Research focuses on testing a hypothesis or deriving future hypotheses. It may also, but not always, involve the testing of an intervention or theory and extrapolation of the findings to another audience or population. Ability to generalize to other populations is frequently an aim in research whereas in program evaluation it is rarely an aim. Finally, research may be removed from 'real-life' as illustrated by laboratory situations whereas program evaluation is always an assessment of extant situations, or work in the field as some say.

Program assessment aims to determine and/or enhance the quality of a specific program rather than raise concerns for other programs. This statement does not imply program evaluations are inapplicable to another site or population. Rather this description indicates the fundamental purposes of research and program evaluation are usually different: extrapolation from research is a common aim program assessment rarely shares.

Although we claim that research is not the primary focus of our discussion in this work, without seeming contradictory, ethics assessment or program evaluation nevertheless *may* be research. Depending on the approach the ethics evaluation takes, the questions raised, and the fundamental purpose, one could construe the assessment or program evaluation as a form of research. If hypotheses or theories were generated and tested as part of the program evaluation, then both research and assessment occur. To return to the point made earlier in this chapter, the criterion for methods relies on the conceptualization of the work. Indeed, a quality program evaluation may sustain a research initiative, as might an ethics audit. The latter could serve as a description of an organization's ethics. However, for the purposes of this work, generally speaking one does not consider an ethics audit research nor would one typically consider a program evaluation a research project. We shall continue with this typical approach as we consider methods and designs. In that regard, the design of the assessment may also differ. Rather than an exhaustive listing of potential designs, the discussion below offers several useful designs for program evaluation for applied ethics.[4]

Evaluation Designs

Design selection is the critical first step following clarification of purpose, and a number of choices are available. One important criterion for ethics evaluation is that designs—including methods, personnel, and instruments—should not exceed the perceived cost-to-benefit ratio obtained by results. Design decisions and the balance between benefit-cost relate directly to the earlier discussion of evaluation effectiveness. If the data collection method, for instance, outweighs the final results proposed, the design should be revised. Design selection also depends on the purpose and extant ethics activities in the organization. If, for example, a hospital has a well-developed ethics initiative, then a program assessment may be more appropriate than an overall hospital audit. In all cases we (always) strive for ethical processes and quality data resulting in response to the questions raised.

Designing ethics audits One-time or stand-alone assessments are not encouraged here because we prefer audits incorporated into an overall program on ethics. Nevertheless, for many organizations, the audit *is* the ethics assessment and obtaining information relevant to the audit is still important. For that reason we give attention to several designs addressing the following questions: What is the current status of ethics in ReallyGood Company? How far reaching is ethics education extending in QualityCare Hospital? Do the employees perceive the culture of Making Products to be ethical (or not)? An ethics audit answers these questions. From them the design is developed. Once the questions (goals) are developed and agreed upon, the design is the next step.

Selection of evaluation designs matches the goals and central questions. The questions posed above could be addressed by surveys among all employees, or to contain costs, a representative sampling could be conducted. If a sample is used, it, too, needs to be developed with the central questions in mind; the recruitment and selection need to follow ethical parameters as well as robust sampling procedures. For instance, if there is concern in an organization the female employees may perceive their work setting differently than the males, or more pointedly, if there has been sexual harassment among females by males, then emphasis is given to attaining a good representation of females and males across all position levels and units in the firm. Good sampling procedures allow one to address central questions.

The design options for the questions posed above are fewer since the questions imply a description of either the entire employee population or a sampling of target dimensions representative of the employee population. In either case, the questions suggest a survey of employees; they also suggest a comprehensive approach. While there is some disagreement about what constitutes a representative sample, if a sampling of the relevant employee population is sought, a 25 per cent sample is considered adequate; it may range upwards from there. Additionally, as implied in the example above regarding males and females, if questions imply attention to specific groups in the employment site, perhaps new hires, to ensure a representative sample and response, the evaluators may need to employ a stratified sampling technique, where relevant groups are designated and from them the sample is attained. One would then group all males and all females, or all new hires, in distinct groups and sample (25 per cent) from each group. This may result in an over sampling among some but ensures adequate representation of the relevant variables of interest.

Expansion upon the above examples is provided. For instance, in a mail survey among all employees, respondents complete the respective forms and return them by mail to a designated site. As discussed under confidentiality and participation, consideration here needs to be given to an off-site return location in order to enhance the response rate. On-line surveys may be developed using the same questions (obtaining copyright permission if purchased) but providing access to all or a sample of employees via electronic avenues. This method reduces costs of mailing and typically allows what is termed a 24-7 response. As with mail surveys, on-line completion dates are needed.

In addition to surveys and contingent on the critical questions to be addressed, follow-up interviews may be conducted to supplement the information obtained on written surveys. The survey is attractive as it allows the evaluator to obtain a relatively broad data-set in a relatively cost-effective procedure. Interviews, while typically more expensive, allow expansion or refinement on survey replies, offering rich narrative information for assessors.

Interviews are commonly developed to follow-up survey responses or expand on comments. A relevant sample of employees may be developed based on survey responses. Evaluators may use interviews to enable employees to expand more than is realistic in writing and so additional questions may be employed as responses. As with the discussion of personnel for conduct of the interviews, consideration clearly needs to be given to interviewers who retain objectivity and confidentiality. Taping of the conversations typically accompanies these interviews. Interviews rendering qualitative data can be assessed with programs developed for qualitative analysis (see below). Interviews may be structured with pre-set questions to which employees respond, semi-structured in which a lead question is provided with relatively open space for response, or open-ended in which the interviewer prompts the employees but remains otherwise noncommittal in the exchanges. Interviews may be combined with surveys, and they may be conducted with individuals or employee groupings.

Participation among employees in group interviews or focus-group formats raises additional considerations for evaluators. Consideration needs to ensure supervisors do not participate with subordinates. It is assumed supervisors present in a group with subordinates would intimidate full and valid responses on the part of the subordinates, and perhaps by supervisors. Likewise, careful selection of group participants attends to confidentiality and the substance of questions raised in the group. Highly sensitive subjects may best be explored with individual interviews. However, careful attention needs to be given to assignment of employees who participate in group interviews.

Designing ethics program evaluation   Below is a listing of issues related to program evaluation. A caveat is added that many a wise director ignores the third point in determining feasibility for evaluation: employees' participation time.

- Goals and purposes; extent of any ethics program involvement
- Personnel for design, contact, communication, and travel
- Participation time of employee respondents (*e.g.*, time from work)

- Supplies in questionnaires, cases, examples, or other paper sources
- Data entry and analysis
- Report writing to completion
- Possible political or public relations issues emerging, both positive and negative

Decisions about design for ethics program evaluation pertain to the importance of the outcomes and the desired control over the results, balanced by access and realistic aspects of the situation to be evaluated. In terms of access, for instance, evaluation of new operating room team procedures is different from assessing new distribution procedures for cars. Control is especially relevant in decisions of a substantive nature such as employee termination, program funding, or education for crucial health care services. Control also pertains to questions of causality. The more significant the decision outcomes, the greater the need for design control in order to assign causality. Design decisions also pertain to the aims of the program, type of data potentially collected, and time and resources allocated to programs and their assessment. The degree of control and thereby resulting data also parallel those designs; they will be examined along those parameters. However, experts in program evaluation argue a good design ensures the potential benefits outweigh the costs (Newcomer, Hatry, and Wholey, 1994:9).

In setting up a design for program evaluation, there are three primary types to consider, discussed briefly below. The discussion highlights considerations for making design decisions and outlines ethical considerations inherent to them. Decision-makers and other leaders could form a decision about ethics program evaluation design based on this discussion.

Non-experimental designs Non-experimental designs are useful for continuous assessment of programs where control over participation is limited. These designs are termed non-experimental because there is no intervention—here denoting an ethics session or event, for instance—introduced in the assessment. Implied by the design is the idea that the entire ethics program is being assessed since no specific intervention is introduced. These designs provide less robust data than the stronger experimental designs (below), in which stronger arguments emerge that the program caused the outcomes measured. Non-experimental designs, however, provide continuing formative useful information. They are often less expensive and can be repeated over time, which segues to two sub-types of non-experimental designs, the repeat measure design, below, and outcome monitoring, both of which are used by program assessors.

Repeat measure designs One form of non-experimental design is repeat measure. As indicated by the design name, the same measurement is repeated a number of instances and over time; the measure itself becomes a form of control. In these designs, one is examining for change in outcome over time using the base measure as a comparison to the ensuing future ones. Either improvement in measure or consistency of measure is anticipated in repeat measure designs. It is important, however, for purposes of comparison that the *same* measures and procedures are used in the repetition assessment. An example of this design might be an ethics in-service education program offered a number of times in an organization for which the same standard survey is used to assess the quality of instruction for each and every offering.

Outcome monitoring To be termed *monitoring of outcomes*, the second sub-type of non-experimental design, the evaluation should obtain information that contains measures of end results; the focus is on the outcomes (results). Several frequently used assessments employ routine measures with central indicators of results reported (Affholter, 1994:96). These systematic reports are typically done in a manner the average 'stakeholder' can understand but with notations providing valid meaning. An example of outcome monitoring might be assessment of the ethics education participants' increased sensitivity to ethical issues at work, using the same method but focusing on the results of the ethics education. One advantage of this form of assessment is relatively quick revision based on sound information—program correction is efficient. It is a form of continuous quality improvement. Again, for purposes of comparison the same measures and procedures are used for each of the assessments.

Quasi-experimental or natural 'experiment' designs The second category of design falls between the less robust but useful non-experimental and the stronger experimental designs.[5] The commonality with non-experimental designs is the assessor has little or limited control over either the intervention or the assignment of participants to the situations, thereby relying on events occurring naturally. The advantage of using natural, commonly occurring events is the ability to contain costs by use of extant situations, and reducing the expense of planned interventions. To obtain a comparison, the design makes optimum use of controls occurring (naturally) in the situation. A relevant example might be the teaching of ethics to physicians on a surgical clinical service compared to physicians on medical services, since both populations are physicians but in different clinical services. Regardless of the population, the design needs to include a comparison in order to assess the aspect desired for measurement. While these designs may appear simpler than the designs with higher degrees of control, in fact these designs require a level of sophistication to ensure useful results without evident and planned or non-naturally occurring controls. The design requires careful thought to attain comparable control groups, yet ones occurring naturally within the situation.

Pre-test post-test control group designs The third design category offers the most robust control and consequently the strongest assessment. Typically termed a *control* or an *experimental control design,* the form is one of the most robust designs used and responds to the question of causality. A classic design identified by Campbell and Stanley (1963:13) provides a strong and valid data-set if conducted well. Briefly, as noted in Figure 5.1, these designs use at least two groups for comparison. More groups may be used; however, among the several groups at least *one* must serve as a control and intervention group, each. Ideally, the group members are *randomly* selected from among potential participants. Assignment of groups through a random selection or similarly strong assignment method is a major component of the pre-test and post-test with control group design, adding to the strength of the plan and its ensuing results. As noted in Figure 5.1, the two (or more) groups are designed to be equal in all ways relevant to the assessment. A director assessing the effect of an ethics seminar—as one part of the ethics program—on attendees wants comparable control groups, for instance, with equal proportions of relevant characteristics represented in all the groups: males and females, short- and long-term employees, those with prior ethics education and those without, to illustrate several relevant variables.

$$RO1 \qquad X \qquad O2$$
$$RO3 \qquad \qquad O4$$

Figure 5.1 Pre-test Post-test Control Group Design*

*Campbell, Donald T., and Stanley, Julian C., *Experimental and Quasi-Experimental Designs for Research:*13. Copyright © 1963 Houghton Mifflin Company. Used with permission.

Once the groups are determined with participants assigned to either an experimental (RO1) or control (RO3) group(s), the (same) pre-testing is conducted for both. Note the results of the initial measure need to be analyzed prior to moving forward with the intervention, because if the initial results differ significantly, adjustments need to be made in the groups (*i.e.*, O1, O3). The intervention (X)— for example, an ethics seminar—is introduced to one (all if more than one is used) of the experimental groups (but not controls), and then the (same) post-test is administered to all groups (O2, O4). What one is anticipating is the ethics seminar—here the X intervention—positively influences the seminar attendees, illustrated by a better outcome among those group participants (O2) than the non-seminar (control) respondents (O4). If the groups are, indeed, similar in initial assignment (*i.e.*, O1, O3 are equal), then theoretically the only difference between participants in all groups is the ethics seminar serving as the intervention. Finally, if the post-test results or outcome scores differ significantly between the experimental (O2) and control groups (O4), the assumption is the intervention (X) caused this difference between groups.[6] One would then conclude the ethics seminar created or caused the result among the participants.

As stated above, the assessor prefers a positive change in the designed results; however, ethically, it is always prudent to remember outcomes may reflect no change (a null result) or the intervention may make things worse (a negative outcome). While the latter two outcomes are undesirable, all results are reported. Ethical parameters surround program evaluation as well as research; data remain unchanged, and outcomes are reported as revealed. The issue of ethics in evaluation also reemphasizes the importance of a robust evaluation process with good outcome measures.

Modifications of this pre-post test design do occur, since random assignment to groups or establishing a control group may be difficult, especially in the 'real world' of hospital services and business transactions. For these reasons alterations may include the following: pre-post test with non-equal groups, pre-post test with an immediate and time-framed post-test, and post-test only design, preferably using equal groups (Campbell and Stanley, 1963). Regardless of the design used, the one providing the highest degree of control is also the design more clearly answering the question: did the program create the outcomes desired? The most robust reply is provided by the third design, Figure 5.1 above. Design modifications of the pre-post test with comparison control group are thereby less robust than the original design but may be used when limits are posed on either the intervention or participant assignment. Modifications in design also need to be reported in final reports along with any other procedures.

From an ethical standpoint, the pressing question is how to assess an outcome or a program in a robust manner when the top management wants everyone to participate in the program. What would constitute a control group, ethically, if all employees should have the program? This issue is especially relevant in health care or business where a troubling event has occurred. One way to plan a pre-post test design with a valid and reliable assessment is to implement the pre- and post-test with a control group by offering the ethics program to a select portion of the employees. Use those not receiving the program as the control group, and then offer the ethics program to those constituting the original control group. Ultimately, in this revised plan all employees receive the ethics program; it is assessed in a robust manner. The author refers to this revision of the classic design a *phased* pre-post test with controls.[7] The caveat of time frame needs to be introduced, however. If the ethics program is highly desirable—even required—for all employees, then the time frame for full implementation with testing needs to be negotiated within that desired time span; the time is relevant to the particular seminar and facility. The challenge might be who constitutes the initial and control group since ideally the participants are randomly selected. Implementing a phased pre- and post-test with control group assessment is another way in which a strong design can be built into the program assessment.

Data Collection, Data Analysis, and Results

Following design selection, the second decision-set regards data collection followed by analysis of data; the two are addressed together in this section. Data collection also influences decisions regarding design. Under the category of data collection we explore two aspects: *procedures* used to collect information and *instruments* on which data are collected. Issues raised previously about participation and confidentiality are extremely relevant here as are questions of design. Regardless of the quality of the design, if the resulting data are not useful and psychometrically sound, the entire design is futile. For that reason the topic of criteria for determining an appropriate data collection procedure is introduced. The criteria pertain to any assessment, whether conceptualized as an audit or program evaluation. Data need to be of good quality, introducing the topic of qualities for useful information.

Critical features to consider include the following:

- Reliability
- Validity
- Adequate response rate
- Feasibility (the link to mission)
- Relevance

Reliability refers to whether the information is consistent and dependable, an assurance the same results will be obtained again, whereas validity refers to whether the instrument measures what it says it will measure.[8] Adequate response rates vary by definition and even by discipline, from the 'gold standard' used by several disciplines of a minimum of 70 per cent to acceptable mail survey responses of around 50 per cent.[9] Even if a response rate is relatively low, there are statistical procedures to implement and confirm fair representation of central variables across the employment.[10] Feasibility balances outcomes with costs; relevance links with the organizational aims. To be a relevant assessment, feasibility must be directly linked to the mission and key questions.

Types of data collection Collection of information in order to address the assessment purpose raises the question of data collection methodology or procedures. The methods selected depend on the purposes of the assessment and type of information desired. There are several collection procedures categorized commonly into two major types: collection based on observations and collection from interviews and questionnaires. We limit discussion to focus on those typical in application of ethics for health care organizations or business corporations. While it may vary, typically the two forms result in either *qualitative* information that can be assessed for content, themes, or patterns, or *quantitative* information that can be numerically manipulated and statistically assessed. Combining the two types to attain both quantitative and qualitative forms of data is also possible and adds strength to the overall assessment. There are sources for additional details on both methods, which are briefly explored here in order to guide decisions about the best procedures for ethics assessments. Below is a listing of examples of common methods of data collection divided into two categories.

- Observations
  Unstructured Observations
     Participant observation
     Records in extant form (historical)
     Anecdotes

Analysis of communication content
Ethics cases (see discussion below)
Semi-structured or Structured Observations
Checklist or forms provided
Focus Groups, may be used as interviews
• Interviews and Questionnaires
Questionnaires
Self-administered, paper or electronic questionnaires
Professionally administered questionnaires
Interviews
Structured interviews
Semi-structured interviews
Open-ended interviews

Observations provide a systematic assessment using previously determined criteria to observe and record behaviors of individuals or groups occurring naturally in the situation, or as some term it, *in situ* (Selltiz, *et al.*, 1976). As with other forms of analysis, observations too are subject to considerations of validity and reliability, linking directly back to the criterion for systematic observation and recording. The advantage of observational procedures for collecting data is that the observations are the actual occurrences compared to hypothetical or laboratory-based ones. Yet another form of data collection relevant to applied ethics might be discussions of relevant cases, to be analyzed regarding their ethical content or processes for decision-making, or observations of both the outcome and the processes participants use to arrive at a resolution. In these situations, cases pre-planned with anticipated outcomes are preferable. Cases for ethics, too, need to be tested for reliability and validity (See: Cases, p.123). In each type above, there are procedures to employ offering unbiased and valid information; experience in conducting observations is also a consideration and needs to conform to quality evaluation standards.

The decision regarding which of the types of observations to use depends on the questions or information desired, the level of expertise and experience required for each, and the situation in which the observations will be conducted; the degree of control is also a consideration, as noted under the discussion of design. For instance, participant observations require an objectively collected set of data on-site whereas reviews of extant records or anecdotes do not interfere with the on-going behaviors; employees' work may not be affected by or interrupted in the latter. Lastly, the degree of flexibility desired is also a consideration, as historical information from records has no flexibility, a checklist or previously determined form has moderate amounts, and the semi- or more unstructured observations offer the most flexibility. Consistency over time using the same methods is also important.

The second procedure for collecting data is through the use of interviews or questionnaires. Within this second type is a common form of data collection for use among employees: systematic surveys of employee participants. This is a commonly used approach when the aim is a comprehensive survey of the entire organization. A related decision is the use of all participants or a method of selecting out a representative sample. Another and increasingly popular form of data collection is focus-group interviews.

Examples of conducting surveys might include the development of several key and untested questions regarding employees' prior ethics education, their level of interest in content of proposed ethics seminars in their corporation, or information about the most frequently observed ethical problems in their particular clinical units. These questions are not formed as a 'scale' or questionnaire *per se* but do elicit useful information for an ethics director or CEO. The questions may also be combined with other questions, instruments, or sociodemographic forms.

A survey might also employ the use of a formally tested scale developed as a questionnaire. The survey is the procedure or methodology through which the questions reach the employees participants, whereas the questionnaire (or observation) is the method of actually eliciting the information. Combinations of observations, interviews, or questionnaire may also be employed, but those selected need to have established standards appropriate to the type of data collection method and form.

One of the challenges in ethics is obtaining an instrument or questionnaire addressing the desired ethics information that has established psychometric properties (especially in a valid and reliable manner). As examined in Chapter One, measurement poses challenges for ethics assessments, primarily due to the lack of valid and reliable measures. Although there are growing numbers of questionnaires emerging, typically an organization has its own assessment measures, or has hired an outside consultant or consulting firm to conduct an appraisement using their own instruments.

Lastly, a third procedure for data collection employs more than one type of method and type of data; combining qualitative and quantitative methods adds strength and depth to appraisements. Multi-method collection reaches a wider range of employees, some of whom may respond preferentially to one methodology or the other. A combined approach also aids in addressing the pluses and minuses of each single approach for qualitative or quantitative data. Thus combined approaches appeal to wider employee populations in terms of response preferences and thereby enhance the possibility of a fuller response. The selection decision relies finally, however, on the initial question and purpose, and second on feasibility: cost, personnel, and time.

Both qualitative and quantitative data are useful in baseline and program evaluations. The criterion for collecting a particular form of data is quality data addressing the desired questions, whether the data are quantitative or qualitative; quality is a continuing consideration for data collection. Pre-tested methods, procedures, and instruments are extremely useful and important and save evaluators significant costs compared to data obtained by untested or unreliable instruments. It is equally wise to select psychometrically tested and sound measures. Likewise, procedures and instruments used in *new* or *quite different* populations may need to be pilot-tested.

In addition to these common forms of data collection, ethics program managers may not recognize the many forms of data available to them in their specific work settings, implied under the first type of collection. Table 5.1, below, displays sample illustrations of extant data sources readily available for assessments, or as complements to evaluations for ethics programs. Several of these data forms are particularly useful for an audit in which comparison between desired and real behaviors is sought, documentation of change is desired, data are needed but difficult to obtain, or the ethics director has cost constraints. Most organizations collect data of many types on an ongoing basis, and it would not require extensive allocation of funds or personnel to gather them in useful formats. In that regard, they also address feasibility. Assessments, while essential, are not necessarily expensive.

Table 5.1 Examples of Extant Data Sources for Ethics Assessment Outcome.*

Desired Outcome	*Data and Source*
• Reduction in number of workers engaging in unethical behavior.	Monthly report of managers; match report with Human Resource and Risk Management data.
• Participation in Ethics Committee.	Member attendance and representation within the firm; number of sessions.
• Expansion of the Ethics Program.	Number of attendees; comparison to base ine; evaluation of sessions.
• Enhanced ability to assess ethically challenging situations.	Minutes of Ethics Committees; time in event deliberations (comparisons).
• Less theft at work. audits	Reports on profits; monthly manager data; of product.
• Enhanced sensitivity to ethical problems in the work setting.	Responses to cases; numbers of cases reported comparing pre-post test time.

*Assumes employees' rights previously addressed for use of materials.

In addition to naturally occurring sources of data, other considerations for relevant information include the following items, each of which provides important information to the results. Contingent upon the comprehensive nature of the plan, each aspect of the organization noted by items on the list in Table 5.1 offers additional information to evaluators. Likewise, evaluators assess not only the item but also the presence and absence of each of the following features.

• Mission statement

- Ethics code
- Product: outcome code
- Policies, Procedures: implementation; communication, employee use
- Employees' perceptions: questionnaires, interviews; written, online, telephone
- Discrepancy behaviors: adherence to policies and procedures
- What has been done to address ethics in the past, prior ethics education
- Stakeholders, board members and customers

Documentation may be complemented by a sociodemographic analysis allowing the evaluator to assess the degree and depth of the item of interest among various important employee groups: males and females, ethnic groups, new and long-term hires, and various positions within the firm. These may be comparatively assessed regarding their perceptions of ethics at work. The analyses allow evaluators to elaborate on special dimensions of ethics within the organization relevant to human resource departments or target areas of concern within a particular organization.

Cost is a relevant issue to consider, since data collection can be expensive. Important to consider are costs of employees' participation time determined, in part, by length of data collection and frequency. Another consideration is efficaciousness: the means to collect data should allow efficient entry of data. Computerized scan forms or collection via on-line surveys, for instance, can ease data collection while enhancing data entry, essentially with minimum error. Most health care and business institutions today have technology in place to support on-line or computerized data collection methods.

Analysis of data collected Analysis of the data parallels the type of data and the assessment aims. If, for instance, focus groups are used, then one assumes analysis of qualitative data obtained from interview notes or tapes. A popular form of analysis method for qualitative data is a program called ETHNOGRAPH, a computerized method of analyzing interview data. A simple means of doing content analysis of communication exchanges, another form of qualitative data, relies upon a 'concept' or 'word check' in a word processing program. Depending on the desired information, the latter may be readily employed and without extensive financial outlay. Other equally valid forms are also available.

In contrast, if the data are obtained on surveys and result in quantitative data, for instance, these data require analysis with relevant statistical methods. Examples of commonly used statistical data analysis programs include, for example, Statistical Package for the Social Sciences (SPSS), SPSS with AMOS, Statistical Analysis System (SAS) or SAS-X, and Bio-Medical Data Program (BMDP). If scan forms or other computer-friendly forms are not used, PARADOX is an accessible data-entry program. Again, organizations often have both programs and personnel on-site to assist with data analysis.

Implementation of the results Once data are obtained and the results analyzed, the focus moves to utilization of the results. This portion of the discussion follows on in Chapter Six, a development of the ethics initiative based on evaluation results. We turn to the issue of developing the program of ethics in order to create (more) ethical environments in the organization, based on the results of the baseline assessment or the program evaluation.

Special Case of Ethics Cases

Thus far, the discussion has explored considerations central to both the foundational and formal evaluation of an ethics program. However, since so much of ethics instruction in various settings and populations relies upon the use of ethics cases, especially in applied ethics, the discussion turns now to a brief exploration of cases: the special case of ethics cases.

As with other forms of assessment, ethics cases, too, represent benefits and losses in their application. Cases, real or hypothetical (or combinations of these), designed to approximate ethics challenges or situations for participants, are frequently used in applied ethics. A well-designed and written case can elicit responses from employees that are extremely comparable to what they would do in a similar real situation. Ethics cases, then, offer unique and useful tools for learning. Likewise, they can be useful for testing. It is for those reasons they are included here with special consideration.

Cases offer many positive dimensions to teaching and thereby to testing the learning of (applied) ethics. Positively, they simulate real ethics situations in which the proposed student, employee, or participate may engage. In this manner they offer an assessor or instructor a close approximation of what employees would do or how health care providers behave in similar situations. Cases may also be written to target or highlight certain ethics issues or specific complex and troubling ethical situations the leaders anticipate employees will encounter. Lastly, employing cases demonstrates the desired consistency between the aims of the program and the learning processes, which is critical analysis. For these reasons, the case has become a very popular tool for discussion and for application of ethics theory and decision making.

Cases also offer a negative side when used singly as a measurement tool raising ethical issues. The first is the amount of time cases take to prepare and to evaluate. Although there are ways to decrease this time investment, such as prepared replies complemented with on-line and computerized responses, overall, cases take more time than other forms of assessment such as surveys or similar objective assessments.

Second, because of their highly contextual nature, cases may be situation-specific; they potentially lack generalizability. Likewise, a case also may lack established qualities or tested standards thereby posing challenges when used as a source of measurement in real-life situations. Used singly, without complementary measures, they potentially pose risks and should be employed with caution. Depending on the desired outcome and use of the resulting information, however, a case may be extremely helpful. Ethically, nevertheless, evaluators need to be extremely cautious about drawing significant conclusions based on participants' analyses of cases, especially decisions based on the results of one or two cases. Employees are contextual in relationship to work, and without additional testing of cases the caveat is constraint in forming decisions based only on cases.

If, however, ethics cases or sets of cases are utilized, the instructor needs to take time to test the cases, compare results across several sociodemographic groups, and discern appropriate outcomes based on multi-analyses. Some instructors weight the critical analysis or the decision process more than the actual outcome of the case analysis, thereby emphasizing the typical aim of ethics education discussed in the first part of this book: critical analysis. Used in this manner, especially with accompanying information, ethics cases provide fruitful responses in the evaluation, for example, of ethics training, in-service education on ethics theories, or assessing employees' abilities to implement critical analysis on ethics. As a special case for ethics, however, ethics cases need the same thoughtful attention other forms of analysis require.[11]

Discussion of cases in applied ethics leads the discussion into consideration of the results of the ethics assessment. As with cases or any other forms of assessment, top management desires information that is useful, reliable, and valid, meeting the stated aims and aiding in enhancing the ethics of organization. These issues suggest the examination undertaken in Chapter Six on ethics development.

Notes

1   For fuller discussion of types of program evaluations, see, for example, D. Grembowski (2001). A modification termed ethicality program assessment (Wholey, *et al.*, 1994), adapted from mainstream program evaluation, focuses on ethical frameworks as articulated in this manuscript. Prior steps in the modification aid in ensuring an optimum outcome, including the following: (1) attention to agreement upon desired goals and questions to be assessed, including those explored in Chapter One; (2) feasibility of the goals; (3) a realistic cost framework for appraisal or efficacious assessment; and (4) final results and their use explored and agreed upon prior to the implementation of the evaluation. Program design parallels the response to each of these considerations. Other terms such as *evaluability assessment* or *modified program evaluation* may approximate this method.

2   An increasingly popular and well-used form of evaluation, utilization-focused evaluation (Patton, 1986) is a modification of program evaluation. Utilization evaluation is specifically related to evaluation goals. Information obtained from this form of assessment aids in making *significant* decisions about a program. Outcome goals are articulated because they affect the type of evaluation to initiate. Utility-designed evaluations aid in assessing the resource use, continuation or termination, and modification of programs. Outcomes are used in critical decisions regarding the program and/or its resources. In most business and health care organizations in contemporary society, the ability to document ethics is important.

3   Some evaluators employ a hidden code to determine relevant units or identify employees. For ethical reasons, this author does not support such use; honesty is essential to ethics assessment and quality.

4   Details of designs may be found in T. Cook and D. Campbell (1979) or J. Wholey (1994). For an extensive discussion of research methods and program evaluation, several resources are noted at the end of Chapter Five.

5   A fuller and more detailed discussion of quasi-experimental designs may be found in T. Cook and D. Campbell (1979).

6   For a fuller explanation of classic experimental designs, refer to discussion in Campbell and Stanley (1963).

7   For a discussion of an application of the design employing an ethics seminar as the intervention with a pre-post-test with control group, refer to C. McDaniel (1998c).

8   For a full discussion of psychometric properties: *Research methods in social relations* (Selltiz, *et al.*, 1976).

9   The 'gold standard,' established by the American Psychological Association (APA) as a minimum 70 per cent, was more recently raised to a preferred 80 per cent. Evaluators implementing mail surveys, in contrast, accept a response rate of around 50-60 per cent. This author prefers the APA criterion.

10   Statistical procedures for ameliorating the issue are provided in Comer's school development program in Prince George's County, MD: A theory-based evaluation (Cook, T. D., *et al.*, 1999).

11   Several universities offer programs on case development, of which one is the Harvard University Business School; they provide additional resources for excellent cases.

References

Affholter, D. (1994). Outcome monitoring. In J. S. Wholey, H. P. Hatry, and K. E. Newcomer (Eds.), *Handbook of practical program evaluation* (pp. 96-118). San Francisco, CA: Jossey-Bass Publishers.

Blake, D. H., Frederick, W. C., and Myers, M. S. (1976). *Social auditing: Evaluating the impact of corporate programs.* New York, NY: Praeger Publishers.

Campbell, D. T., and Stanley, J. C. (1963). *Experimental and quasi-experimental designs for research.* Boston, MA: Houghton Mifflin Company.

Comptroller General of the United States. (1988). *Government auditing standards.* Washington, D.C.: Government Printing Office.

Cook, T. D. and Campbell, D. T. (1979). *Quasi-experimentation: Design and analysis issues for field settings.* Boston, MA: Houghton Mifflin Company.

Driscoll, D., and Hoffman, W. M. (2000). *Ethics matters: How to implement a values-driven management.* Waltham, MA: Center for Business Ethics.

Grembowski, D. (2001). *The practice of health program evaluation.* Thousand Oaks, CA: Sage Publications, Inc.

Harrison, M. I. (1994). *Diagnosing organizations: Methods, models, and processes.* Thousand Oaks, CA: Sage Publications, Inc.

Hultman, K., and Gellerman, B. (2002). *Balancing individual and organizational values: Walking the tightrope to success.* San Francisco, CA: Jossey-Bass /Pfeiffer.

Joint Commission on Standards for Educational Evaluation. (1994). *The program evaluation standards* (2nd ed.). Newbury Park, CA: Sage Publications, Inc.

Kraut, A. I. (Ed.). (1996). *Organizational surveys: Tools for assessment and change.* San Francisco, CA: Jossey-Bass Publishers.

Newcomer, K. E., Hatry, H. P., Wholey, J. P. (1994). Meeting the need for practical evaluation approaches: An introduction. In J. P. Wholey, H. P. Hatry, and K. E. Newcomer (Eds.), *Handbook of practical program evaluation.* San Francisco, CA: Jossey-Bass Publishers.

Patton, M.W. (1986). U*tilization-focused evaluation.* Newbury Park, CA: Sage Publications, Inc.

Shirom, A., and Harrison M. (1995). Diagnostic models for organizations: Toward an integrative perspective. In C. L. Cooper and D. M. Rousseau (Eds.), *Trends in organizational behavior* (V. 2, pp. 85-107). New York, NY: John Wiley and Sons, Ltd.

Wholey, J. S., Hatry, H. P. and Newcomer, K. E. (Eds.). (1994). *Handbook of practical program evaluation.* San Francisco, CA: Jossey-Bass Publishers.

Worthen, B. R., and Sanders, J. R. (1973). *Educational evaluation: Theory and practice.* Worthington, OH: Charles Jones Publishing Company.

Chapter Six

Developing the Ethical Environment

Introduction

As excellent leaders know, it is not enough to merely desire a renewed organizational ambience. Ethics does not simply emerge. Specific plans need to be implemented in order to create the desired outcome. These plans constitute the process of developing the preferred result, an ethical environment. Development builds upon the information garnered in the prior chapter on assessment. Now comes the challenge of putting the ethics program in place. It raises the question: What is development? Development actualizes the aim of attaining an ethical, or more ethical, environment in the desired organization. If successful, the ethical environment involves change of organizational values and puts the ethics program in place, resulting in revision of the previous ethos of the firm. Development also requires other ethics initiatives in addition to the foundational audit. If the audit provides information on which to make decisions, the next question is what to do in order to instill ethics among employees and develop a more ethical organization.

This discussion is not, however, about training and development of any program, nor is it a 'how to' on ethics programs *per se*. It explores, in particular, the need for development of an ethos in organizations pertaining to ethics, whether health care or business organizations. For that reason, the focus is on strategies most germane to an ethics program. As will be seen below, not all situations result in the desired outcome.

Allen Anderssen, an ambitious and young mid-level manager, was hired by Serving Customers Company three years ago. Top management recognized his eagerness to move forward. To that end, they asked him to assume the task of developing a program for ethics education in their main office. If it were successful, then he would have the opportunity to extend this programming to other sites, thereby also ensuring him a promotion. He would be rewarded for his efforts.

Anderssen was eager to begin. The first step was to talk with several of his peer level coworkers in management. 'What did they think was the main problem?' was his primary question. With the various replies in hand, he then moved forward to develop a program responding to their concerns. The program would be offered as an intensive three-day on-site workshop, and all persons in the target department would be required to attend. The managers of the respective units were asked to inform their employees. A confirming note was sent to them.

On the first day, 37 employees showed up out of an anticipated 55. Not only was Anderssen puzzled, so were the managers. As the program progressed with Anderssen and one outside person presenting material in lecture format, employees asked few questions. Presentations covered the most common theories of ethics, described problems with them, and posed the one most useful for Serving Customers Company. That afternoon the employees took more coffee breaks. During the second day, the presenters noticed that after lunch several attendees did not return and others drifted slowly back from lunch. One brought a book to read. By the end of the third day, about ten employees were present and of those, few looked interested.

Although reluctant, near the end of the three-day session Anderssen distributed an evaluation form developed at the company, one top management required of all on-site company offered programs, formal or informal. The results of these evaluations were calculated by the central human resources office, out of which most training was offered. Not surprisingly, the employees who were present and completed the evaluations did not rate the newly developed program highly. They thought the material boring and irrelevant to their ongoing work; they wondered where the material 'came from' since it had nothing to do with their work. Employees also complained about the intensity of the offering and the lengthy time away from their work. One employee pointed out that no one replaced her at her office, requiring her to work a weekend to make up for lost time and work. Her family was not pleased, nor was she. The new ethics program was doomed to fail. In an attempt to rescue the program and adjust for the overall negative results, Anderssen pointed out the evaluation was skewed since only ten persons out of the anticipated 55 completed the form. That only raised questions, however, about the low number of attendees. Anderssen was dejected by this outcome and feared he would never be promoted.[1]

Characteristics of Programs of Excellence-Development Phases

What are the common characteristics of a quality ethics program? Or, put another way, what aspects of the Anderssen program are missing? Are there aspects of an ethics program requiring specific attention? The items listed below indicate ethics programs of excellence take time and intentional planning. Additionally, programs need buy-in from top management and need to be tailored to the particular firm. Constructive settings do not merely happen, they result from well-designed work. Development of a positive organizational ethos is needed along with the specific ethics value. Miller (1986:199) identifies dimensions important in the development of a positive environment: 'Only by taking the responsibility for environmental design and implementation can managers ensure the environment supports the goals of the organization.'

Obviously a specific firm's ethics program depends on the organization. Furthermore, the ethics program differs by the identified mission and needs of the organization; no two ethics programs look exactly alike, affirming the ethics initiative needs to be tailored to the particular organization. Even acknowledging organizations share many characteristics and dynamics in common, each company or hospital has its own unique style and culture. The ethics program will be more successful and remain a viable endeavor within the organization if the identified needs and particularities of each organization are acknowledged and addressed through the ethics program.

Having expressed the opinion that programs of excellence reflect the organizational mission and goals, it is also suggested consideration be given to the functions initially outlined for ethics committees in hospitals (Cranford and Doudera, 1984). Borrowing from research on hospital ethics committees suggests corporations employ their three primary functions of ethics case or situation review, ethics education, and ethics policy development. Missing from this list, however, is the responsibility for overseeing to ensure continuing ethics activities within the organization, added below.

Primary Potential Functions of an Ethics Committee:

- Review of situations or events among employees or with patients and customers, posing ethical challenges.
- Ethics education to enhance critical thinking, analysis skills of employees.
- Development of policies or other standards to support organizational ethics.
- Overseeing, review, and monitoring of ongoing ethics program and offerings.

If the above were adapted, and providing examples of each, the ethics program would aid health care providers and employees in business in analyzing and resolving critical ethical dilemmas they encounter in their work. The program would also offer relevant education to further the organizational ethics and support the employees in their ethical pursuits. Lastly, the ethics program would keep records on the various dilemmas among employees and recommend or develop polices emerging from the analyzed issues, themes, or patterns in the respective organization. Overseeing the ethical activities is also needed and integrates the three former functions. An additional function, combining any of the above, could be lectures or external speakers to provide supportive illustrations of companies of ethical excellence, and areas of excellence in one's own firm. The three functions initially suggested for hospital ethics committees, plus the addition of overseeing, suggest functions potentially also relevant to ethics programs generally.

Having identified that ethics programs need to be tailored to a particular firm, we now turn to the shared characteristics of programs of excellence leading to success, *i.e.*, the common traits for success. In contrast to the course pursued by Anderssen, good program development requires significant (pre-implementation) planning, as well as thoughtful implementation. Ethics programming requires additional care, especially since some persons may consider the information sensitive and even confidential in nature. Likewise, ethics programs require attention to design, planning, and implementation aspects others may not require, or at least not to the same degree. Excellent ethics programs contain the following characteristics in one form or another:

- Goals, clear and linked to a realistic time-frame
- Finances, other indicators of support
- Well-planned design, with ethics in mind

- Relevance for employees' work, linking the desired goals to the work
- Ethical program consistency and accountability
- Measurable outcomes with documentation

Pre-Implementation Phase

As most employees know, each organization has a unique aesthetic feel that is almost palpable; when people enter a company, it does not take long to obtain a sense of place. If managers desire their firm's aesthetic feel to be positive, and the aim is to establish an ethical environment, the goal becomes the 'gold standard' for the organization. To further the conversation about creating an ethical environment, ethics program development is divided into pre-implementation and implementation phases while addressing the characteristics of programs of excellence. The first phase is foundational to the second, but both include features of a quality ethics program. We now turn to the aims, using the above list as an organizing frame and treating them as *pre*-implementation phases for program development.

Goals One assumes development of an ethics program begins with implementation. In reality, however, implementation actually begins when top management expresses a desire for a more ethical environment. Desire for a different ethics paradigm implies change and development. Once the CEO decides the organization needs a new ethics paradigm, the change begins. Desires need to be translated into measurable goals.

The first aspect of any program of excellence is its goal. To be differentiated from the goals of evaluation examined in the prior chapter, we now explore goals for the ethics program. What is the mandate of the ethics program and what will it attempt to achieve? The answers to these questions become the program goals. The critical question is how the program links with the organizational mission and conduct code, a point Anderssen missed in his preparation. The overarching goal of an ethics program is to meet the goals and needs of the organization through its workers and their work as they pertain to ethics; the program addresses ethics in the daily activities of employees in their organization. The goals of ethics programs of excellence are inherently linked to the corporate mission and strategic plan. In that regard, one aim is an organization exhibiting a comprehensive and cohesive ethics value throughout the system. An excellent ethics program aids in meeting and retaining those aims.

Goals also provide a frame for the rest of the ethics programming. The goals, objectives, or aims of the ethics program offer guides to the manner and type of program designed and implemented within an organization. Therefore it is impossible to move forward toward enhancing the organizational ethic without a clear statement of goal. Anderssen, for example, could have explored what top management wanted out of the program: what were the key objectives in initiating an ethics program? These typically come from the CEO, top management, or corporate board and surely need their affirmation.

Resources of personnel and finances Goodpaster (1989:213) notes the challenge of addressing ethics and implementing the appropriate strategies in the corporation are myriad and identifies lack of attention to the bottom line as primary. The perceived split between approaches developed by the academy and the actual application of ethics is suggested as one reason for this challenge. Attention to budget, finances, and relevant supports is primary for programs of excellence. However, using research and theory for application in implementation can redress this issue. Even with research and theory, no program of quality can advance and develop over time without adequate financial backing and future plans. Commonsense narratives suggest an initial program needs sound funding for at least the first year. Strategic time frames allow a director to plan and develop additional funding if needed for future resources. Thus the key resource is financial; however, it is not the only form of resource an ethics director should address strategically; others, including personnel, are explored below.

Work done prior to implementation includes excellent planning, attention to relevancy, and consistency to ethical dimensions of the program. We explore key areas to consider for facilitating implementation and garnering personnel and financial resources for the program. Well-planned and executed programs are also forms of prevention. Good ethics programs implicitly or explicitly strive to prevent problems on the job prior to their emergence, illustrating that ethics programs are preventive as well as responsive endeavors. Below we explore two resources illustrated by personnel and finances.

Personnel No group is more essential to develop as a resource than the organization's employees. Some might refer to this as gaining employee buy-in or ownership. Regardless of the terms used, what is important is the level of cooperation with the ethics program among workers. Gaining the investment of significant proportions of the workforce, including central individuals, aids in addressing a major constraint: lack of participation and investment among them. If employees can see the direct benefits from ethics programs, the overall cooperation and investment will be enhanced; management-only initiatives may not succeed in the long run. Below we explore four considerations to enhance cooperation among employees:

- Pre-Planning: Anticipate questions and concerns; explain the purpose of the program and roles and expectations of employees. Include a statement about future use of the results.
- Feedback Loop: Obtain and give feedback regarding the plan, as well as the anticipated outcome, including revision of designs based on employee feedback.
- Pay-off: Make the direct and immediate benefits of the employees' work obvious; draw the connections for employees who may not see the links. Also work with Risk Management or Human Resource Offices to obtain relevant data to support claims.

• Communication: Open continuous communication, with feedback.

Another way to enhance investment in the ethics initiative is to communicate to employees the costs of *un*ethical behaviors. Below is a short list of possible areas in which employees' unethical behavior is costly to the company, resulting in financial loss. This information is especially compelling if these losses prevent employee raises, additional benefits, new office furniture, reduction of company travel, or other attractive work components in companies or hospitals. In one consultation, this author suggested a trainer translate the revenue losses into annual salaries of managers; it got their immediate attention.

Unethical Behavior	*Calculation to Document Loss*
• Inappropriate use of company property.	Use profits as a base, subtracting losses attributed to theft times frequency.
• Damages to property owned by company.	Costs of replacement times frequency.
• Slow-down response to patients or customers.	Provide results of patient or customer satisfaction surveys; graphically display; translate into profit loss.

In addition to support from employees, development and implementation are basically impossible without the support and continued encouragement of the organizational leadership. The sustained support and buy-in of and communication about CEO and top management support are crucial for developing the ethics endeavor. While most acknowledge the importance of the central leadership, exemplified by the CEO and top management, the role of mid-level managers is also important. Employee support is important; however, support of management is vital—another point Anderssen missed.

Anderssen missed several major considerations in setting up the ethics program for Serving Customers Company. In fact, by their reactions the participants conveyed the opinion that if the company is serving customers, the program was not serving them! Anderssen would have been wise to solicit a written statement to all employees from management, notifying them that Serving was planning to offer an ethics program which Anderssen would be implementing. As with any corporate statement, mandates from the CEO are necessary for the success of ethics programs.

Although the managers at Serving Customers were engaged in the initial conversations Anderssen had about the proposed program, steps were missed: only a few coworkers participated, and they may not have been representative of the company. Employees reported dissatisfaction not only with the format in terms of its intensity and length but also with the absence of plans for replacement of missed work and tasks not addressed. One might ask: Is it ethical to waste employees' time? Coordination is a manager's responsibility, as is conveying respect for other workers' time and tasks. Directors in charge of the ethics program, especially a newly developed one, can coordinate missed work, obtaining support of employees and managers and confirming the director is savvy about the realities of participants' work life.

Finances Many ethics programs are begun with the assumption that because ethics is (somewhat) abstract in contrast to technical programs, resource needs will be minimal. This is not accurate. Developing a successful program for ethics takes the same thoughtful approach and resources in place as any other program. While it may not take as much financial outlay as, for example, an extensive computer-training program requiring technological equipment or a clinical lab, ethics programming requires resources. Anderssen did not get commitments for support and resources, nor does it appear he had a budget. Financial supports and budgets with future projections are essential. Additionally, to 'kick-off' his program, it would have been prudent for Anderssen to have involved experts in the field of ethics, indicating the company's financial commitment and support for the value placed on ethics.

Program Plan and Design

Attaining a high quality program requires the ability to anticipate and implement quality designs, coordinating with, and reflective of, the organizational need. It also requires consideration of other departments to sustain ongoing appraisal activities, behaviors, or problems occurring in the organization regarding ethics, a point Anderssen missed. Understanding the emergence of ethical issues on-site is a challenge, however. The complexity of organizational life is a major reason given for the inability to ascertain the causes of organizational problems (Shirom and Harrison, 1995:93). Difficulty in linking symptoms with their causes is based on the lack of accumulation of research and attention to organizational life; the indeterminacy and complexity of typical organizational life also contribute to the difficulty. For these reasons, this discussion attempts to make the complex work of development more manageable by linking characteristics for program excellence to relevant strategies.

Keeping it Relevant

Of all the errors in planning, none could be more telling than the lack of information about what employees consider to be relevant issues. Similar to this lack is programming unrelated to the mission, noted earlier. One way a moral or ethical environment is understood is the '...investment for reasons other than ...economic return in the quality of life with the corporation itself' (Andrews, 1989:258). Theorists and economists who argue the primary aim is maximization of profits among corporations, of course, counter this perspective. Argued in this book is that the two are complementary: ethics is good business. The central question, then, is why the ethics program in the first place? To what is the CEO responding? If Anderssen did not know, he should have inquired about signal events on-site, in competing companies, or changes in the external climate. The bottom line is why: What is the problem, and to what is this ethics program responding?

The response to these questions above links the program to perceived needs and they back to the program goals. It links the ethics program to the organizational mission and strategic plan, creating relevancy. If employees do not perceive a need, then they need to be informed. What is occurring globally to which their CEO is responding? What is happening in their company that employees are encountering or of which they are unaware? Perhaps with planning and care, Anderssen could have informed employees about factors that make the program relevant, such as a single egregious event at their site. Employees need a context in which to understand new programs and their relevance to them, their work, and organization.

Regrettably, the employees with whom Anderssen was working saw the ethics program as *ir*relevant. Presentations offered on-site by a business, hospital, corporation, or clinic need to be practical, addressing the ethical challenges employees are encountering or will encounter in their day-to-day work. Like most employees they are busy, take time from work, and are ultimately frustrated with the lack of relevancy to their concerns, as noted in the Anderssen case. In the pre-planning stage the person responsible for the programming needs to gather information from participants. What are the key questions these employees have? Have they had prior ethics training, perhaps in school or another firm? If so, what was it like, and what did it cover? These are questions for pre-planning the program.

How does an ethics director ensure connection to mission and employees' work, to relevant issues in the work site? A *job analysis* is one means to ensure relevance. Matching the program, its offerings, and foci to an analysis of a specific job or several clusters of jobs aids directors in ascertaining relevancy; it serves as a check on the objectives of the offering. This applies to lectures on ethical theories, ethics cases for discussion, seminars on ethical analysis, or any ethics event the director plans. Ethics offerings are linked to the work of employees, and a job analysis ensures direct connection.

To respond to these questions of relevancy, employees of a firm might be asked to submit examples of problems they encounter in their daily work. Another buy-in strategy uses a detailed analysis of the ethical assessment recommended in Chapter Five, focusing on the top concerns among the majority of the employees, or focus on the concerns occurring most frequently. *Frequency* refers to the number of problems occurring most among employees whereas *prevalence* refers to the most widespread ethical concerns within the organization; while related, these two concepts differ. Information from risk management or human resources assists in coordinating and complementing ethics development activities addressing and confirming frequency and prevalence. Whether using frequency counts or prevalence reports, a rational approach to addressing organizational ethics concerns among health care and business employees aids in sustaining a strong development approach.

Another strategy to gain relevancy—either in addition to the first strategy or as a substitute—is to conduct a system-wide survey to solicit input, differentiated from the survey conducted as an ethics audit. Surveys address several needs. They communicate to the target audience that the program is underway, supplementing any message sent by the CEO. A survey can convey to employees that a responsible person takes their work concerns seriously and has expertise in program development. Survey input also communicates that information planned and presented emerges from the concerns of the employees. The comments provided by participant employees suggested that the approach used by Anderssen was more abstract than employees desired and thus did not meet the perceived interests and needs of employees.

Once data from the employee surveys are gathered, the director would be wise to use them as the basis for the first ethics presentation, thereby linking the presentation to concerns among employees and concerns to the desired outcomes. The ethics director could, for example, wisely introduce the newly developed program, highlight the purpose, and then convey the results of the employee survey about their own ethics concerns, issues, or needs. The results become the basis of the newly developed program, keeping the ethics program relevant to employees' needs. The director will probably not be able to address all concerns noted by employees, but this gap can then serve as a plan for follow-up sessions, which plans may be conveyed to employees.

Career benefits represent another form of relevancy. Research reveals employees participate best when they perceive the program to enhance their career benefits (Tharenou, 1997:24). Typical participants in training are younger rather than older employees, have higher position levels of employment, tend to be better educated, and have more occupational skills. They also are more motivated than those who do not participate in development programs, conveying an interest in learning on the job. What this does, however, is to preference employees with better employment situations, compared to all employees. Results of the research suggest attention needs to be given to attracting the participation of employees who represent *other* domains: those who have had less education, are lower on the position ladder, and are less motivated. Attracting these less motivated employees is an asset to a company wanting to develop a system-wide and consistent employee approach for ethical concerns. The approach attends to equality, parity, and justice on the job by including all employees in education.

Employees are not the only ones who desire a relevant ethics program; management also wants to know programs are relevant to the employment situation. Employees participate in development when they perceive the environment in which they are working supports training resulting in growth (Tharenou, 1997:21). For both employers and employees, development needs to pay attention to enhancing the program by offering relevance to employment.

Ethics Program Consistency and Accountability

Consistency in ethics programming refers both to content and pedagogy. Ethics education's primary mandate is furthering understanding about ethical theories and concepts. It also wants employees to apply ethical theories and concepts to their daily work life. Most books, articles, and therefore most presentations about ethics appear compelled to cover the most frequently used theories of ethics. While this may be useful, since it is a common approach, planning needs to ensure attendees are not receiving material repeating prior education. If so, then a different or combination format is needed. From an ethical standpoint, the content, format, and pedagogy need to be consistent with the program aims.

The format Anderssen selected did not build on these concepts. For instance, discussion about practical information regarding issues emerging at work should be illustrated in ethics cases derived from work situations. In this way the program consistency also illustrates relevance; programming is consistent with the organization's goals as exemplified in the activities of the ethics program. There is an inherent contradiction between the program aim of skill enhancement on the job and the presentation Anderssen designed: lecture format on theories. This is not to suggest lectures or ethical theories are irrelevant but rather that they serve as a background for addressing the program aim, which is skill in thinking about ethical situations emerging in the workplace of Serving Customers Company.

The point is not to inform participants of a 'right' way to resolve problems but to instill confidence and enhance competency in addressing troubling ethical issues emerging at work. Therefore, the pedagogy used in the ethics program needs to substantiate the aim, and participants need an opportunity to engage in the form of analysis implied by the program. These convey consistency between program objectives and methods.

Select cases relevant to the *type of work* the particular employee group is engaging in at the time. As Anderssen discovered, employees want cases representing situations relevant to their work, and top management desires cases or seminars addressing events and situations to reduce the number of problematic events at work and ultimately enhancing the organization's work. These are complementary aims. Cases do not have to be derived from Serving Company but should represent the type of work. If employees are being asked to discuss cases, clearing the case is also important. An equally effective approach is to select cases, illustrating the issue to be discussed, but from another company-type. This removes the situation and therefore the discussion from the company in which the participants are working, offering a safety net for engaging in discussions.

Consistency is an ethical issue. A firm desiring to develop an ethical framework needs to address consistency, integrating the firm's stance among individual employees with their participation in the ethics program. Since the ethics program must illustrate ethics in its development, to ignore a portion of the company's employees or treat them unevenly implies a less than ethical approach. Corporations also need to consider program mandates, along with the personal integrity of the employees in the firm. If employees perceive the goals of the firm are widely disparate from their own, the chance of a truly integrated approach sustained over time is greatly reduced. Such discrepancy also needs to be discussed with employees. This goes to the core of respect for persons and fairness in treatment and supports consistency in the program.

Accountability and a related concept, responsibility, raise another set of considerations. Those of us working in the field of ethics may forget the manner in which others approach the subject. When planning a program on-site among coworkers, the director needs to consider the material and what is being asked of the employee. In addition to format and pedagogy other issues are particularly relevant to ethics. Ethics programming raises concerns explored below under the headings of accountability and responsibility, representing three levels of employment relationships: among participants in ethics events, between the director and attendees, and between the director and management, respectively.

The first level is the accountability of participants to each other during the ethics sessions: presentations and discussions among one's own coworkers. What if another employee recognizes a situation presented for discussion? What if the case—although Anderssen, alas, did not use cases—happens to touch on a sensitive topic or an event similar to one an employee experienced? How much can employees say in such situations? What will employees do with information presented in this company forum? These questions get to the core of confidentiality with sensitive information (See: Chapter Five), as well as the accountability of employees to each other.

Second is the question of what directors assume are their responsibilities if information about problematic issues, albeit vague in detail, emerge in the session? Do directors have a responsibility to seek out an employee and follow on a potentially problematic case presented in a session, or should he/she encourage the employee to follow-up? What if the presenter is an external consultant hired for the particular session? In addition to the relationships among employees, the role and responsibility of the director of ethics programming needs to be clear. The pre-planning phase is when these issues need to be addressed. Since the ethics director is also an employee, participants may have assumptions about actions he/she would take. Nevertheless, as with the discussion regarding the client in Chapter Two, these key relationships need to be clear and explicit. For the director, the continuation of his/her employment may be at stake, thereby requiring more emphasis on clear lines of communication and responsibility.

The third level is the relationship between the program director and organization regarding accountability. What accountabilities do the Anderssens of ethics programming have to CEOs who initiate programs? What responsibility to the Risk Management Office in a hospital? Although relevant to many programs, it is necessary in ethics programming to clarify relationships. Personnel responsible for ethics programming need to spell out the relationships between the program and top management. For instance, what understanding does the CEO have about material presented during discussions? What about 'cases' or 'events' emerging during the discussions? Will information be conveyed to managers or CEOs? Will identifiers be used if anecdotes are retained? Realistically, employees might not fully engage in a discussion unless clarity is provided regarding responsibility, accountability, and work relationships.

One assumes Anderssen would be asked to report back on the outcomes, including the evaluation results, of the program. Beyond that, is Anderssen expected to report on cases, themes, issues, or other material emerging in the sessions? These questions raise the issue of what Anderssen reports back to the top management, including attendance. Do reports include only themes and issues without any identifying material? Most employers who provide training also want to know who attends. While the latter may be more commonplace, keeping attendance needs to be clarified if it is not a company-wide policy.

Some situations occurring at work—fraud, stealing, and similar behaviors—are clearly unacceptable and need to be reported; some actions are not only unethical but are also illegal. Organizations typically have procedures for handling challenging illegal issues at work. Even so, these issues, too, can be addressed and 'talked through' in an ethics program. In addition, the person to whom an employee can turn with questions needs clarification. Such matters as harassment on the job, either to self or other employees, need a clear line of communication and action for resolution. Unless the program developer communicates these approaches clearly, employees may be left puzzled about how to move forward on ethical issues observed at work. Employees need to know these lines of communication and action, which also support the developing ethics value.

However, as human resource personnel know, sensitive information may emerge in the most unexpected contexts. Since ethics assumes potentially confidential information, it requires program developers to be proactive in anticipating and thereby preventing additionally difficult situations from emerging; those caused by unclear lines of authority and relationship boundaries. We anticipate that serious and unplanned situations may emerge. What we need to consider is the manner in which they are addressed when they arise, assuring that handling of the situation is ethical and appropriate. Once problems regarding the ethics program emerge, the potential for its success evidenced in continued support, attendance, and employee participation is almost surely undermined; prevention is ethically prudent.

Measuring and Documenting Outcomes

The ability to measure and the ability to document change created by the ethics program are critical. Balance between a specific overall measure within the firm and the desired outcomes may be difficult to attain but is critical for program success.

A program aiming to develop an ethical environment typically desires to enhance the ability of employees to respond to ethical dilemmas. Changes in behavior or enhancement of abilities, however, need to be documented in the organization. Research reveals behavioral changes pertaining to decision making among employees in organizations are understandably complex and sensitive.

Linda Treviño (1997:4) has examined a model of ethical decision making among employees, suggesting three facets need to be addressed: the ego strength, the field dependency, and the locus of control. Of importance for a developing program is attention to ego and dependency. Employees who have confidence in their abilities to make ethical decisions ultimately move forward to enact them. Lack of either confidence or competency erodes the ability to make ethical decisions on the job. It opens employees to the potential of succumbing to negative influences, as did the drivers of food delivery trucks in the case explored in Chapter Two. The support and cooperation of one's peers on the job add support for ethical decisions. The organizational culture plays an important role in the ethics development of employees. A common set of assumptions, values, beliefs, or norms shared by the workers goes a long way in supporting employees to act in ethical ways. The ethics program also enhances these behaviors. According to Treviño (1997:13), the culture of the organization influences the thoughts and feelings, and guides behavior of organizational members illustrating ego strength and considering field dependency of decision making.

The importance of ethics development is supported by results revealing that reference to others is important to employees (Treviño, 1997:14-15), corroborating the consideration of ego strength and field dependency. Increased responsibility for the consequences of actions increases employees' ethical behaviors, a finding related to the discussion on control. Training programs are important avenues for increasing employee awareness and understanding in order to develop ethical behaviors on the job. Role taking is one means of enhancing ethical decision making on the job. In making an ethical decision, most persons 'search' outside of themselves for guidance. In sum, this research on ethical decision making among employees reveals it is prudent for successful development of an ethics program to address the education of the individual employees and provide organizational support for enhanced ethical decision making.

Likewise, employees in organizations prefer a workplace in which there is a supervisor who can support them in their ethical concerns and in which the culture is deemed ethical (McDaniel and Schoeps, 2003a). Employees desire working conditions and situations supporting their ethical concerns. As noted in earlier chapters, employees leave situations in which their ethical concerns about the challenging and troubling situations in their daily work life are ignored, dismissed, or neglected. Therefore documenting the important changes occurring in the organization as a result of the ethics programming is critical to program development and its success. It is critical for the director, top management, and employees to know the influence of the ethics program, and, as will be explored in more detail in Chapter Seven, it is foundational to sustaining ethics programming.

Implementation

Once the planning for the ethics program has been completed, the focus turns to implementation of the program activities. Development relies in part on prior work in the organization. There is no codified body of knowledge for identification of causes for organizational problems (Shirom and Harrison, 1995:93). Relevant etiology is missing from many discussions for diagnosing problems in the organization. Fruitful aspects for advancement of understanding organizational life are abilities to identify etiologies for organizational *in*effectiveness. In every organization there is a creative tension between the implementation of an ethics initiative and acknowledging the implicit organizational concerns. Several of those tensions are addressed below under considerations for developing the new ethics program. This discussion attempts to address the challenge of balancing competing tensions by exploring five strategies for successful implementation: incremental, small implementation; a multi-faceted program; control and responsibility; collaboration and communication with personnel; and ethics program committees.

Incremental, Small Implementation

Implementation for new programs typically employs two approaches. One approach is to select a few departments or sub-units and implement change in phases, taking incremental and small steps. The advantage of this approach is more control over the initial endeavor. With incremental implementation, if revision in the program is needed, the program can be altered prior to creating a change in all departments, linking back to the discussion on program evaluation designs. The analysis and effect of few and small changes can enhance the development among the remaining units of the corporation. A contrasting and second method is to implement the new initiative within the system all at once, creating system-wide and significant change simultaneously. The advantage to this method is that employees share a common change at the same time—there is potentially less unevenness within the corporation. Another advantage contingent on size of the system is the need for fewer staff.

Similar to the above discussion is the tension of incremental versus major or significant change. Employees want to see evidence of change; nevertheless moving more slowly and involving a small number of employees may get everyone on board since it then becomes a collective action rather than an initiative of one or two. It is also unrealistic to assume developing an ethics code or setting up an office on ethics will change an entire organizational culture. Changing to an organizational ethic that is desirable takes time. Change in the ethical ethos is essentially a paradigm shift in the organization. In this regard, it is often wise not only to start small and garner success with each step but also to do so in incremental steps ensuring enduring change over time.

An additional reason for starting small and gaining success is conveying the impression that top management is in the business of supporting ethics over the duration of the organization. Employees need to know management is committed for the lifetime of the company or health service. This is where the CEO and top management play an important role—they need to champion the ethics initiative.

Both of these methods have advantages as well as disadvantages. How would the director of an ethics program know which to select? One selection criterion is size of the corporation. Large firms might benefit from the first approach whereas a smaller firm in which manageable implementation can be accomplished might benefit from a one-time and significant implementation. Even here, however, it is prudent to create change for long-term effect in incremental steps to allow assessment as development unfolds. This also allows for assessment of employee reaction to the proposed change.

A second consideration for determining where and how to start is the magnitude of the need. Was this new ethics initiative the result of dire need, perhaps gross negligence in a clinic or major profit loss due to theft? If these are the stimuli for attention to ethics, it may suggest a need to move quickly throughout the company but with smaller parts implemented. Obviously, if the change includes aspects raising ethical issues such as a new accounting system to replace a prior, ineffective one allowing fraudulent and unethical practices to continue, it would be unwise to delay implementation in the entire organization. In such situations, one would best move forward quickly to eradicate *un*ethical practices adversely affecting the firm and its employees. Directors of ethics programs may not have a choice of methods when these adverse situations are present in their organizations.

For the ethics program, similar analysis is needed. Select the one aspect of the program ensuring success, or for which there is greatest employee interest and support. Introduce that part first. Use an evaluation, test out the receptivity, and, once it is underway, move to the second phase. Evaluate each step, gathering employee feedback at each point. Another consideration is to treat the phase as a pilot test or exploratory one; implement a part, then test to determine the receptivity of the ethics program offering. Although phasing the program in small steps may take more time, once the program catches on and others capture the enthusiasm for the usefulness of the program, it will expand and grow. Directors of ethics programming are typically enthusiastic about their initiatives; however, taking on more than can be managed well and with high quality is a mistake. A few moral or invested persons cannot change a whole corporation, especially large ones. The implementation of and attention to the institutionalization of the program can incrementally and ultimately change a company's overall perspective regarding ethical values.

Similar to incremental and small approaches is a comprehensive and integrated approach. A comprehensive and integrated approach is preferred, in which the ethics initiatives are conceptualized as a program. With clear goals in mind, the director plans and makes necessary decisions for phasing in the program. The opposite of comprehensive programming is fragmentation, an approach detracting from development. Prioritizing or phasing in various dimensions is not the same as fragmentation. They are rather the opposite, since planning requires priority setting and decision making about what relevant steps to take and in what order. This leads to the next consideration.

A Multi-Faceted Ethics Program

The numbers and types of facets in an ethics program, the second consideration, are contingent upon two issues: purpose of the program and perceived need. A multi-faceted program, one with various aspects within one program, reaches more people and has a broader appeal to wider employee audiences. Multi-faceted programming uses varied pedagogies, styles of presentations, and responses to employees' concerns, as well as different program offerings. For instance, in a hospital setting, an Ethics for Lunch program appeals to a large range of employees; they can drop in during a lunch break, gather information they need, and slip away. Clinical Ethics Rounds focused by occupation—doctor, nurse, physical therapist, or social worker—serve an educational need and guide decision making. Even more appealing in contemporary health care is a multi-disciplinary ethics round. Or a hospital may offer in-service training for ethics education.

In the corporate world, team meetings focused on discussions of challenging ethical issues serve to support employees and educate them about ethical standards in their firm. Likewise, an outside speaker to whose presentation many employees could be invited exhibits corporate support for ethics and confirms the standards set by top management. A popular format among many corporations is a breakfast discussion with either the CEO or keynote speakers with expertise in business ethics, or a facilitator who engages all participants in a discussion of compelling or widespread ethics problems. In tandem with any of these is the possibility of offering similar program or events to sectors of the organization illustrated by administrators, delivery personnel, front-line service workers, managers, or salespersons.

Control and Responsibility

Since one of the goals of the ethics program is development of a program sustaining ethical behavior in the organization over time, it also implies eradication of *un*ethical and problematic behaviors, raising the question of control, the third consideration. Such expectations introduce the tension between control, even coercion, monitoring with sanctions, and freedom and responsibility of employees. These issues were explored in Chapter Three. However, here it is important to note the issue of control as a potential and implicit issue surrounding the ethics implementation. It is wise to move this implicit issue to the forefront and engage management in conversations about the expectations regarding control. Implied is consideration of criteria for assessing the morality of individuals in the firm. Likewise, how much monitoring does management of the program expect? Is the director expected to monitor behavior of employees in a hands-on manner or delegate this to other personnel? What, if there is one, is the link with the Human Resource and Risk Management Departments? Are such expectations realistic? Clarity about these interpersonal and interactive facets of the evolving ethics program helps in moving the initiative forward and gains more trust from other managers or directors in the organization. In that way it also clarifies unrealistic expectations preventing potential resistance and problems with colleagues.

Collaboration and Communication with Personnel

The Anderssen case serves to illustrate the importance of collaboration and communication with company personnel, a fourth aspect. Most training offered, to date, at Serving emerged from the Human Resource Office. One wonders what Anderssen was assuming when he moved forward without engaging the personnel in human resources, training and development, and risk management offices. Not only would seasoned human resource personnel know about program planning, but they may have had useful suggestions based on years of experience with presentations, and perhaps even expert presenters. If for no other reason than collegial relationships, human resources should have been consulted. Anderssen, upon assuming responsibility for this initiative, could have asked the CEO what collaboration occurred with other relevant offices in the firm, such as training and development. Clear communication is essential as an illustration of respect for coworkers.

Communication style is another aspect to consider. Nash (1989:244) points out the need for consideration of the manner in which an initiative is stated: it needs to be written for the layperson, not for philosophers or academicians. The average employee needs to be able to grasp and understand ethics concepts and situations suggested for a hospital's or corporation's ethical mandate. Furthermore, statements need to be linked to the daily work of employees with clear, consistent, and direct communication, as noted under the discussion regarding support of CEOs for the ethics program. Ethically, the accountability relationship expected among employees needs to be communicated in language employees appreciate prior to initiating a session.

Ethics Program Advisory Committee

The fifth and last strategy is to establish a representative ethics advisory committee, differentiated from a hospital or institutional ethics committee. Rather than solicit information from one's peers or friends as Anderssen did, develop a system-wide committee to advise the ethics program and its director. Even though it may be either *ad hoc* or ongoing, broad input is required regarding the needs of the potential attendees.

An important strategy for development success used by several firms is representative teams of employees from across the company or health facility, gauging employees' interests, support, and continuing feedback. If leaders responsible for implementation of the plan note relatively high degrees of resistance, or even lack of motivation for the plan, selection of employees who represent strategic areas within the firm to serve on implementation teams may increase the acceptance of the project (See: resistance, below). An ethics advisory committee serves as a direct link to coworkers, explaining the new initiative and serving as a good-will ambassador to workers. It may also serve as a group in which ethics dilemmas emerging from programs are examined for relevant patterns, themes or issues in the organization, serving as the basis for policies reflecting employee concerns through the hospital or company.

Committee members may be 'elected' from among discrete categories, or they may be appointed. It may also be prudent to ask managers at mid-level positions to select or nominate key persons in their respective departments. Not only do such strategies enhance a broad view of the corporate-wide personnel pool, but these members may also provide useful suggestions regarding ethics events relevant to the entire organization. Overall, such teams enhance acceptance of new ideas which ethics programs may illustrate.

As an aside, various terms are used internationally, and at times interchangeably, for the ethics program, including ethics office, panel on ethics, ethics committee, institutional ethics committee, and hospital ethics committee, and in some cases the institutional review board, committee on integrity, ethics platform committee, or ethics project (group). Generally, ethics office or ethics program is a more universal term to represent these other concepts.

Resistance: An Important, Often Ignored, Aspect

Development of an ethics program leading to a system-wide and comprehensive ethics ethos requires sustained effort on the part of many. Because development of an ethics environment means change from less to more attention on values, it involves value change. Furthermore, it implies planning realistically for implementation, allowing for (some) resistance or backward slippage. Creating a holistic model means the overall plan needs to be broken down into realistic steps that can be implemented, assessed, and then revised.

There is no one response to the issue of ethics implementation, although sources discuss resistance to implementation of programs. Causes of resistance are located in cost, time, personnel, expertise or lack thereof, and perceived need. We turn now to explore several reasons why resistance may occur and negatively influence the development and eventual implementation of an ethical environment for management and its employees.

Implementation of an ethics program implies organizational change. Research documents the opinion among employees that they prefer to work in an ethical rather than a non-ethical setting, but not all employees share this perception. Rarely is the need for ethics totally shared as a common perception in today's organizations. Some of the reasons are *unrelated* to ethics *per se*. When a culture changes, at the very least it alters patterns of interaction in the organization; it changes relationships among employees and between supervisors and employees. It may also alter the power balance ingrained in the firm. The latter is one of the most prevalent and robust sources of resistance to change.

Ethics provides organizations dimensions many may not realize. With its emphasis on justice and resulting fairness to all employees, and by providing a language shared across disciplines or professions, ethics supports conversations among employees. Ethics offers an inclusive means of engaging in conversations and deliberations about morally difficult situations emerging at work, rather than an exclusive language owned by one discipline or profession. It is therefore a subtle means of re-allocating the power or authority in interpersonal relationships. In this way, ethics programming becomes the focus of resistance since it threatens prior relationships based on implicit power, informal authority, or other manifestations of power *im*balance in the work setting. It is the nature of humans to seek, and probably to prefer, power and use of power, as well as preferring prior patterns of interaction. These formations of power may include company cliques, exclusive and cohesive work groupings illustrated by the food drivers, or groups formed by varied sociodemographic features. Additionally, the interactions may enact power extending to clusters of employees engaging in bribes, paybacks, product theft, or forms of *quid pro quo* in which the employees use power to exert or extract behaviors or favors from employees, even supervisors. Power in the workplace is a significant consideration in both interpersonal relationships and employee work groups.

A wise director of ethics also pays attention to areas of resistance in his/her organization, in order to address them and create ways to ease the implementation of the ethics program. To return to the discussion in Chapter Five, we remind ourselves of how important a full assessment is; the caveat to explore political issues is relevant to this point. Another reminder is the case example in Chapter Two regarding the culture surrounding the food delivery personnel; they did not want the culture to change, revealing evident resistance during the interviews. Resistance takes many forms. Sage ethics directors, minimally, assess potential sources of resistance and use top management to support the continued development and implementation of positive value change. The need for involvement of the CEO or other top management leads directly to the topic of the next chapter: sustaining ethics programs in organizations.

Note

1   Appreciation is expressed to Robert Hall for helpful comments on the case of Allen Anderssen.

References

Andrews, K. R. (Ed.). (1989). *Ethics in practice: Managing the moral corporation*. Boston, MA: Harvard Business School Press.

Cranford, R., and Doudera, A. (Eds.). (1984). *Institutional ethics committees and health care decision making*. Ann Arbor, MI: Health Administration Press.

Goodpaster, K. (1989). Ethical imperatives and corporate leadership. In K. R. Andrews (Ed.), *Ethics in practice: Managing the moral corporation* (pp. 212-238). Boston, MA: Harvard Business School Press.

Miller, D. B. (1986). *Managing professionals in research and development*. San Francisco, CA: Jossey-Bass Co.

Nash, L. (1989). In K. R. Andrews (Ed.), *Ethics in practice: Managing the moral corporation* (pp. 65-72). Boston, MA: Harvard Business School Press.

Shirom, A., and Harrison, M. (1995). Diagnostic models for organizations: Toward an integrative perspective. In C. L. Cooper and D. M. Rousseau (Eds.), *Trends in organizational behavior* (V. 2, pp. 85-107). New York, NY: John Wiley and Sons, Ltd.

Tharenou, P. (1997). Determinants of participation in training and development. In C. L. Cooper and D. M. Rousseau (Eds.), *Trends in organizational behavior* (Vol. 4, pp. 15-27). New York, NY: John Wiley and Sons, Ltd.

Treviño, L. (1997). Ethical decision making in organizations: A person-situation interactionist model. In T. Donaldson and T. W. Dunfree (Eds.), *Ethics in business and economics* (Vol. II, pp. 601-617). Aldershot, UK: Ashgate Publishers.

Chapter 7

Sustaining Organizational Ethics

Introduction

In the first two chapters of Part Two we explored assessment and development as phases in the progress toward an improved ethical environment. The third step is sustaining the ethics work. As with other initiatives in an organization, CEOs and managers want to confirm the effort and financial outlay result not only in positive outcomes but also in ones that are continued. To be anticipated, however, changes in behavior and attitude are difficult to attain, much less to sustain. For that reason, explicit attention needs to be given to strategies keeping the ethics development in place and preventing regression of the development efforts.

Fundamental to sustaining the ethics work is its conceptualization as a *program*, explored in Chapter Five under the discussion of program and program evaluation. Sustaining activities need to consider the wide range of activities currently comprising the ethics program. It takes consideration beyond the initial ethics audit to include the information obtained in the audit, the plans for response to the audit, and ultimately the programmatic work on ethics.

According to Goodpaster (1989:222), the leader's agenda is defined as having three broad imperatives for the ethics agenda: orienting, institutionalizing, and sustaining corporate values. In Chapter Eight we explore the first imperative of orienting and here explore the need for institutionalizing and sustaining values, recognizing these behaviors as leader activities. Values are conveyed by the director of the program but may be delegated to and carried out by others. It is important, however, to provide documented results of any change in values. Positioning them parallel to other mandates within the organization recognizes the importance of the last two agenda items. Thus value takes on increasing importance for the anticipated ethical corporation. In particular, orienting suggests leaders need to first determine the direction for the future. These become maps for leadership initiatives, or as this author prefers, the *ethics path*.

Foundational activities also offer means for identifying and keeping record of future ethics challenges; keeping record becomes a way to continue gathering information as found in the feedback loop process. Results may also indicate important patterns, themes, or concerns common to several individuals or groups of employees; they in turn lead to company-wide policies and procedures. These were explored in Chapter Three under the discussion on ethics and compliance. Related to this aim of documenting results is the ability to measure the desired outcome, discussed in Chapters One and Five. Management leadership of the firm needs a cohesive approach to the development because fragmented and divided approaches may do more harm than good to the organization.

An important aspect of the move toward a more ethical environment is the ability to effect change in and among employees. Kilmann and Covin (1984:303) point out effecting change in an overall system requires two aspects: locating controllable variables and action steps to adjust those (controllable) variables. Once these two are addressed, change becomes likely. This chapter explores those steps to ensure established change.

Effecting change by itself is not adequate, however. Change without accompanying supports will not remain (Dawson, 1994). An ethics program not planning for sustainability is anticipating its own future demise. Common mistakes in maintaining a developed ethics programming are ignoring needs for sustainment, ignoring goals developed as part of the program, or both. Critical to retaining a program is integrating the program outcomes with the aims and measuring advancement of the program. Measuring the advancement of the program is also linked to documentation of the outcomes, explored later in this chapter. Leaders want to sustain programs and keep them evolving in a forward direction. Continuing the ethics program is necessary and needs to be explicitly addressed.

> Susan Simpson was an energetic manager with good ideas. The CEO asked her if she would take on the responsibility for an initiative in the firm, one the CEO referred to as *Ethics for Lunch*. What the CEO initially envisioned when the program was developed was an opportunity for employees to gather informally and discuss their issues of an ethical nature arising at work. The CEO wanted employees as well as employers to participate in ongoing discussions about business ethics. As a far-sighted and visionary leader, she remembered the importance of such programs in her own early career. Simpson was now being asked to ensure the CEO's vision continued.
>
> Simpson picked up where the former ethics program director stopped; she read over the reports, attendance records, and program agendas. She began her work with an informal committee, gathered a few key persons, and developed a plan on which there was initial agreement. She kept notes of possible discussion topics and listed the various suggested potential presenters. The current list was compared with those from prior sessions. Simpson also made plans for another meeting and wisely asked for feedback from the persons gathered.
>
> A time and place were developed for this first *Ethics for Lunch*, including an invited presenter to 'kick off' the sessions. Simpson introduced the presenter and briefly reiterated the program aims reported in early committee minutes. The first lunch brought in about 15 interested employees. While sparsely attended, those present reported it good and the topic interesting. Simpson's first lunch session seemed to go well.
>
> Even with all of these initiatives, however, Simpson never did clear with the CEO the formal resources allocated for this program. Budget and reporting were both unclear. Perhaps even more important, Simpson failed to create a formal committee institutionalized into the company; there was never a formal structure with reporting and feedback mechanisms within the organization regarding ethics programming. As this relatively new company became increasingly busy, the topic and the program offering were shuffled into another room, then into another time slot. Simpson had no

recourse for the program other than the CEO, now quite busy and traveling a lot. The morning of an ethics event, a top manager suggested the ethics program be melded into another initiative on training and development occurring on the same day. Simpson, unaware of this other offering and the implications of this shift, agreed.

Within six months, *Ethics for Lunch* was absorbed into other programs offered in the organization; the topic and its title disappeared. Susan Simpson's responsibility for this initiative also disappeared. At the end of the year, approximately one year from her initial conversation with the CEO, Simpson reported topics were being discussed but the program had been melded—morphed might be more to the point—into other programs. She presented this revision in a positive manner, but the point is made: *Ethics for Lunch* disappeared for lack of planned sustainability.

It might be argued a revised program is a positive step. Perhaps, but such was not planned. In this instance, it 'just happened' rather than resulting from intentional and strengthened revision. Other strategies could have either retained the program or provided for joint program planning. The final blow came when Simpson went to a meeting for training and development about 18 months later and heard a colleague comment, 'Where did that discussion called *Ethics for Lunch* go? I thought it was a good idea, and it seems to have just disappeared from sight.'

Unfortunately, Susan Simpson, like so many well-meaning and enthusiastic employees, learned a hard lesson from this experience. As a bright talented person, she will not repeat this mistake. In fact, in private among trusted friends, Simpson wondered aloud what happened and whether lack of resources and support had anything to do with the departure of the former program director. The results of the Simpson case could have been prevented, however, and *Ethics for Lunch* would now be a well-respected ongoing ethics program in the firm. This blunder draws attention to the controllable variables for change. Lack of sustained programming pertaining to the controllable variables contributed to the ethics program departure. Let's use the Simpson case as a test point for exploring ways to sustain ethics programs, desired changes, and ethical environments sought by top management.

Strategies for Sustaining

What is sustaining? What would a sustained ethics program look like in organizations? Sustaining refers to the permanency and endurance of a program: the ability to maintain viability and remain in existence for a lengthy, if undefined, period of time. A sustained ethics program is an integral part of the organization and evident in the formal dimensions of the work; it withstands (some) erosion, resistance, or 'attack' if it occurs. Ethics programs that are developed, implemented, and sustained are 'in the minds of the employees.' Representing programs of time and standing in the organization, the ethics initiative is not only recognized by top management but is also acknowledged and used by a wide range of employees in the firm.

Sustaining an ethics program building upon and resulting from the ethics program development implies that it attains acquired status within the firm. It does not, however, imply a static or changeless endeavor. Although ethics programs may be continued over time, as part of an open system viable programs also respond to changes internal and external to their organization; they are responsive and therefore change in ways enhancing their goals. Indeed, an ethical value system will in reality never be 'fully developed.' The implication of a continuing development is a primary reason why attention to sustaining the endeavor is so important.

Leaders and others in positions of responsibility for implementing a system need to realize development as an ongoing and continual process. Value change and employee attrition require constant monitoring and reinforcement. New employees are hired as old ones retire, resign, or are let go. Novel initiatives and new challenges continuously face the contemporary corporation, an open system also constantly changing and responding to its context. Fresh ethics initiatives need to attend to sustainability because they are especially vulnerable to erosion. Leaders who assume they can implement a new value system and then leave it are unrealistic. Such a system is doomed to decline almost immediately.

One dimension of sustaining ethics programs is the manner in which the program is conceptualized. Related to the discussion in Chapter One in which we explored the creative relationship between the individual and the corporate is the need to switch from individual approaches and concepts to those germane to the collectivity. If the objective is a more ethical ambience in the system, then a paradigm shift needs to occur in all facets of the organization: structures and processes, including language. A transition occurs to 'shift' from thinking about individuals to thinking about organizations and ethics. In that light, several concepts common to work with individuals are listed with possible organizational corollary. For many directors, this list highlights the need to think more institutionally about their work.

Individual	*Collective*
Honesty	Policies and procedures supporting consistency, monitoring and follow-through.
Justice	Fair, just policies and procedures, trustworthy organization, accountability measures.
Respect	Consideration, communication, deliberations; consumer (patient, or customer) satisfaction.

The parallel listing of suggested concepts encourages management to think about the collective or corporate parallel. Many a firm continues to talk about organizational ethics yet discusses concepts relevant to individuals, not the whole. While individuals, as examined in Chapter One, are part of the whole, the point is developing a collective ethics, not just a collection of individual ones. The aim is a collectively shared and supported organizational ethics.

As Kilmann and Covin (1984) suggest, the assessment explored in Chapter Five is foundational in determining which variables, which aspects of the organization, can change. Once those have been identified and the program designed (examined in Chapter Six) the next step follows: affecting those controllable variables to sustain the change.

Sustaining a program implies approaches pertaining to controllable variables, divided into two major categories. One is attention to the *structures* of the ethics program, and the other is attention to the *processes*, or, some might say, the substantive efforts of the work. For heuristic purposes, we treat the two approaches as dichotomous, *i.e.* each approach is considered separately from the other. In order to be truly successful, however, the approaches must be addressed in a complementary fashion. One without the other will not result in sustained quality ethics programming, as they supplement and support each other over time.

Structural Strategies for Sustainability

Let us turn now to the step of exploring structures as strategies to sustain programs. What are structures? What do we mean by sustainability structures in organizations? Structures represent the evident or institutional dimensions of the program. In other terms they are the hardware in contrast to the software. The structural dimensions institutionalize the ethics program, keep it stabilized within the organization, and continue its existence within the firm. Structures are indicated on a company's formal organizational diagram. Structures can be changed within the organization, yet they are formal aspects of the ethics program. They include, for example, organizational groups offering discussion and deliberation, ethics committees providing oversight or advising the director on the program, policies and procedures, formal reports, written goals, or the written evaluation of the ethics program. We move now to several examples of structural sustainment strategies.

Training Education for ethics and ethics training are both important dimensions of any sustained ethics program. Education also poses a complex way of thinking about continuity because the ethics educational initiative illustrates both structures and processes; here we explore ethics training as structure. In many organizations, there is a designated office for on-site training and development. As suggested earlier, some collaboration and coordination needs to exist between this and the ethics work. Whether the ethics input is understood as education or training, the organization needs to continuously instill ethics, convey the value message to new employees, impart the ethics message consistently to all workers, and indicate the consequences of unacceptable behaviors at work. This requires education as one of the responsibilities of an ethics-training program and is a central sustaining strategy.

Another area for education is the relationship between supervisors and employees. As noted earlier, employees value work situations in which their supervisors support them. Relationships between supervisors and subordinates raise an obvious question: Can supervisors engage in fruitful conversations with their subordinates to instill more desired ethics behavior? It is pointless to develop a program of ethics if supervisors who interact with employees on a daily basis either do not support it (raising yet another set of issues for top management to address) or cannot aid in implementing the desired behaviors. Managers too need training and education.

Difficult behaviors need to be discussed, and training programs may serve as sources for those challenging conversations. Employees can be encouraged to explore and discuss problematic behaviors at work in order to achieve understanding of acceptable and unacceptable responses. A straightforward mechanism is to ask employees what they observe in their daily work. For example, they might be asked how much unwarranted sick time is used in their department, if moonlighting occurs, or if conflicts of interest are present between other positions and the firm. Use of bribes, careless behavior surrounding confidential patient care or financial information, and removal of hospital property constitute poor activities. Unethical behaviors also include use of company equipment for personal use. This is inappropriate; however, the use of irreplaceable company property, such as food or stationery, constitutes theft. Employees rarely conceive of such use as theft, instead considering it an extension of their paid work or perceived recompense due to them. Regardless, hospital or company rules need to be conveyed in writing to employees as noted in earlier chapters.

Conversations can also attempt to uncover acts of outright fraud and corruption; however, it may be difficult to get employees to openly identify individuals engaging in such behaviors. Initially, it might be more fruitful to inquire about the presence of such activity in the firm generally and move to conversations about the problems it poses, ways to report it, or ways in which the present employees can address it if the situation occurs. The fact that the hospital or company is having a discussion about these unethical behaviors puts employees on guard: behaviors are attracting the attention of top management. Explored later in this chapter are ways in which sanctions can both prevent and decrease such unethical behaviors; consequent sanctions are needed for these inappropriate acts. Using information from the foundational audit, the evaluator can also introduce behaviors he/she notes in the firm. Given these activities occur in your organization, how often do you observe them in your unit or department, and how much of a problem are they?

There are also procedures encouraging dialogue among employees to explore commonly occurring ethical challenges. These include discussion of excessive call-in for sick time, continued lateness on the job, use of company property, delays in response to patients' needs, and use of patients' medications. Some researchers suggest that conversations about one's own 'friends' are often revealing, based on the theory that what one perceives in others is similar to one's own behavior or situation (Katz and Allport, 1931). The underlying question about these assessments, however, is their reliability and validity. As asserted in earlier chapters, reliance upon only one form of intervention poses risks, suggesting that a multi-pronged approach is more plausible.

An educational strategy to convey the importance of ethical behavior to employees is to relay ways in which an ethics ethos has payoff: image, reputation, inventoried products or patient care, and reduction of error. Allied Holdings, in

Decatur, Georgia, reduced company insurance claims by attention to the ethics values of respect and consideration for each employee, repaying the firm in reduced liability claims, insurance costs, and turnover, noted in Chapter Eight. Education and training are central strategies to sustain ethics in organizations and may be broadly or narrowly construed to meet organizational needs.

Personnel The role and position of directors of ethics programs are critical to the ethics work. What is the position of the director, and is the position established within the institution? Directors of ethics who are not located on organizational charts, for example, might have cause to ask whether the ethics program is well situated. Permanent positions in health care and business are evident on company charts, complemented by listings on the main directory, offices accessible to employees, and other manifestations indicating the centrality of the ethics initiative.

> Recently, in an attempt to locate the central person for a hospital ethics program, this author traveled through the tunnel of a hospital to find a small and obscure room in which the ethics initiative was housed. The impression conveyed: ethics is not central to the health care system, which is also experiencing numerous staff and patient care conflicts.

The person assigned responsibility for ethics within a health care or business system needs to be located in a central and accessible position for employees throughout the organization. For health care systems accessibility extends to patients and their families, as illustrated by the case in Chapter Four. As with any other key position in a firm, the complementary accoutrements of office, mailbox, phone, or secretary are available. This is not to suggest an ethics office or program demands large outlays of staff and facilities. Rather what is suggested is a central location making the ethics office readily accessible to personnel.

Committees as deliberation structures Employees in health care and business firms prefer work settings in which they have some access to discussions regarding the troubling and challenging ethical issues emerging in their daily work, documented by research (McDaniel and Schoeps, 2003a). If leaders want to develop a strategy enhancing and sustaining ethics in their various clinical areas or business departments, a structure through which employees may participate in deliberation about the morally difficult situations they experience at work is one strategy. A sustainment strategy includes institutionalizing structures to support ethics deliberations.

Committees and similar structures can be used to continue a new ethics program. The committee is formal rather than informal and is listed in written materials in the company. Sporadic committee structures implying the program is not established or is tentative in nature are to be avoided. Structured committees are illustrated on the formal organizational chart, and unlike informal gatherings occurring occasionally, deliberation structures and committees addressing ethics have written schedules available to all employees; the discussions need to be accessible. The initiatives, once developed and put into place, need to be formalized so they become constant aspects of the daily life of the firm. Sporadic, occasional, or intermittent approaches do not work over time.

An ethics committee institutionalized and structured into the organization is in contrast to the example explored in Chapter Four, in which physicians were unconcerned about access. A well-structured committee exhibits a planned schedule of meetings and a realistic time frame known within the firm; employees know how to access the committee to submit ethics problems for discussion. The committee also has appropriate links to other relevant departments within the firm, such as the Training and Development Department, the Office of Human Resources, or Risk Management.

Parallel to the development of a formal ethics committee is selection of committee members. Placing a few key persons on a committee can enhance its stature in the organization, strengthen the ethics program, and gain access to needed lines of communication or resources. Important to the ethics committee are members with expertise or interest in ethics. Also important is consideration of representatives from other relevant and related aspects of the firm noted above (*e.g.*, Risk Manager, Director of Human Resources, Director of Training and Development, or their designated representatives). If the committee is composed of personnel without experience, or those who demonstrate lack of commitment to ethics, a program administrator needs to be alert to adverse behaviors. Requesting additional representative personnel would be wise.

Because key personnel are typically also busy, if the program director is asked to consult about individuals to place on the ethics committee, the initial negotiation for committee membership can be time-limited. This form of negotiation often secures active participation within a set time frame. Most staff members are pleased to offer expertise and advice when they know the requested time investment represents a realistic expectation; time parameters also allow busy managers and employees to plan realistically and ahead on their own time commitments and schedules, respectively.

Lastly, the ethics committee needs to maintain written documentation of its activities. While retaining confidentiality requisite to its work, minutes or reports can also be conveyed in summary manner to employees. These forms of communication keep the work of the committees or similar structures before the employees and management and provide formal documentation of decisions and results of their work.

Policies and procedures   Development of an ethical framework also implies (implicitly and explicitly) the development of policies and procedures aiding in identifying appropriate behaviors, offering a guide for those behaviors, and determining consequences of the behaviors, both positive and negative. These various policies and procedures need to include hire and fire procedures, the full range of human resource activities, as well as those involved in the interactions with customers.

Some policies emerge from federal regulations including those addressing diversity, persons with disability, and harassment. Policies either need to be included or assurance needs to be provided that employees are aware of these mandates. What does an employee do when a customer offers him/her a bribe? To whom may he/she turn for advice or counsel? What happens to employees who 'blow the whistle' on other employees? These situations need to be clearly addressed by written policies and procedures system-wide in the company. Written policies and procedures attest to permanent and sustained ethics activities in organizations.

Reward system Essential to an ethics program is recognizing positive *ethical* behaviors on the part of employees, especially those going beyond the mere obedience to regulations. The reward system recognizes and affirms activities other than, or in addition to, those of its primary aims of making money (Miller, 1986). An employee returning money to a customer or correcting a company error— mistakes occur in all organizations—and letting the customer know are only two examples of employees who demonstrate ethical excellence. The behaviors should be recognized. These positive behaviors become the listing of 'best practices' among employees and serve as exemplars of desirable employee behaviors. Employees need positive role models and examples to emulate, especially when employers are seeking changes in behavior among workers. Corporations and hospitals need to develop clear statements of value and reward employees who enact those values.

Rewards for recognition of ethical behavior and values need to be linked to the ethics program. An 'Employee of Excellence Award' also affirms ethical behavior among employees, as do 'Most Valued Employee' recognitions; these rewards link employee behavior with company values and express them directly to employees. They become annual events, representing strategies making preferred values sought in the ethics program tangible and explicit for employees. Awards to individual employees and other forms of recognition provide complementary reinforcement of the desired values in the firm. Considering team or group awards is also important to support collaborative and cooperative work among employees. Researchers know outcomes need to be connected through a feedback loop to the desired behaviors with rewards to reinforce and support them (Kirkpatrick, 1985:255).

Related to the reward system to sustain ethics is consideration of corporate fit. The policies and rewards related to and affirming of the ethics program need to be consistent with the corporate culture of the organization. At the same time and not suggesting a contradiction, the revision in system ethics to one emphasizing values, may counter a formerly negative culture or a climate in which values are *dis*valued. These, too, need to be considered and perhaps countered. In some firms, however, a highly systemized approach is not as effective as one less structured and informal yet interwoven into the ethos of the organization. Whatever the chosen approach, the ethics initiative best complements the culture of the firm; it needs to fit the normative patterns and interactions of the corporation, or the chance of its survival as a program is lessened.

As Goodpaster (1989:227) suggests, the form of reinforcement for ethical values needs consideration, pointing to the paradox of motivation for ethical values. For example, he notes the need to attend to apparent contradictions in using punishments in order to instill and encourage employees to assimilate a more ethical set of interactions and behaviors. The '... leader who is mindful of this. . . [apparent contraction w]ill approach the task ... with a special kind of circumspection.' Ethics needs to be communicated in ways enhancing conformance with the desired outcomes, suggesting positive rewards and reinforcement for ethical values. Another way of examining the concern is to reiterate an earlier claim supported here: the work of the ethics program needs to be consistent with the content and processes of the program. These activities confirm ethical consistency.

Communication In consort with the awards noted above, some means of communication needs to be developed within the firm to convey consistently the message about ethics to all employees. It may not require separate forms of communication such as newsletters, but it does require a means of communication with employees about the ethics program, the processes and works of the program, and, especially, results of the effort. Laura Nash (1989) points to the need for communication not only for academics or top managers; communication needs to be written for, and engaging to, the layperson in the organization.

Communication includes brochures, fliers on events, biographies on speakers, and examination of ethics situations typically occurring at the site. Several successful programs always include one illustrative problematic ethics case in each written communication, to reinforce core values and aid employees' analyses of ethical issues. Written reinforcement is important to continue the ethics program, because the activities need to be made evident for employees. Included in this communication is information on hot-lines or other ways of obtaining support when employees require it.

Some organizations are developing consultations for troubling moral situations as part of their ethics programs. Consultation extends communication to the actual engagement with employees and customers, or providers and patients and their families on-site. This facet of the ethics program is similar to the ethics consultation services hospitals and other health care facilities employ. Likewise, in health care systems, the activities of the ethics program may complement an on-going ethics committee or consultation service, requiring both to work together cooperatively. In addition to consultants, on-call experts for resolution of ethics cases can be helpful in health care and business settings. Continued reinforcement about the work and results of ethics programs and management are important to sustaining the ethics program. Communication makes the ethics program salient to employees and illustrates a controllable variable in the system.

Realistic goals Being realistic is also important to sustain a new ethic. Realistic goals are essential to development of a sustained ethical organization. A philosophically fine but difficult-to-reach goal is not realistic. Neither is a social view not taking into consideration avoidance of injury and affirmation of beneficence. Limiting corporate ethics development to a few well-selected key rules is more successful in the long run than difficult-to-understand mandates or impossible sanctions. The ethics program also needs to offer managers and employees ethics guidance for work with their departments and employees who occupy those departmental positions. This, too, is realistic. These steps connect back to the organizational goals, and they in turn to the reward system noted above. The interconnecting links between company goals, employee behaviors, and rewards for ethical activities need to be clear and explicit for employees. Making these connections explicit is a management responsibility and realistic goal, which organizational leaders and directors of ethics programs need to assume, examined fully in Chapter Eight.

Processes for Sustainment

In contrast to structures sustaining ethics programming, processes are dimensions that flesh out the structures. If the ethics program serves as the hardware, the processes illustrate the software side of the enterprise. While difficult to describe explicitly, the processes are important to the daily work life of employees. One structure for sustaining the ethics program that overlaps with processes is education, which is commonly conducted in a formal program or training service in the organization. Education or training also represents processes for imparting knowledge or demonstrating new behaviors to employees. Imparting ethics theories and conveying ethical analysis are illustrations of processes. Nevertheless, processes are an essential and important aspect of the ethics initiative and should not be overlooked.

Processes are dimensions sustaining trust over time, instilling new meaning in ethical behaviors, and sustaining the values of the business or health care corporation for the long term. Processes include the various conversations, exchanges, and discussions of an ethical nature occurring in the daily work life of employees. Informal and casual conversations regarding ethical issues are processes. Examples also include ethics discussions, teaching on-site, or communications surrounding the ethics program; informal gatherings, *ad hoc* committees, or task forces emerging to aid in meeting ethics program goals. They also include the rhythms of the company anticipating weekly discussions on ethics, and ethics rounds providing avenues for learning; conversations occurring in the company regarding ethical behaviors, and resulting solutions or decisions.

The brief case illustrates how companies are sustaining ethics:

Both UPS and Chick-fil-A attend to sustainability processes. Leaders of the former discuss the company ethics code and policies regularly in meetings, whereas Chick-fil-A's CEO gathers their 'Operators' and other key directors together for annual information exchanges and supports, including family members. Consistent, repeat, and explicit value messages attend to the sustainability of their companies' ethical values.

Processes of ethics programming may include sensitivity to ethical issues when they arise and identification of a problem needing to be addressed for the betterment of the organization. Ethics processes also include the reactions of employees when they observe harassment on the job, stealing, or other forms of unethical behavior, such as disrespect shown to a coworker. These employee reactions become the palpable forms of understanding the ethics ethos of any specific organization. Processes become dimensions of the organizational culture. They are foundational to the organizational ethos and aid in communicating the core values and attitudes of any endeavor. Certainly, both structures and processes are important to establish, in order to sustain the ethics program.

Challenges to Sustained Programming

The case of Susan Simpson illustrates an ethics program, like any program, is open to challenges of establishing a vulnerable new endeavor. A critical issue illustrated by Simpson's case is the lack of planning to sustain the program. Attention to the process side of planning the initiative is missing, especially the political dimensions resulting from a lack of collaboration with other employees and departments. Not only are the formal structures ignored, including resource allocation to sustain the program, but Simpson also allows the program to meld without a fight. Relatively new initiatives are always vulnerable to 'takeover' by others or simply by tight schedules, highlighting the importance for sustainability activities for ethics programs. Several challenges anticipated for ethics programs and their directors are listed below; these are specific challenges to sustained ethics programming.

1. *Takeover*. As Simpson learned, creative initiatives are always vulnerable to 'takeover.' This may occur intentionally, arising from equally energetic, visionary, and competitive employees who are eager to expand their power if not their prestige. It may also emerge in unintentional ways from lack of planning or protection.

    As explored in Chapter Three, a significant challenge for ethics takeover is the blending of ethics into compliance or subsuming ethics under the company compliance program. Other examples of integration may occur with the same result. We have already explored the issues inherent in such decisions, but the point needs to be reiterated here: watch for (individual and) system takeover or competing program takeover.

2. *Schedule Conflicts*. Point number one, always a threat in contemporary hospitals and businesses, will more than likely emerge from the typical organizational schedule: too much to do, too many other competing initiatives.

Schedule conflicts were an apparent problem for the event Susan Simpson planned. These, however, are forms of 'takeover' if for no other reason than new initiatives not yet 'welded' into the company structure are vulnerable to 'schedule squeeze.' Protecting one's new program or new initiative is critical for continued success. Simpson needed to protect *Ethics for Lunch*.

3. *Waning Enthusiasm*. Most persons recognize new or relatively new initiatives get the attention of key persons. Newness is nice, so to speak. Some persons thrive on new rather than established programs. This statement is not an evaluative one but merely describes the reality of life in busy organizations with any program. However, keeping this caveat in mind is critical for sustaining an ethics program. Program managers need to be aware of and prepare for waning enthusiasm. Without referring to empirical studies on the topic, wane appears to occur about six to eight months out from the time of initiation. Sage program planners anticipate and thereby prevent program wane.

4. *Resistance*. In all formal organizations there is resistance to new programs. Sometimes this resistance is against any new initiative, a new program competing with 'mine,' or a new program reallocating company or hospital resources. Resistance was explored in more detail in Chapter Six; suffice it to reiterate here, resistance is a consideration in the continuation of an ethics program. Resistance comes in several forms: implicit and explicit, intentional and unintentional. Regardless of the forms, the result is counterproductive to the aims of the ethics program and its continuation. In whatever manner this new initiative is understood, sustaining a program means attending to various forms of resistance.

5. *Sabotage*. As much as all of us would like to think others welcome our creative initiatives, this is often not the case. In fact, resistance, as explored in number four, may escalate into forms of sabotage of a new ethics initiative. While the reasons for sabotage may be similar or even the same as those for resistance, sabotage takes resistance to a new level; sabotage is intentional. Undermining the program, undercutting the program developer, or short-circuiting resources are only a few of the means used to sabotage new programs. Rerouting of memos to exclude new ethics directors, using up or lack of allocated funds, or negative comments about the program to others rather than to the director are all potential forms of sabotage; some of these are also unprofessional and unethical behaviors. The seemingly helpful suggestion to meld or include one's program in an ongoing one can become a form of sabotage. Persons who work in ethics may assume merely because a program concerns ethics it is welcomed. This assumption is naive. A relatively new ethics officer in a long-standing firm said about some quite active and overt sabotage of a similar program, 'But how could they? The programming has to do with ethics!' Indeed, an additional cautionary note is to state just because

the program or the topic is ethics does not mean it is immune to sabotage. Ethics aside, program developers need to be aware of the potential for challenges. Awareness leads to prevention of sabotage.

6. *Lack of Resources.* Any new initiative needs resources allocated to keep it running. If budget allocation, adequate space, or other forms of resource allotment are not forthcoming, wise program planners need to inquire further about the level of commitment for the ethics program. A lack of resource within the company is the first step on the path to discontinuation of a program, since lack of resources decreases potential for sustainability.

   If the CEO or visionary manager wants an ethics program to succeed, then adequate resources need to be allocated to ensure success. At a minimum, most planners suggest 'seed monies' provided for one year out. A second step related to garnering resources is clear expectations about the follow-up. Is the director, for example, expected to acquire additional or follow-up funding? What are the plans for support beyond the first year? While a program like *Ethics for Lunch* would not necessarily require high levels of financial support, resources are needed and serve as indicators of projected commitment for the program. Regardless of the amount, resources to sustain the ethics program for a realistic time frame need to be forthcoming.

7. *Lack of Documentation.* Implicit in the discussion above of strategies for sustainment, is the need for goals, plans, resources, and other important aspects regarding the program to be placed in writing. These include committee minutes, goal statements, and desired outcomes. While it may seem unnecessary to mention this, experience indicates planners often overlook this aspect for sustaining programs, especially as it pertains to ethics. It is equally important to get important aspects of the program in place early in the negotiations. Strategies sustaining ethics are like any other program in a company, requiring the same written documentation.

   Although explored more fully below, it would be remiss not to mention the need to document the results of the ethics program explored in Chapter Six. Outcomes of the ethics program work, important advancements on the part of employees, or other contributions all need to be documented.

8. *Lack of Institutional Commitment.* The above are also indicators of the degree of organizational commitment for ethics. The CEO and top management need to 'buy-in' to the ethics program; they need to be on-board. CEOs or managers who shy away from formal committees, plans, resources, and personnel to support a program are giving key negative messages about the endeavor. At this point, the director (or person responsible) needs to assess the next step. Lack of commitment needs to be confronted directly. Wavering commitment may need to be enhanced with demonstrated need or outcomes; even here, caution is the word for preparing well for the future. Obviously, adequate resources suggest strong levels of commitment. Addressing the point should

ensure sustained ethics programming over time, which is the goal of this discussion.

Feedback Loop

At various points in this work we have referred briefly to feedback loops. The discussion below details the feedback loop and connects it directly to the activities for sustaining the ethics advancement.

What is a feedback loop? Why is it important? What is the relationship to sustaining ethics advancements? Feedback is a concept originating in organizational studies during the 20th century. The feedback mechanism is one part of a larger overall 'loop' or continuous information flow, serving as a *self-correcting* mechanism within organizations. This self-correcting quality is why a feedback loop is important in advancing systems of excellence. CEOs need to know that mechanisms are in place to provide the information necessary for rational and informed decisions. Directors of ethics programs need the same assurance, especially in health care systems and business systems so reliant upon quality employees and front-line activities between providers and patients and employees and customers.

Technically, the feedback loop includes four steps and refers to information resulting from an earlier process which is 'fed back' to the original source, becoming another means of assessment. In open systems—an assumption about organizations used here—feedback provides evaluators information about the 'transformation' aspect of the system. The four parts are the initial input or information on ethics, the processes or transformation, the outcomes, and using the outcomes to 'feed back' to the initial input on how well the steps succeeded in meeting (initial) goals. Theoretically, the feedback loop is continuous; the initial outcome then becomes the fourth step or more input. The process occurs again, repeated continuously in quality systems over time.

An excellent example is an ethics seminar with mandates to enhance sensitivity among employees about ethical issues occurring at work: the input is ethics information and the transformation is the pedagogy or teaching. The outcome desired is determined by asking the following: Did employees readily or more readily identify ethical issues at work? Was the new ethics information applied in their daily work life? The response to the questions (outcome) is feedback about the ethics program. The concept of 'loop' is a means of conceptualizing the input (ethics), the transformation (teaching), and output (learning or change in behavior) as one continuous circle or loop. The results of the process, or the outcome, become, in part, the information upon which to base continuing evaluation thereby becoming the input for a second phase of the 'loop.' To some this may seem like a cumbersome way of examining the typical process of formative evaluation, or using review and revision. However, since many organizations rely solely on ethics audits, used to reference a one-time or stand-alone ethics analysis, it is important to highlight the need for continuous flow of information on which to base sustained ethics assessment. Indeed, continuous assessment is the primary means to achieve and maintain a quality organization with an ethics environment.

Because we are assuming organizations are open systems, the assumption also implies information from the external environment influences the internal environment. Serious ethical situations emerging externally such as those during the WorldCom debacle, or the Duke University organ transplantation with incompatible blood type, serve as examples from which changes are made in other similar organizations, as well as their own. In such cases the changes are transformations to prevent the same outcomes from occurring in one's own system. To return to teaching of ethics as part of the ethics program, in addition to creating new policies and procedures, the director of ethics programming may be asked by the CEO to ensure the firm's employees are aware of new rules, can identify and address ethical challenges, and know the channels for reporting relevant unethical behaviors.

Organizations as open systems also illustrate equifinality, referring to the fact systems achieve similar ends with different means (processes). Meeting the goal of preventing a problem may be achieved by several or a combination of several methods (processes). Equifinality also connects back to the discussion in Chapter Six regarding the multi-faceted approach to ethics programming and supports the importance of diverse methodology.

Other reasons exist for the importance of a feedback loop. As a method of instilling continuous and self-correcting feedback in an organization, feedback loops imply work of the ethics program is inherently related to the mission of the organization; they establish feasibility and relevance explored earlier. Furthermore, feedback loops connect the work of the ethics program with *all* aspects of the organization. Linkage also serves as a method of institutionalizing the ethics program within the system and thereby enhances the sustainability work of the ethics program.

Given the exploration of Chapter Three in which it is evident natural attrition among a company's employees creates an unending need for ethics education, the work of the ethics program and education is continuous. So, too, is the work of assessing and sustaining the ethics program. Finally, it should be evident that an ethics program sustained within the system is one integrated in and related to the mission, relevant to employees system-wide, and providing outcomes connecting back to goals of the organization. In this manner, ethics programs also contribute to the creation of an organizational culture in which evaluation is part of company life; contributing to quality improvement is concomitant with employment. Feedback also affirms respect among employees as their comments and concerns are implemented within the evaluation system of the organization. As highlighted early in this work, an ethical organization is one where consistency is evident throughout the system. Ethical behavior woven throughout the organization is one illustration of ethics consistency and enhanced sustainment.

Outcomes for Sustainment

In addition to establishing the feedback loop explored above, the evidence of feedback needs to be explored. We begin with the evidence of the initial result displayed in documentation.

> Kaija Suominen was the new director of the hospital ethics program. Eager to do a good job, she implemented, with the knowledge of the CEO, an ethics evaluation and discussed it with the Risk Management Director, who was also working to reduce hospital errors. When Suominen obtained the results of the initial audit, one to be built into a continuous feedback monitoring system, she found some alarming replies. Several staff in the critical care units commented short-cuts were being taken in medication procedures and it bothered them; short-cuts were becoming prevalent. These 'short circuits,' as they were termed, had the potential for significant damage to patients and hospital.
>
> With this documentation in hand, but hiding the identity of the employees, Suominen arranged a meeting with the Director of Risk Management and legal counsel. Together they developed a plan in which a complementary program was designed to address both risk issues and related ethics issues. She then documented the process and resulting changes in behavior among the staff. Finally, she met privately with the staff to let them know changes were occurring, and assured them of risk management's involvement. To her knowledge, further 'short circuits' were prevented.

Documentation to Sustain

According to Miller (1986:169), the environment is an important component in the orchestration of organizational success when striving for change. Attention to the ethos is key to sustaining organizational effectiveness. Of four points Miller raises, documentation of goals is relevant to this chapter on sustainment. Documentation is especially critical for the phase of change explored here, sustaining the desired ethical ethos. Documentation establishes evidence of desired outcomes, sought changes, goals met, or all of these. Once the ethics program is implemented, information substantiating the desired changes needs to be gathered and compiled. Documenting desired outcomes is critical for a sustained ethics program.

As Kilmann and Covin (1984:303) note, effecting and documenting change among employees is critical to sustaining a new program. Change may be documented as simply as recording the number of attendees at *Ethics for Lunch* from initiation to present (See: Table 5.1). More formal assessment may rely upon evaluation of sessions or documentation of situations of an ethical nature that have emerged and have been addressed. The latter are especially important if employees who participate in ethics programs resolve ethics situations and do so well.

Rather, a model for diminishing *dys*functional acts or *un*ethical behaviors is the examination of the dynamics contributing to them. Assessing and analyzing the antecedents for unacceptable behaviors include listing the individual unethical activities of employees. Common but unethical activities serve as an illustration of unacceptable and sanctionable behavior in the organization. By critically analyzing behavior initially by frequency of occurrence and prevalence, patterns or themes may emerge which can be addressed institutionally. Unethical behaviors also represent lack of values or values ignored. Values—whether positive or negative—that employees enact represent individual or group choices, decisions made in employment.

Researchers divide outcomes of harmful and unethical acts into two major categories according to level of effect. Outcomes may be primarily injurious to the individual, or to the organization. Instances given for individual effect include examples of sexual harassment, physical violence, or unsafe work practices. Those affecting the organization include examples of theft of property, violation of company rules and laws, or breach of confidentiality, including communication of sensitive or proprietary information important to the firm and its patients and customers.

While most would recognize the behaviors listed above as injurious, researchers have also found a major deterrent to *in*appropriate behaviors is knowledge the behaviors will be revealed and will have consequences (Robinson and Greenberg, 1998:23). Included on the documentation lists are activities to eradicate unethical behaviors, and the various consequences and sanctions of those behaviors. Behaviors going unnoticed are, according to researchers, behaviors that will probably continue within an organization. While it is important to list and reward positive behavior and changes in behavior, it is also important for employees to know the consequences of poor behaviors. Monitoring with follow-up sanctions is important to decrease undesirable behaviors among employees. These activities and their documentation are part of the ethics program. These actions are also forms of respect and justice for employees as they go about their daily work.

Recent attention has been given to behaviors harming the firm. Most of this literature focuses on financial losses incurred by organizations. It is also important to understand and not underestimate, especially in terms of the ethical nature of the behaviors, the damage to psychological, emotional, or other aesthetic features of work life, including employees' esteem and pride in their work. Loss of cohesion among work groups, lack of trust, fear of retaliation, or loss of reputation are aspects of work life representing a large toll, albeit quite difficult to measure. These behaviors represent enormous losses for a company or industry, yet in many ways are immeasurable; they are also ethics losses at work, undermining the degree of respect and justice in the organization. The old adage that it takes years to build but seconds to destroy a good reputation is pertinent to *un*ethical behavior.

Unacceptable behaviors also raise ethical issues for the organization and its leaders. A firm with a mandate for ethical behaviors and developing an ethical environment, yet doing little to deter unethical behaviors among employees might be considered unethical in approach. Promise keeping, attention to issues of justice on the job, and creating a work setting commensurate with the policies, procedures, and mandates of the organization all attest to the organization's observance of ethical practices. These practices are desired by employees and substantiated in research results (McDaniel and Schoeps, 2003a). They extend beneficence, respect, trust, and honesty on the job. To do otherwise not only undermines the ethics program but also sends a counter-message to employees. Sustainability is a close cousin to results, follow-up, documentation, and consequences, or attention to them in ways acceptable to and illustrative of ethics in the firm.

Obtaining data to substantiate the results is part of the feedback loop. Feedback begins with the initial audit explored in Chapter Five, followed by the development explored in Chapter Six; reassessment with documentation allows substantiation of the outcomes explored in this chapter. Leaders of organizations want data to confirm desired changes, as well as ethics program effectiveness. Sustainability depends on clear statements of anticipated outcomes and evidence outcomes are met. Sustaining also enhances a culture of excellent, one in which quality improvement is a continuing part of hospital or company life. The proposed aim needs to be clearly articulated, preferably by the leadership of the corporation in tandem with the director of the ethics initiative.

Characteristics of a Sustained Ethics Program

An ethics program is designed for a particular organization. It is also useful, however, to learn from others what succeeds and is helpful to employees. What do exemplary programs include? Are there essential components included in every program, given the uniqueness of each organization? Below are several dimensions of ethics programs culled from a number of organizations. The director of the program needs to decide which of these are helpful to his/her employees and aid in meeting the goals of his/her firm. This list offers possibilities for the future.

- Stated mission and purpose for ethics program found in written material
- Administrator (program director, ethics officer) located on the chart of the firm
- Calendar of events, written, distributed, known in organization
- Budget and resources, clarified and included in operating budget
- Communication mechanisms for all employees
- Structures to facilitate ethics; discussions, deliberations, rounds
- Education (training) on ethics
- Employee access for guidance, support, or information when ethics issues arise (might include consultation on-call, ethics 'hot-line,' '24/7' supervisor available, ethics committee)

Whether large or small, rural or urban, health care or business oriented, organizations investing in the time and effort to assess and develop organizational ethics reap benefits by sustaining the ethics initiative. Regardless of how complex or what dimensions are included, attending to the ethical activities of the firm enhances an organizational culture of excellence, attracting and retaining desirable employees. How to move the health care system or the business endeavor forward on these goals is one of the key roles of management, leading us to the discussion of the final and eighth chapter regarding leaders as advocates for ethics.

References

Andrews, K. R. (Ed.). (1989). *Ethics in practice: Managing the moral corporation.* Boston, MA: Harvard Business School Press.

Cooper, C. L., and Rousseau, D. M. (Eds.). (1998). *Trends in organizational behavior* (Vol. 5). New York, NY: John Wiley and Sons, Ltd.

Dawson, P. (1994). *Organizational change: A professional approach.* London, UK: Paul Chapman Publishers, Ltd.

Goodpaster, K. (1989). Ethical imperatives and corporate leadership. In K. R. Andrews (Ed.), *Ethics in practice: Managing the moral corporation* (pp. 212-238). Boston, MA: Harvard Business School Press.

Katz, D., and Allport, F. H. (1931). *Students' attitudes: A report of the Syracuse University reaction study.* Syracuse, NY: Craftsman Press.

Kilmann, R. H., and Covin, J. (1988). *Corporate transformation: Revitalizing organizations for a competitive world.* San Francisco, CA: Jossey-Bass Publishers.

Kirkpatrick, D. (1985). *How to manage change effectively.* San Francisco, CA: Jossey-Bass Publishers.

Miller, D. B. (1986). *Managing professionals in research and development.* San Francisco, CA: Jossey-Bass Publishers.

Nash, L. (1989). Ethics without the sermon. In K. R. Andrews (Ed.), *Ethics in practice: Managing the moral corporation* (pp. 65-72). Boston, MA: Harvard Business Press.

Robinson, S. L., and Greenberg, J. (1998). Employees behaving badly: Dimensions, determinants and dilemmas in the study of workplace deviance. In C. L. Cooper and D. M. Rousseau (Eds.), *Trends in organizational behavior* (Vol. 5, pp. 1-30). New York, NY: John Wiley and Sons, Ltd.

Chapter 8

Leaders as Ethics Advocates

Introduction

Examining employees who strive to do the right things, work well and productively, and engage with their coworkers in deliberations to resolve ethics disagreement and conduct their work in an ethical manner, leads naturally to the parallel concern of their employers. The various CEOs, top managers, and other decision makers in health care and business provide leadership for these many employees in today's global organizations. We would like to assume that in most instances these men and women lead well, and they, too, attempt to serve ethically, providing quality leadership, and offering examples to be emulated among their employees. While many around the globe do just that, exemplary leadership is not always the case. Despite less than appealing models in contemporary organizations and among their leadership, most leaders continue to strive for a more productive workplace, instill better work situations for their employees, and consider how to develop an ethical environment for their workers. Since we have explored the mutual yet distinct responsibilities of employees and employers for ethical parameters in work, this chapter explores the very important role of leaders in health care and business organizations, recognizing their central role in establishing ethical environments.

When the topic of organizational ethics arises, the question about organizational leadership closely follows. Substantive research and many scholarly writings have focused on leadership, exploring the historical question regarding what makes a good leader. Whether applied to business or health care, the search for leadership excellence continues. Studies on leadership include examination of the relationships between leaders and employees, types and quality of supervision, characteristics and styles of effective leadership, and the means by which good leaders aid the formation of positive work groups (Hackman, 1990; Stodgill, 1984). However, agreement on definitive characteristics comprising leadership excellence and ability to predict good leadership has eluded theoreticians and researchers for several decades.

A related and equally compelling question for our purposes pertains to leadership resulting in ethical organizations. What makes an ethical leader? What are the characteristics of leadership excellence that instill ethics in organizations? Ironically, few leadership studies explore ethics in work settings or anticipate ethics as a component of quality leadership, although the foundational nature of an ethical workplace is a continuing and compelling issue for millions of leaders and workers. Given the public outrage surrounding recent situations such as Enron, WorldCom, or Tyco, attention to ethical leadership in organizations is overdue.[1]

Leaders have long been recognized as persons of influence in their systems; leadership quality is central to the health of the employee workplace, organizational environment, and outcomes. Leadership excellence is exemplified in professional and productive organizational change (Kirkpatrick, 1985:255). Authors also note the importance of good leadership for moral and ethical values. Examining large corporations in the northeast U.S., Aguilar (1994) and Darr (1991) address concerns for business and health care organizations, respectively. Hans Wolf, the former Vice Chairman of Syntex Corporation in Mexico City, affirms the need for CEOs to provide excellent examples (Conference Board, 1994:8). Writings and personal interviews regarding business corporations, health resource departments, and universities attest to the importance of the role of leaders as critical to an ethical ethos (Gulley, 2001). As one executive commented, if you want an ethical situation, it '...will not happen without the top person' (Miller, Personal Communication, June 11, 2003).[2] Leaders of corporations espousing high values and integrity are cited in U.S. publications and are among the renowned leaders of top companies. These leaders are recognized for their contributions to the company and its ethical corporate environment, and attending to values is affirmed by their corporate reports. To that end, leaders emerge as ethics advocates in their respective organizations.

The following discussion explores ways leaders in organizations enhance the behaviors of employees and aid in creating an ethical environment. Leadership excellence and ethics go hand-in-hand therefore identifying strategies instilling ethics is central to understanding ethical advocacy among leaders in contemporary society. This chapter examines the very important role of health care and business organization leaders as ethical advocates in their firms.

Ethics Advocates

The above discussion above begs the question of what is meant by an ethics advocate in the organization. What is an ethics advocate? How would an employee know if he/she observed a leader performing as one? Are there certain characteristics CEOs, managers, and other leaders of organizations exhibit so providers and employees or patients and customers, respectively, identify them as ethics advocates? It is one thing to say a leader is an ethics promoter in a firm. It is yet another to discuss explicit behaviors constituting ethical advocacy. What is missing from this discussion are strategies health care and business leaders use to instill an ethical framework.

The term advocacy is used here rather than other emerging terms, such as ethics agent. An agent is one who is a representative, manager, or negotiator, among others, whereas an advocate is a promoter, supporter, sponsor, and even an activist (Random House, 1999). Representation is important, as is the management of ethics in the firm. To develop and sustain ethics in organizations, however, particularly among the large and highly integrated ones typical of many business and health care systems today, a leader needs to do more than manage. He/she needs to promote, advocate, and actively support ethics in the system. The more active and assertive role of an advocate is needed in today's organizations if ethics is to become the norm in the system. Advocacy for ethics is, just that, an active rather than a passive role. Thus an ethics advocate is needed among the CEOs and top management of firms in our global endeavors.

Leaders as ethical advocates are ultimately responsible for developing and sustaining the ethical environment. The leader of an organization, serving as an ethics advocate, 'frames' the organizational ethics. Similar to building a house, the ethics advocate provides a foundation and frames the concrete actions. Some of these features are explored in Chapter One regarding the relationship between the individual and collectivity. Leaders put into place structures and processes for employees to work ethically. As advocates they ensure the written parameters for the particular firm are in place and the message about ethics in the endeavor is conveyed to the employees throughout the firm. Leaders are the ones hiring— either directly or indirectly—employees to support the desired values of the firm. While other employees add remaining parts to the house, without the foundational frame it will not be completed. The leader is therefore an essential component for ethics and serves as an ethics promoter in the organization.

As advocates of ethics leaders not only champion the cause, they make it happen. In order to advocate ethics, sage leaders create links between individual and corporate activities instilling ethics in their firms. Although leaders have their own unique styles and strategies, nevertheless some characteristics are shared in common by ethical leaders. The following discussion highlights key features ethical advocates demonstrate, some of which may be described as characteristics and others as strategies. However, ethics advocates combine several dimensions in their important role in organizations. But what is it about leaders that attracts our attention? What is *Fortune* magazine recognizing in ethical CEOs?

Allied Holdings is the largest car-haul trucking company in the United States and Canada, continuing the family-owned endeavor begun in 1934. As CEO, Robert J. Rutland vowed to retain high values at Allied. Indeed, attention to this dimension of the corporation has aided Allied Holdings to reduce liability claims, related insurance expenses, and training and turnover costs for the nation-wide company. Their values, expressed from the beginning, are, 'From day one, ours has been a company that treats people with respect. The commitment to protect that caring attitude has never diminished' (Allied, 2003).[3]

The CEO of Allied, Robert Rutland, believes this attitude of respect for persons is central to their company's current success. Indeed the values are effective, substantiated by the fact that in an industry in which turnover is extremely high and ethics is rated lowest (National Business Ethics Study, 2001), the turnover at Allied is less than five per cent (Allied, 2003). Values pay, according to Allied's CEO. There is a clear company message and a consistency between message and behaviors supported at Allied. Values guide the CEO and company interactions, and top management espouses and articulates the vision. These interactions link the CEO with organizational values. With this excellent example in mind, the discussion focuses now on the various ways in which leaders of organizations serve as ethical advocates. Ethics advocates take action and those actions can be observed in organizations. The following discussion explores nine components illustrative of ethical advocacy.

Personal Ethic

Ethical advocates are the stewards of ethics and they champion the values. But, from where does this advocacy arise? The first characteristic for the concept of ethical advocacy, to speak out and act responsibly regarding ethical concerns, emerges from a personal ethic, according to Darr (1991:145). This claim is supported by the Ethics Resource Center (2003), which cites the importance of the leader's personal value system as foundational to integrity at work.

Personal ethic is also related to the way in which these leaders perceive the world. Managers are ethics advocates with independent duties to patients in health care and customers in business. They are able to analyze systems and acknowledge the link between their personal ethic and the system. Central to the role of ethics advocate is *de*creasing the 'disconnect' between mission and reality of ethics in the system. In that regard, continuity prevails. Leaders are both initiators of and accountable for ethics. Thus managerial actions and decisions may be judged in that context.

The leader's integrity is important. Surveys report a link between company loyalty among employees and employees' perceptions regarding the integrity of senior leaders. When integrity among senior leadership is perceived as high, employee loyalty is (also) high, about 40 per cent, whereas, among leaders with lower integrity, only six per cent of the employees exhibit strong company loyalty (National Business Ethics Study, 2001). To reiterate earlier reports, employees want their bosses to support them in their ethics pursuits (McDaniel, 2003a). Leaders who attempt to establish a company ethics without addressing their own personal ethics also run the risk of presenting an *ethics charade*. Personal ethics matters to employees, especially among their senior leaders; it starts with top management.

Leaders face inherent challenges in moving the firm forward ethically, according to Carr (1989:29), and they face the growing mistrust and suspicion of the general public. This mistrust and suspicion has accelerated in the U.S. during the 21st century in the wake of Enron, Arthur Andersen, and WorldCom to name a few. The public is mistrustful of many businesses and executives themselves indicate concern. A survey (Carr, 1989:27) reveals that 90 per cent of the leaders responding report themselves as ethical, while 80 per cent confirm the presence of unethical activities in their firms. Included on this list of unethical actions are price rigging, bribes, or contract bidding with conflicts of interest.

Indeed, organizational ethics starts with top management and leaders' own personal ethics, especially in the face of challenges. However, personal or individual ethic alone is not enough. An individual ethical stance needs to be conveyed throughout the organization in explicit, written, and clear ways, complemented and supported by other characteristics and strategies exhibited by ethics advocates.

Exemplar

CEOs who serve as ethical advocates, a second strategy, take seriously their roles in the firm as ones who have responsibility for illustrating the company values. They exemplify the very values and standards they desire in their firms. Advocates illustrate honesty, integrity, respect for others, and fairness in approach. While a CEO may never be labeled an ethics officer *per se*, he/she serves that function. There is an implied advocacy about the role of the CEO; the ethics advocate serves as an ethics role model, and in the role conveys the central message about ethical values of the firm. As leaders, they know the importance of being 'out in front' on ethical issues, including the ethics assessment. An ethical advocate seriously considers the ethics of the firm as a concomitant part of the leadership role. Ethics is not an addition to but rather an inherent part of the exemplary leadership role.

Ethics advocates as exemplars also serve as standard setters. Synovus Chairman and CEO, Jim Blanchard, is a standard setter; he is an exemplar. As leader of a multi-billion dollar company since 1971, Blanchard was recently recognized by *Georgia Trend Magazine* as 'Georgian of the Year.' This affirmation follows acknowledgement of Synovus as *Fortune*'s ninth in '100 Best Companies to Work, having ranked among the top ten for the sixth straight year, and fifth best-performing bank by U.S. *Banker Magazine* (Synovus web page, 2003).[4] Indeed, a speech to a local college notes 'Blanchard places tremendous emphasis on leadership education at Synovus' (Southeastern College, Web, 2003) and treating employees right. He exemplifies good leadership in every way.

Leaders of excellence noted here—Blanchard, Rutland—set the standard for their companies. While not all employees have the opportunity to interact with top management in day-to-day functioning, the leaders' reputations and exemplary actions surely permeate their firms. Personnel see them perform on the job and comment on their activities on-site. The reputation of leaders precedes them as persons of quality and high standards. Actions they take in the wake of a crisis, for instance, serve to illustrate standards for other employees. A classic and well-known example is the way in which the CEO of Johnson & Johnson addressed the Tylenol threat in the 1990s (Kuhn and Shriver, 1991:314), following the tampering of a package of Tylenol. The Chairman, James Burke, played a central role in leading the response to public concerns and for corporate responsibility. He decided to pull Tylenol from the shelves of thousands of stores across America, at an estimated loss of $100 million dollars. This explicitly ethical action paid off in consumer respect and knowledge: Johnson & Johnson is a company customers trust. Trust flows from Burke's behavior as an exemplar.

Ethical Visionary

The CEO, top managers, and other senior leaders promote the ethical vision of the company; a third strategy. They cheerlead the company vision and its ethics. Ethical advocates also ensure the ethics programs in their respective organizations are part of the vision. While most organizations have a mission statement and goals and objectives, if the top management does not state the ethical vision, it will not happen. The ethical mission of the company is as important as the statement about the product itself. An important role for the ethical advocate is thus to express, talk about, and cheer on others in their own roles as members of this evolving ethical environment. The ethics advocate thereby creates the ethical vision.

A visionary also markets ethics. A well-designed marketing strategy needs to be developed for ethics as well as for company products. It is importance, however, to add that an ethics marketing strategy based on lack of substance will appear to be merely that: only a marketing strategy. Ethics needs to be conveyed and sold, and in that regard it needs to be marketed throughout the firm; it needs to be backed up with actions, hence the role of ethics advocate rather than agent.

While codes of ethics—discussed below—and similar messages regarding ethics are communicated internally to employees, the external communication needs to be conducted differently. A company logo claiming excellence, integrity in products, and other compelling value messages conveying the ethical intent to the customer are essential. As many managers of local franchises know, the message may precede the product. Ethics needs to be marketed along with the vision.

Logos, and other forms of explicitly eye-catching communications illustrate the value and offer specific statements about organizational values. They serve to extend the mission statement in ways customers may not otherwise see. Once associated with excellence and integrity, they are valued and protected, as illustrated below.

> In the Midwestern United States, a hardware manufacturing concern started in the mid-1800s developed a reputation for quality. Its hardware, with classic logos, was instantly recognized as a quality product. This firm, the Shapleigh Hardware Company of St. Louis, Missouri, also owned the Diamond Edge and Keen Kutter brands and accompanying slogans. On the Diamond Edge emblem, a large circle in bright yellow with a marker of equally bright red cutting across the circle, is the slogan: 'Diamond Edge is a Quality Pledge.' On its sister emblem for Keen Kutter the top part of the circle reads: 'The Recollection of Quality,' while the bottom half of the circle reads: 'Remains Long after the Price is Forgotten' (Shapleigh Hardware Company, 2003). At one time Shapleigh had the largest tool and cutlery distribution in the Midwest and more than a century of service excellence to the public. These slogans, stated on signs found throughout the Midwest, reminded people they, the customer, were of first concern and integrity was important to this corporation. Today, those tools and cutlery are sought-after items, albeit in antique markets since the company sold its major holdings in the 20th century. However, the original owners initially retained copyright to the Diamond Edge and Keen Kutter emblems. Shapleigh heirs want to retain the

association of quality reputation with their products. Hard won reputations for excellence are to be protected and revered.[5]

Ethics Affirmation

Not only does the ethics advocate express the vision and serve as a positive example, but he/she also affirms ethics in terms of central ethical concepts, the fourth strategy. Among several important ones emerging most frequently in research on corporations are honesty, trust, integrity, justice as fairness, and respect; we explored these concepts in Chapter Two. These concepts are grounded in ethics. Of these, two of the most universal concepts are justice and respect for persons. Jim Blanchard of Synovus and Bob Rutland at Allied recognize the importance of affirming these concepts and instilling ethics in their firms.

Justice raises the issue of fair treatment—or presence of *un*fair or discriminate treatment. Justice is a key issue for most managers since appropriate treatment of employees, diversity, and allocation, are central. Nowhere is this truer than in the medical systems of contemporary society. Assignment of personnel in organizations is a form of allocation in health services, and is clearly an ethics leadership issue. Rarely do hospitals, clinics, or public health facilities have enough personnel to provide the desired services for the populations under their assignment. Justice and the allocation of scarce resources is a fundamental tenet for an ethical organization.

> Smalltown Hospital was experiencing significant financial instability and the CEO, Kris Thomas, decided to reduce the workforce. The single largest personnel cadre was under nursing service. He decided to cut these staff by 20 per cent. However, in contrast to several hospitals in surrounding communities serving the same region, Smalltown's CEO decided not to lay off more than five per cent and allow early retirement, natural turnover, and other attrition to adjust for the remaining 15 per cent. For the five per cent reduced, he worked out a volunteer lay-off system. Lastly, rather than escort personnel who would be laid off, he called them to his office, talked with them honestly and arranged a discrete strategy for them to leave the hospital, avoiding the use of police and pink-slips which can be damaging to personnel and community relations. This set of actions ultimately resulted in more patients. One year later Smalltown resumed hiring personnel. Respect, justice, and integrity have their rewards.

A criterion for ethics is the leader's approach in resolving ethical problems and whether criteria are applied consistently to demonstrate justice. This criterion of justice is foundational to a system in which fairness prevails. When similar ethical problems are considered, justice requires uniform application of the criteria for assessing and balancing the relevant decisions. Persons in similar situations should be treated similarly, regardless of their social standing or position, in order to affect a fair decision process for ethical problems.

Respect for persons is also foundational to work with dignity and treating others as one would want to be treated—in a respectful and considerate manner. Respect is foundational to treatment of personnel to avoid discrimination or harassment on the job. Respect is linked to integrity at work, and integrity is a foundation for a 'fully realized life' (Hodson, 2001:xiii). Immanuel Kant (1963) was foremost in articulating the role of the ethical advocate with attention to respect. Persons have rights in and of themselves arising from duty to one another as moral agents. Persons, according to Kant, are not to be treated as other than ends or as means to an end, but as ends alone. Thus respect and its sister concept of justice are two central tenets ethics advocates convey to their employees. Indeed, respect is central to the philosophy of Allied Holdings.

Lack of tolerance for disrespectful behaviors or unjust actions is also important, and top management sets the tolerance level. Each of these ethical concepts, however, may comprise other related concepts management uses. For instance, under respect some managers put truth telling (Darr, 1991:21) as a key tenet. Regardless of how the term is used, respect for employees and customers is foundational to an ethical organization and is affirmed by the ethics advocate. Ethics advocates affirm ethics and value concepts.

Value Message

The value statements of Allied Holdings, Synovus, and Shapleigh Hardware companies convey clear messages. Furthermore, the companies take pride in their messages. The value message, the fifth aspect of ethical advocacy, is an important part of the company culture, one interwoven into the daily fabric of the firm's work. However, closely related to the value message of an ethical organization are three other aspects, discussed here because they are linked to the value message: consistency, value reach®, and ethics code.

Consistency Merely having a value message is not enough. The value message needs to be explicit, clear, and *consistent*. Leaders in the role of ethics advocate articulate the ethical position in numerous ways; they communicate to and with other managers, employees, and customers. As noted in Chapter Three, statements of company standards and principles are consistently interwoven through the letterhead, logo, mission statement, and other communications; they are a consistent message. Consistency is illustrated between verbal and written communication, and the message is related to the company mission. Ethics advocates recognize change illustrated by an emerging ethics program takes consistent reinforcement (Dawson, 1994). Regardless of how values are conveyed, the message pertaining to ethics needs to be consistent, reinforced in many forums throughout the organization. Messages are also reinforced and retold in stories throughout the company. As this case conveys, the message and its consistency influence the company reputation.

> A small firm in the Northwest had a CEO who wanted to signify uniqueness, and to set her firm apart. Rather than rely upon feedback from outreach personnel, however, the CEO attracted attention by painting the company cars different colors and each car wheel in yet other and varied colors—purple, orange, flashy red, flame yellow. She

attracted attention while alienating personnel and drawing derision from customers. When a manager was asked about the unique colors on the cars, especially the wheels, he could not give a clear answer: 'Wish I knew,' was a typical reply. The common question, why the colors, was never integrated with the company product, its logo, or motto, and surely not the mission. As personnel continued to turn over in high numbers, the CEO wondered what was wrong. A firm conveying such a unique—even ambiguous—message is also sending a meta-message about the respect and value of workers, customers, and ultimately the company product. The lingering question: What is the message?

Ethical consistency in a firm is also exhibited by behaviors starting at the top. Organizations exhibiting an ethical environment display consistency throughout the endeavor. In an analysis of the organizational culture, Rob Cooke (Cooke and Rousseau, 1987:245) reports an organization in which the culture is consistent throughout is termed a 'dense culture.' Similar approaches are preferred for an ethical ambience: a dense ethics ethos. Ethical consistency links directly back to the personal ethic and examples set by the CEO and top management.

Firms displaying *in*consistency are typically firms in which uneven rewards and difficult behaviors occur. These may lead to overt discrimination on the job. Recall, too, employees prefer to work in situations in which there is an ethical culture; turnover in such organizations is significantly lower than in those in which employees perceive the ethics to be elusive (McDaniel and Schoeps, 2003a). An ethical ethos enhances company loyalty (National Business Ethics Study, 2001). Consistency also means employees may err; in situations in which the company needs to pull a product off the shelf, as James Burke at Johnson & Johnson did, they acknowledge or recant to remain consistent with the stated values. Ethical advocates also admit mistakes, because admission of error is consistent with their ethical principles.

Value Reach® Leaders who serve as ethics advocates strive for value communication throughout the company, including the outer-most dimensions of the firm, the components intersecting with patients and customers. They enhance *value reach®* which is the second aspect under clear value message. It does little good to have an ethics code or high standards if they are not communicated from top to bottom in the corporation. This communication needs to reach providers and employees and be evident to patients and customers. As Peter Drucker (2001) well knows, walking around the company and talking with employees at all levels of the firm are important activities. Interacting with employees provides an opportunity for leaders to convey the ethics message and assess the degree of value reach®. Messages such as 'I am glad you support our values,' 'Ethics Company surely values high standards,' or '...integrity is central to our firm,' are important messages for leaders to convey to employees. However, research also reveals as one moves away from the core of the organization, the central figures of the system, the appreciation for and recognition of ethical values tend to wane (McDaniel and Schoeps, 2003a). Value reach® typically decreases incrementally as one transitions from top to bottom or inner core to outer periphery of employees.

For this reason continued attention to value reach® is an important function of ethics advocates.

Interaction with employees is an opportunity to test out the extent of the value reach®. In large corporations with multi-branches or stores, it is essential to monitor and reinforce the values of the firm. One reason it is important to assess one's employees on a regular basis is to obtain feedback on how far reaching and embedded the ethical standards are within the organization. An ethics assessment discussed in Chapter Five, determines the degree of *value reach*®. The example below tells it all. Chick-fil-A has a policy that stores are closed on Sunday, conveying a value important to Truett Cathy, CEO of this family-owned, multi-billion dollar business.

> We have it written in our lease with each shopping center that *all* Chick-fil-A restaurants be permitted to remain closed on Sunday. Some developers inject in their lease that Chick-fil-A may close on Sunday 'as long as *all* Units are closed on Sunday.' One Operator could cause us a lot of problems over that issue. And in one instance, an Operator did cause us trouble.
>
> It started when we received disturbing reports from several people. 'I thought you never opened on Sunday,' a friend said.
>
> 'We don't,' I replied, 'and never will.'
>
> 'I saw one of your stores open on a Sunday afternoon,' our friend said, and he named the place. He's mistaken, I thought, but I passed the word on to Jimmy Collins, then Chick-fil-A's executive vice president.
>
> I've heard the same report from two other people,' Jimmy said. 'I'll find out the truth.'
>
> Jimmy dialed the store. A young man answered. 'What are your store hours on Sunday?' he asked, not identifying himself.
>
> 'Twelve to six.' 'Thank you,' Jimmy said and hung up.
>
> The next morning Jimmy told me about his phone call. I thought about it a few seconds. I wanted to be sure of what had happened. The month had almost ended.
>
> 'Let's wait until we get this month's report,' I said. I decided that if the Operator wrote down sales from Sunday, I could believe he had not understood our iron-clad policy of never opening on Sunday. I wanted to give him every possible benefit of the doubt. 'But if he doesn't show sales for Sunday, then we'll know.'
>
> A few days later, Jimmy brought in the monthly report. The Operator had not listed the Sunday business. He had, apparently, divided his sales between Saturday and Monday. We believed the totals came out right, but he had broken a trust with us and had violated one of the company's basic policies.
>
> We called him to Atlanta and terminated his Operators' Agreement. 'I'm not dismissing you for opening the store on Sunday,' I told him. 'I'm terminating you for deceiving us. Your records are not true. You have lied to us, and that's why we're asking you to leave.'[6]

As an ethics advocate for Chick-fil-A, Cathy appreciates value reach®.

The aim of an ethical organization is shared understanding of the ethics of the whole. If only part of the employees are working under the preferred value system, while the remainder are working under another set of values, the organization will be perceived as fragmented and uncoordinated by the customers with whom the employees interact. Trust informed by a consistent message, is therefore important to the ethos of a firm. Lack of coordination and unevenness throughout a company is unethical, since it serves as a lack of promise keeping. When an organization promises customers it will be open six days a week, then it needs to demonstrate value reach® and promise keeping. It needs to demonstrate ethics. Cathy, as an ethics advocate, recognizes this.

Ethical code The third aspect to support a clear value message is ethical codes or statements of standards. When the CEO of a major service company wants the endeavor to have an ethics code the CEO makes it happen, thereby serving as an ethics advocate for the international concern referenced in the case from the introduction. Development of an ethics code serves as a guide for employees in the firm. Corporations without a code of ethics are often those in which there are problems. Major organizations of excellence frequently acknowledge a system-wide set of standards. An ethics code is one of these standards and becomes a strategy for keeping ethics alive.

Codes of ethics by themselves, however, are not enough. A code of ethics needs to be supported by the CEO, referred to in company-wide messages and speeches, and complemented by other forms of communication. The ethics code needs to be reinforced and rewarded. A code that is not reinforced, as Truett Cathy recognizes, does little to instill ethics in a firm. In addition to these key messages about organizational values, the reward system for employees in the firm supports these important core values. Companies valuing ethics convey the value system to their personnel and customers. Interactions between employees and customers conveying these values are noted and rewarded. The reward system of the firm is not only directed to high productivity, but also to employees aspiring to high standards who illustrate them in their work. It is not just customer or employee appreciation, but rather the manner in which customers and fellow employees are treated. Ethics pertains to actual behaviors supported by an ethics code. When ethics is of concern, the behaviors are also rewarded within the company. It is the ethics code that sets the stage for other statements.

Ethics Guidance

The sixth related means of serving as an ethics advocate is for CEOs of hospitals and corporations to take firm stances on ethical situations and offer guidance for critical ethical issues. While the CEO may not be the person with whom the majority of employees interact, the CEO ensures guidance is available in the corporation. Research substantiates employees' desires for a place in their work site to talk about morally challenging issues emerging in workplaces (McDaniel and Schoeps, 2003a); other research supports this finding (National Business Ethics Study, 2001). Guidance on ethically challenging issues is a form of support.

United Parcel Service of America, Inc., (UPS), typically referred to as 'brown,' is a global firm operating in more than 143 countries. Their CEO and top managers know the importance of ethical guidance. At the opening of each business meeting, a company policy affirming their principles is read along with their ethics code; this is followed by a manager-led discussion of how UPS understands the code and policy, and their application to employees and customers. The results are substantiated with UPS' consistently high ratings for principled (ethical) actions by their employees, and equally high customer ratings. UPS illustrates the importance of consistent and continued ethical guidance and the central role leaders play in its promotion.[7]

Managers in a company rarely agree with all other managers, or may not agree completely with the CEO; thus guiding principles need to be clearly articulated for the firm. Never has this been more accurate than in our global and increasingly diverse organizations of today. The same is true for hospitals and hospital administrators. Guidance needs to occur in verbal and informal means, and in formal written policies and procedures implemented throughout the firm. Guidelines also need to conform to federal, state, or relevant regulations. Guiding actions need to be provided for all employees, as UPS illustrates. The ethical advocate makes sure guidelines are present, followed-up, and monitored. Serving as ethics advocates means leaders provide guidance, by ensuring guides are in place as one example of framing the organizational ethics of the system. Ethics advocates provide the ethics frame on critical moral issues. This is an excellent example of the important CEO role in articulating the ethical standards adhered to in the firm, as Jim Blanchard of Synovus knows. In contrast, a lack of ethical leadership is conspicuous by its absence.

Proactive

CEOs as ethics advocates recognize instilling ethics in employees is a challenge. The seventh strategy, being proactive, requires constant attention and monitoring; ethical problems need to be anticipated with a proactive organizational stance. Health care and business corporations are well served by being proactive in exhibiting ethical advocacy. Rather than focus on what the firm will not do or is unacceptable as a negative position—which clearly needs to be stated—firms also state what they affirm. Firms via their leaders need to articulate what they adhere to, and what they represent; they need a constructive stance provided by their leaders rather than a negative or destructive one (Kelley, 1988:190).

> Kirk Stuart, the Medical Director of a local community hospital, was returning from a meeting with his physician colleagues. As he mulled the news of one of his medical classmates embroiled in a tragic ethical situation, he wondered how he could prevent what could be a similar situation at his community hospital. Not sure of what to do, he realized there was no ethics committee or consultation available to all personnel. Thinking this was also a good example of a preventive measure, upon returning he called a team together and asked them to design a solid ethics committee followed by a consultation service. 'If we have a similar issue,' he stated at the final meeting, 'It will not be due to lack of preventive ethics effort.'

Wise leaders do not wait for a problem to emerge. They are not naive. Leaders are sage enough to know sooner or later an error will occur. In anticipation of the possibility, and knowing prevention is less costly than cure, ethics advocates put proactive measures in place to avert ethical problems. Not only do ethics advocates as leaders of excellence attempt to avoid problems, they develop ethics codes, create clear organizational messages, and reward employees for ethically consistent behavior. Ethics advocates encourage and support ethics actions. Many of the activities, already discussed in early chapters and noted above under ethical advocacy, also serve as illustrations of a proactive stance on ethics. Proactive and constructive approaches to ethics are always preferable to one of error, correction, or punishment.

Personnel and Delegation in Ethical Advocacy

Ethical advocates, especially in large concerns, know they cannot do it all or do it alone. Ethics advocates need the support of delegated others, and reinforcement of other personnel, representing the eighth strategy. Reality prevails, suggesting leaders who serve as ethics advocates look for others who demonstrate ethics behaviors in their work. They recruit and hire personnel to enhance and extend the ethical stature of the firm, as explored in part one of this work. Ethics advocates seek a team of collaborators to whom they can delegate ethical advocacy and who will support them as well. Ethics advocates develop a team with shared values, seeking opportunities to reward those who demonstrate the values they desire. They are watchful monitors of personnel who enact principles and values important for the company. They also suggest parameters, providing boundaries for good behavior. There are clear messages regarding what is acceptable and unacceptable in the firm and they reinforce it among company personnel. Thus hiring others who exhibit ethics in the organization is central to serving as ethics advocates, as is dismissing those who do not. Surrounding oneself with others who share those important values is an equally important strategy for ethical advocacy.

Ethical hires provide support and sustainment for the leader(s) and serve to build an ethics team. Indeed, developing a team is tantamount to creating a more ethical ambience in the organization; leaders are central, but they cannot do it alone. They need a team and they need one to whom they can delegate dimensions of ethics advocacy. Included in this team is (potentially) an ethics officer, in charge of the ethics standards of the organization. However, just as it is unrealistic to assume CEOs can do it by themselves, it is unrealistic to assume ethics officers can evolve a company ethos alone.

The ethics officer may have designated responsibility for ethics and more typically for compliance but, as examined in Chapter Three, ethics and compliance are distinct company-wide endeavors requiring layers of support and involvement. Furthermore, an identified ethics officer is not an excuse for others to relinquish responsibility for supporting and sustaining ethics. The officer—with other leaders—articulates the means to evaluate the situation assessing whether the problem has been resolved, needs to be further addressed, or finalized. Thus along with consistent and wide value reach® throughout the organization, the ethics advocate assembles a range of personnel who attend to ethics, including in many instances an ethics officer.

Actors in the positions of clinical directors, unit managers, or department heads, for instance, are hired on behalf of organizations. While it may seem logical to separate the roles of hire and delegation, in fact, every employee hired has an inherent delegated function of advocating for ethics within the firm, especially those employees hired in any clinical administrative or corporate management position. Mid-level managers are ethics advocates in their respective positions. They are not excused from the results of their actions merely because they are following directions. Managers who behave only as technocrats are ignoring their role as ethics agents, according to Darr (1991:13).[8]

Managers are responsible for actions, and the consequences of those actions. Every individual who accepts an administrative appointment occupies a supervisory position as a potential ethics advocate. The willingness and courage to speak out on important ethical matters is needed as a component of personal ethic for ethics advocacy, a responsibility also delegated to others in the firm. Additionally, recent U.S. laws protect those who engage in whistleblowing and support strong advocates of ethical behaviors (Sarbanes-Oxley Law, 2002). Research reveals this is extremely important to employees (McDaniel and Schoeps, 2003a). As Truett Cathy and James Burke demonstrate, also needed is follow-up action on *un*acceptable behaviors. Identifying key personnel and citing ethical issues—explored in Chapter Three—is worth very little if corrective action is not taken in those situations and supported by key personnel throughout the endeavor. This leads to the last feature for ethics advocates.

Accountability

Accountability is the ninth aspect of ethical advocacy in organizations. The recent regulation by the U.S. federal government requiring CEOs to sign-off on financial records signals the importance of accountability in organizations. No longer can leaders in organizations assume financial accounting is accurate. U.S. leaders are now being required to indicate corporate accountability, calling into question the direct responsibility central decision makers play as ethics advocate in their firms, and supporting the discussion of Chapter Two. It also implies a more direct, hands-on relationship is emerging in these firms.

It is more difficult to hold managers and other leaders of the organization accountable if the CEO has not provided clear statements of ethical standards and acted consistently with those standards. CEOs functioning as an ethics advocate serve as foundations for accountability. Leaders cannot assume employees whom they hire know the principles of the firm; those principles need to be made explicit and evident throughout the organization. Likewise, when standards are broken or misused, then employees also need to know, as a delegated ethics advocate, her/his supervisor will follow-up with corrective actions. Explicit consequences communicated to employees serve as strong deterrents to undesirable behaviors on the job (Robinson and Greenberg, 1998:28). The action Truett Cathy took provides an excellent example. In similar manner, when excellent ethical behavior is demonstrated it needs to be rewarded. Mid-level managers, too, serve in the role of ethics advocate, and they, too, should have exemplary behavior rewarded. Ethical advocates affirm and demonstrate accountability.

Continuing Challenge

Taking action and following up are not easy, nor is it easy to serve as an ethics advocate; it may not be a popular position. Consistent honesty, respect, and fairness resulting in trust take time, discipline, and attention on the part of ethics advocates and their employees. It is a continuing challenge assumed by leaders of excellence. As Carr (1989:26) notes, each advance in business ethics is the result of 'pain and protest.' It further substantiates that advances may pave the way for a more humane workplace and ultimately a more humane society. For these reasons, the importance of key leaders as ethics advocates in society is central. In contrast, the position of the executive who fails to take strong positions on ethical issues is defined as ambiguous (Andrews, 1989:28) with leadership excellence in question. To fail the test of ethics is to fail the challenge of leadership excellence.

Leaders, according to Norris (1989:36), also face certain tests. Accountability for a firm and its ethical actions are included among the challenges of those who aspire to be ethics advocates. Norris suggests one challenge is ability to live with compromise; others are being able to only disclose part of the information, and making final decisions on less than complete information, living up to expectations while not being trapped by them, and being a person of thought as well as action. Badaracco claims compromise is not 'splitting' the ethical decision into either-or, but approaching an ethical dilemma in creative ways; ethics is not split into parts. It is not a halfway endeavor. They [ethics and principles] 'should be defended, with courage and determination....' (2002:148).

On the other hand, Badaracco (2002:117) also states ethics endeavors are best judged like 'Olympic diving.' Ethical advocacy should be judged against the degree of difficulty presented by the ethical challenge, as James Burke at Johnson & Johnson illustrates. The other reality is the necessity on the part of leaders to succeed at the profit margin while also instilling ethical values within their organizations. Executives need to make difficult decisions, including 'sitting in judgment' of one's colleagues and peers: a 'measure of aloofness becomes the price of objectivity' (Norris, 1989:40).

Instilling ethical environments in organizations also requires attention to change, explored in earlier chapters as a continuing process requiring dedicated attention (Kessen, 1990:4-6). Ethics change, as leaders of excellence know, takes time and dedication. With these sobering comments in mind, we return to the central role of the CEO, top management, and other organizational leaders as the central ethics advocates in their respective organizations. It is to ethics advocates we turn to establish the ethical environment. Health care systems and business companies rely upon them. Their leadership excellence is foundational for developing and sustaining organizational ethics in the many endeavors, small and large, complex and multi-faceted, far and wide that exist in our contemporary global society. Ethical advocacy is today's challenge for the benefit of tomorrow's organizational ethics, an ethical ambience also enhancing employees who work and reside in society.

Notes

1   Since these events, attention to the issues has increased. This change should be noted in recent publications providing more details on the subject. A report on the Enron investigation and related entities on federal tax and compensation issues may be found on-line under U.S., Congress, and Joint Committee on Taxation, 2003.

2   Appreciation is expressed to Alice Miller, Executive Vice President for Human Resources, Emory University, Atlanta, Georgia, for comments on this chapter.

3   Appreciation is extended to Robert Rutland, Chairman of the Board, Allied Holdings, Inc., for his review of this material, and for his continued support of organizational ethics.

4   Jim Blanchard, via Rob Ward, is noted with appreciation for his review of the material related to Synovus.

5   Shapleigh logos were recently purchased by Val-Test, which company retains ownership.

6   Appreciation is expressed to Chick-fil-A, via Helen Garner, Executive Assistant to T. Cathy, for a review of references to their firm and CEO, Truett Cathy, and permission to reprint the case from Mr. Cathy's book, *It's Easier to Succeed than to Fail*, pp. 76-77.

7   Appreciation is extended to Peggy Garner, United Parcel Services (UPS), Atlanta, Georgia, for review of this case.

8   Kurt Darr uses the term ethical agent rather than ethical advocate.

References

Aguilar, F. (1994). *Managing corporate ethics*. Oxford, UK: Oxford University Press.

Andrews, K. R. (Ed.). (1989). *Ethics in practice: Managing the moral corporation*. Boston, MA: Harvard Business School Press.

Badaracco, J. L., Jr. (2002). *Leading quietly: An unorthodox guide to doing the right thing*. Boston, MA: Harvard Business School Press.

Carr, A. Z. (1989). Can an executive afford a conscience? In K. R. Andrews (Ed.), *Ethics in practice: Managing the moral corporation* (pp. 26-35). Boston, MA: Harvard Business School Press.

Conference Board. (1994). *Business ethics: Generating trust in the 1990s and beyond* (Report #1057-94-CH; S. J. Garone, Ed.). New York, NY: Author.

Cooke, R., and Rousseau, D. M. (1987). Behavioral norms and expectations: Quantitative approach to assessment of organizational culture. *Group and organizational studies 13*:245 ff.

Darr, K. (1991). *Ethics in health services management* (2nd ed.). Washington, DC: Health Professions Press.

Dawson, P. (1994). *Organizational change: A professional approach*. London, UK: Paul Chapman Publishers, Ltd.

Drucker, P. (2001). *The essential Drucker: Selections from the management works of Peter F. Drucker*. New York, NY: Harper Collins.

Ethics Resource Center. (2003, May 13). What's important to business ethics? Washington, DC: *Ethics Resource Center On-Line Report*. Retrieved Sept. 22, 2003, from: http://www.ethics.org/today.

Gulley, S. (2001). *The academic president as moral leader: James T. Laney at Emory University 1977-1993*. Macon, GA: Mercer University Press.

Hackman, J. R. (Ed.). (1990). *Groups that work (and those that don't)*. San Francisco, CA: Jossey-Bass Publishers.

Hodson, R. (2001). *Dignity at work*. Cambridge, UK: Cambridge University Press.

Kelley, C. M. (1988). *The destructive achiever: Power and ethics in the American corporation*. Reading, MA: Addison-Wesley Publishing Company, Inc., pp.183-201.

Kessen, R. (1990). *Managing corporate culture*. Aldershot, UK: Gower Publishers, Ltd., pp. 4-6.

Kirkpatrick, D. (1985). *How to manage change effectively*. San Francisco, CA: Jossey-Bass Publishers, pp. 255-256.

Kuhn, J. W., and Shriver, D. W. (1991). *Beyond success: Corporations and their critics in the 1990s*. New York, NY: Oxford University Press, p. 314.

McDaniel, C., and Schoeps, N. (2003a). Ethics in corporations: Employee position and organizational ethics. In process.

National Business Ethics Study. (2001, May). *Walker Loyalty Report: Loyalty in the Workplace*. WalkerInformation Online Report. Retrieved July, 2003, from: http://www.walkerinfo.com/ resources/report.

Norris, L. W. (1989). Moral hazards of an executive. In K. R. Andrews (Ed.), *Ethics in practice: Managing the moral corporation* (pp. 35-45). Boston, MA: Harvard Business School Press.

Random House Webster's college dictionary (2nd ed.). (1999). New York, NY: Random House, 1487.

Robinson, S. L., and Greenberg, J. (1998). Employees behaving badly: Dimensions, determinants and dilemmas in the study of workplace deviance. In C. L. Cooper and D. M. Rousseau (Eds.), *Trends in organizational behavior* (Vol. 5, pp. 1-30). New York, NY: John Wiley and Sons, Ltd.

Sarbanes-Oxley Law. (2002). Pubic Law No. 107-204, 116 Stat. 745. Regarding reform legislation covering governance of public corporations, including protection of whistleblowers. See: U.S. Government, 107th U.S. Congress.

Shapleigh Hardware Company. (2003, August 5). Retrieved on July 15, 2003, from: http://www.shapleigh-hdww.html.

Southeastern College. (2003, June 11). Retrieved on August 10, 2003 from: http://www.secollege. edu/News_Events/html.

Stodgill, R. M. (1974). *Handbook of leadership: A survey of theory and research*. New York, NY: Free Press.

Synovus. (2003, June 11). Retrieved on August 10, 2003, from: http://www. synovus.com.

Bibliography

Affholter, D. (1994). Outcome monitoring. In J. S. Wholey, H. Hatry, and K. E. Newcomer, (Eds.), *Handbook of practical program evaluation* (pp. 96-118). San Francisco, CA: Jossey-Bass Publishers, pp. 96-118.

Agich, G., and Youngner, S. (1991). For experts only: Access to hospital ethics committees. *Hastings Center Report 21*:17-25.

Aguilar, F. (1994). *Managing corporate ethics*. Oxford, UK: Oxford University Press.

Alderfer, C. (1972). *Existence, relatedness, and growth: Human needs and organizational settings*. New York, NY: The Free Press.

American Society for Bioethics and Humanities (ASBH). (2002). Annual meeting. Report from Affinity Group, Organizational Ethics and Compliance, October 22-26. Baltimore, MD.

Andrews, K. R. (Ed.). (1989). *Ethics in practice: Managing the moral corporation*. Boston, MA: Harvard Business School Press.

Applebaum, E., Baily, T., Berg, T., and Kalleberg, A. (2000). *Manufacturing advantage: Why high-performance work systems pay off*. Ithaca, NY: Cornell University Press.

Argyris, C. (1993). *Knowledge for action: A guide to overcoming barriers to organizational change*. San Francisco, CA: Jossey-Bass Publishers.

Argyris, C. (1964). *Integrating the individual and the organization*. New York, NY: John Wiley and Sons, Inc.

Argyris, C. (1962). *Interpersonal competence and organizational effectiveness*. Homewood, IL: Dorsey Press.

Argyris, C. (1953). *Executive leadership: An appraisal of a manager in action*. New York, NY: Harper and Brothers Publishers.

Badaracco, J., Jr. (2002). *Leading quietly: An unorthodox guide to doing the right thing*. Boston, MA: Harvard Business School Press.

Baier, K. (1992). Class notes. Theories of ethics (Fall semester). University of Pittsburgh Graduate Program, Department of Philosophy. Pittsburgh, PA.

Baumeister, R., and Leary, M. (1995). The need to belong: Desire for interpersonal attachments as a fundamental human motivation. *Psychological Bulletin 117*(3):497 ff.

Baumgartel, H. (1957). Leadership style as a variable in research administration. *Administrative Science Quarterly 2*:344-360.

Bayley, C. (2002, October 25). Addressing Errors. Presentation, American Society of Bioethics and Humanities (ASBH). Chicago, Il.

Beauchamp, T., and Childress, J. (1994). *Principles of biomedical ethics* (4th ed.). Oxford, UK: Oxford University Press.

Bebeau, M., Rest, J., and Yamoor, C. (1985). Measuring dental students' ethical sensitivity. *Journal of Dental Education 49*:225 ff.

Best corporate citizens, The 100. (2001). Corporate social responsibility report. *Business Ethics 15*(2):12-16.

Blake, D. H., Frederick, W. C., and Myers, M. S. (1976). *Social auditing: Evaluating the impact of corporate programs*. New York, NY: Praeger Publishers.

Bourbonnais, R., and Mondor, M. (2001). Job strain and sickness absence among nurses in Province of Quebec. *American Journal of Industrial Medicine 39:*194-202.

Brown, M. T. (1998). Concepts and experience of the 'Valuing Diversity and Ethics' workshops at Levi Strauss and Company. In B. N. Kumar and H. Steinmann (Eds.), *Ethics in international management* (pp. 243-257). Berlin, GR: Walter de Gruyter.

Callahan, D., and Bok, S. (Eds.). (1980). *Ethics teaching in higher education.* New York, NY: Plenum Press.

Campbell, A., Converse, P., and Rodger W. (1976). *The quality of American life: Perceptions, evaluations, and satisfactions.* New York, NY: Russell Sage Publications, Inc.

Campbell, D. T., and Stanley, J. C. (1963). *Experimental and quasi-experimental designs for research.* Boston, MA: Houghton Mifflin Company.

Carr, A. Z. (1989). Can an executive afford a conscience? In K. R. Andrews (Ed.), *Ethics in practice: Managing the moral corporation* (pp. 26-35). Boston, MA: Harvard Business School Press.

Cartwright, D., and Zander, A. (Eds.). (1968). *Group dynamics:Research and theory* (3rd ed.). New York, NY: Harper and Row Publishers.

Chadwick, R. F. (Ed.) (1992). *Immanuel Kant: Critical assessments.* London, UK: Routledge Publishers.

Charns, M., and Schaefer, M. (1983). *Health care organizations: A model for management.* Englewood Cliffs, NJ: Prentice-Hall, Inc.

Churchill, L. R. (1987). *Rationing of health care in America: Perceptions and principles of justice.* Indianapolis, IN: Notre Dame Press.

Cohen, R. I. (1986). *Justice: Views from the social sciences.* New York, NY: Plenum Press.

Coke settles lawsuit with employees. (2000, July 1). *Atlanta Journal Constitution,* p. A5.

Comptroller General of the United States. (1988). *Government auditing standards.* Washington, DC: Government Printing Office.

Conference Board. (1994). *Business ethics: Generating trust in the 1990s and beyond* (Report #1057-94-CH; S. J. Garone, Ed.). New York, NY: Author.

Conference Board. (1992). Corporate Ethics: Developing New Standards for Accountability. New York, NY: Author, p. 8.

Cook, T. D., Habib, F-N., Phillips, M., Settersten, R., Shagle, S., and Degirmencioglu, S. (1999). Comer's School Development Program in Prince George's County, Maryland: A theory-based evaluation. *American Educational Research Journal 36*(3):543-597.

Cook, T. D. and Campbell, D.T. (1979) *Quasi-experimentation: Design and analysis issues for field settings.* Boston, MA: Houghton Mifflin Company.

Cooke, R., and Rousseau, D. M. (1987). Behavioral norms and expectations: Quantitative approach to assessment of organizational culture. *Group and Organizational Studies 13:*245 ff.

Cooper, C. L., and Rousseau, D. M. (Eds.). (1992-1998). *Trends in organizational behavior* (Vols. 1-5). New York, NY: John Wiley and Sons, Ltd.

Cranford, R., and Doudera, A. (Eds.). (1984). Institutional ethics committees and health care decision making. Ann Arbor, MI: Health Administration Press.

Darr, K. (1991). *Ethics in health services management* (2nd ed.). Washington, DC: Health Professions Press.

Dawson, P. (1994). *Organizational change: A professional approach.* London, UK: Paul Chapman Publishers, Ltd.

Dence, R. (1995). Best practices benchmarking. In J. Holloway, J. Lewis, and G. Mallory (Eds.), *Performance measurement and evaluation* (pp. 124-151). London, UK: Sage Publications, Inc

Donaldson, T. (2002, February 25). Global Ethics. Panel Presentation, Association of Practical and Professional Ethics (APPE), Cincinnati, Ohio.

Donaldson, T., and Dunfree, T. W. (Eds.). (1997). *Ethics in Business and Economics* (Vol. II). Aldershot, UK: Ashgate Publishers.

Driscoll, D., and Hoffman, W. M. (2000). *Ethics matters: How to implement a values-driven management.* Waltham, MA: Center for Business Ethics.

Drucker, P. (2001). *The essential Drucker: Selections from the management works of Peter F. Drucker.* New York, NY: Harper Collins.

Dubler, N., and Marcus, L. J. (1994). *Mediating bioethical disputes.* New York, NY: United Hospital Fund.

Durkheim, E. (1965). *The rules of sociological method* (8th ed.). G. E. G. Catlin (Ed.). (Trans. by S. A. Solovay and J. H. Mueller). New York, NY: Free Press.

Elling, R. H. (1980). *Cross-national study of health systems: Concepts, methods, and data sources.* Detroit, MI: Gale Research Company Book Tower.

Ethics Resource Center. (2003, April). *Ethics Resource Center Online Report 1(8).* What's important to business ethics? Retrieved August 18, 2003, from: http://www.ethics.org/today.

Federal Sentencing Commission. (1991). *Federal Guidelines.* Washington, DC: United States Government.

Fisk, G. (1979). Issues, priorities and sanctions for enforcing social responsibilities in European business firms. In G. Fisk and E. Korsvold (Eds.), *Social responsibility in business: Scandinavian viewpoints* (pp. 158-169). Lund, Sweden: Studentlitteratur.

Fortune' Best. (2002). Listing of best companies in U.S. *Fortune 154(2):111.*

Fortune Global 500. (2000). The world's largest companies. *Fortune Global 500 142(3):232-312.* Frederickson, B. (1998). What good are positive emotions? *Review of General Psychology 3:*300-319.

French, J., Caplan, R., and Van Harrison, R. (1982). *The mechanisms of job stress and strain.* New York, NY: Wiley Publishers.

French, P. (1984). *Collective and corporate responsibility.* New York, NY: Columbia University Press.

Gilbert, J. A., Stead, B., and Ivancevich, J. M. (1999). Diversity management: A new organizational paradigm. *Journal of Business Ethics 21:*61-67.

Goodpaster, K. (1989). Ethical imperatives and corporate leadership. In K. R. Andrews (Ed.), *Ethics in practice: Managing the moral corporation* (pp. 212-238). Boston, MA: Harvard Business School Press.

Green, B., Miller, P., and Routh, C. (1995). Teaching ethics in psychiatry: A one-day workshop for clinical students. *Journal of Medical Ethics 21:*234.

Greengard, S. (1997, October). 50% of your employees are lying, cheating and stealing. *Workforce 76:*44-53.

Grembowski, D. (2001). *The practice of health program evaluation.* Thousand Oaks, CA: Sage Publications, Inc.

Griffin, R. W., Kelly, A. O., and Collins, J. (1998). Dysfunctional work behaviors in organizations. In C. Cooper and D. M. Rousseau (Eds.), *Trends in organizational behavior* (Vol. 5, pp. 65-82). New York, NY: John Wiley and Sons, Ltd.

Gulley, S. (2001). *The academic president as moral leader: James T. Laney at Emory University 1977-1993.* Macon, GA: Mercer University Press.

Hackman, J. R. (Ed.). (1990). *Groups that work (and those that don't).* San Francisco, CA: Jossey-Bass Publishers.

Hall, R. T. (2000). *An introduction to healthcare organizational ethics.* Oxford, UK: Oxford University Press.

Harrison, M. I. (1994). *Diagnosing organizations: Methods, models, and processes.* Thousand Oaks, CA: Sage Publications, Inc.

Hart, J. (1997). *Ethics and technology: Innovation and transformation in community contexts.* Cleveland, OH: The Pilgrim Press.

Harter, J. K., Schmidt, F. L., and Keyes, C. L. M. (2003). Well-being in the work place and its relationship to business outcomes: A review of Gallup Studies. In C. M. Keyes and J. Haidt (Eds.), *Flourishing.* Washington, DC: American Psychological Association.

Health Care Compliance Association (HCCA). (2002, August 4). *Corporate compliance for the health care professional.* Retrieved August 4, 2002 from: http://www.hccainfo.org/html/compliance.html.

Hébert, P., Meslin, E. M., and Dunn, E. V. (1992). Measuring the ethical sensitivity of medical students: A study at the University of Toronto. *Journal of Medical Ethics 18:*142-150.

Heller, J. C. (2001). Preface. In J. C. Heller, J. E. Murphy, and M. E. Meaney (Eds.), *Guide to professional development in compliance* (pp. xi-xii). Gaithersburg, MD: Aspen Publishers, Inc.

Helsingin Sanomat, International Edition. (2002). Business and Finance Report. Finnish officials least corrupt once again. August 30:A1.

Hodge, B. J. (1988). *Organization theory* (3rd ed.). Needham Heights, MA: Simon and Schuster Publishers.

Hodson, R. (2001). *Dignity at work.* Cambridge, UK: Cambridge University Press.

Holloway, J., Lewis, J., and Mallory, G. (Eds.). (1995). *Performance, measurement, and evaluation.* London, UK: Sage Publications, Inc.

Hultman, K., and Gellerman, B. (2002). *Balancing individual and organizational values: Walking the tightrope to success.* San Francisco, CA: Jossey-Bass/Pfeiffer.

IBE Survey. (2003, May 13). *Ethics Today Online, 1*(9). Retrieved August 3, 2003, from: http//www.ethics.org/today.

Joint Commission on Accreditation of Healthcare Organizations. (1994). Accreditation Manual. Oakbrook Terrace, IL: Author.

Joint Commission on Standards for Educational Evaluation (1994). *The program evaluation standards* (2nd ed.). Newbury Park, CA: Sage Publications, Inc.

Kahn, J. (2001). Special report: America's 50 best companies for minorities. *Fortune 144*(1):114.

Kant, I. (1964). *Groundwork of the metaphysic of morals* (H. J. Paton, Trans.). New York, NY: Harper and Row (Original work published 1785).

Katz, D., and Allport, F. H. (1931). *Students' attitudes: A report of the Syracuse University reaction study.* Syracuse, NY: Craftsman Press.

Kelley, C. M. (1988). *The destructive achiever: Power and ethics in the American corporation* (pp. 283-201). Reading, MA: Addison-Wesley Publishing Company, Inc.

Kessen, R. (1990). *Managing corporate culture.* Aldershot, UK: Gower Publishers, Ltd.

Keyes, C., Hysom, S., and Lupo, K. (2000). Positive organization: Leadership legitimacy, employee well-being, and the bottom line. *The Psychologist-Manager Journal 4*(2):143-153.

Khushf, G. (2001). Organizational ethics and compliance. In J. C. Heller, J. E. Murphy, and M. E. Meaney (Eds.), *Guide to professional development in compliance* (pp. 157-188). Gaithersburg, MD: Aspen Publishers, Inc.

Kilmann, R. H., and Covin, J. (1988). *Corporate transformation: Revitalizing organizations for a competitive world.* San Francisco, CA: Jossey-Bass Publishers.

Kirkpatrick, D. (1985). *How to manage change effectively.* San Francisco, CA: Jossey-Bass Publishers.

Kitson, A., and Campbell, R. (1996). *The ethical organization.* London, UK: Macmillan Press, Ltd.

Koehoorn, M., Lowe, G. S., Rondeau, K. V., Schellenberg, G., and Wagar, T. H. (2002). Creating high-quality health workplaces. *Canadian Policy Research Networks' Discussion Paper No. W/14.* Ottawa, CA: Canadian Policy Research Networks, Inc.

Kraut, A. I. (1996). An overview of organizational surveys. In A. I. Kraut (Ed.), *Organizational surveys: Tools for assessment and change* (pp. 1-14). San Francisco, CA: Jossey-Bass Publishers.

Kuhn, J. W., and Shriver, D. W. (1991). *Beyond success: Corporations and their critics in the 1990s.* New York, NY: Oxford University Press, p. 314.

Kuhn, T. S. (1996). *The structure of scientific revolution* (3rd ed.). Chicago, IL: The University of Chicago Press.

Landeweerd, J. A., and Boumans, N. (1988). Work satisfaction, health, and stress: A study of Dutch nurses. *Work Stress* 2:17-26.

Lavelle, L. (2002, October 7). The best's worst boards: Special report. How the corporate scandals are sparking a revolution in government. *Business Week* (European ed.), p. 58.

Levering, R. I. (2000). *A great place to work: What makes some employers so good (and most so bad).* San Francisco, CA: Great Place to Work Institute, Inc.

Lowe, G. (2000). *The quality of work: A people-centered agenda.* Toronto, CA: Oxford University Press.

Lowe, G., and Schellenberg, G. (2001). What's a good job? The importance of employment relationships. *Canadian Policy Research Network (CPRN) Study W-05.* Ottawa, CA: Canadian Policy Research Networks, Inc.

McDaniel, C. (1995). Organizational culture, ethics work satisfaction. *Journal of Nursing Administration* 23(11):15-21.

McDaniel, C. (1998a). Enhancing nurses' ethical practice: Development of a clinical ethics program. *Ethics for Nursing Practice* 33(2):299-311.

McDaniel, C. (1998b). Hospital ethics committees and nurses' participation. *Journal of Nursing Administration* 28(9):47-51.

McDaniel, C. (1998c). Ethical environments: Reports of practicing nurses. *Nursing Clinics of North America* 33(2):363-373.

McDaniel, C. (1999). Clergy contributions to healthcare ethics committees. *HEC Forum* 11(2):140-154.

McDaniel, C., and Schoeps, N. (2003a). Ethics in corporations: Employee position and organizational ethics. In process.

McDaniel, C., and Schoeps, N. (2003b). Physician perceptions of ethical environments: Study of Finnish health care providers. In process.

McDaniel, C., Schoeps, N., and Lincourt, J. (2001). Organizational ethics: Perceptions of employees by gender. *Journal of Business Ethics* 33(3):245-256.

McDowell, B. (2000). *Ethics and excuses: The crisis in professional responsibility.* Westport, CT: Quorum Books.

May, W. F. (2001). *Beleaguered rulers: The public obligation of the professional.* Louisville, KY: Westminster John Knox Press.

Mill, J. S. (1993). Utilitarianism. In G. Williams (Ed.), *Utilitarianism; On liberty; Considerations on representative government; Remarks on Bentham's philosophy* (pp. 1-43). London, UK: J. M. Dent. (Original work published in 1910).

Miller, D. B. (1986). *Managing professionals in research and development*. San Francisco, CA: Jossey-Bass Publishers.

Murphy, J. E. (2001). The compliance officer: Delimiting the domain. In J. C. Heller, J. E. Murphy, and M. E. Meaney (Eds.), *Guide to professional development in compliance* (pp. 19-35). Gaithersburg, MD: Aspen Publishers, Inc.

Nash, L. (1989). Ethics without the sermon. In K. R. Andrews (Ed.), *Ethics in practice: Managing the moral corporation* (pp. 65-72). Boston, MA: Harvard Business School Press.

Nash, L. (1990). *Good intentions aside: A manager's guide to resolving ethical problems*. Harvard Business School. Boston, MA: Harvard University Press.

National Business Ethics Study. (2001, May). *Walker Loyalty Report: Loyalty in the Workplace*. WalkerInformation, online report. Retrieved July, 2003, from: http://www.walkerinfo.com/resources/report.

Niebuhr, R. (1932). *Moral man and immoral society: A study in ethics and politics*. New York, NY: Scribner's Sons.

Newcomer, K. E., Hatry, H., and Wholey, J. (Eds.). (1994). Meeting the need for practical evaluation approaches: An introduction. *Handbook of practical program evaluation*. San Francisco, CA: Jossey-Bass Publishers, pp. 1-10.

Norris, L. W. (1989). Moral hazards of an executive. In K. R. Andrews (Ed.), *Ethics in practice: Managing the moral corporation* (pp. 35-45). Boston, MA: Harvard Business School Press.

Parsons, T. (1964). *Social structure and personality*. New York, NY: Free Press of Glencoe.

Patton, M. W. (1986). *Utilization-focused evaluation*. Newbury Park, CA: Sage Publications, Inc.

Pellegrino, E. (1979). *Humanism and the physician*. Knoxville, TN: University of Tennessee Press.

Peters, T. J., and Waterman, R. H. (1989). *In search of excellence*. New York, NY: Harper and Row.

Petterson, I-L., and Arnetz, B. B. (1997). Perceived relevance of psychosocial work site interventions for improved quality of health care work environment. *Nursing Science* 18:4-10.

Porter, L. W. (1964). *Organizational patterns of managerial job attitudes*. Washington, DC: American Management Research.

Räikkä, J. (1997). On disassociating oneself from collective responsibility. *Social Theory and Practice* 23(1):93-108.

Random House Webster's College Dictionary (2nd ed.). (1999). New York, NY: Random House, p. 1487.

Rawls, J. (1971). *A theory of justice*. Cambridge, MA: Harvard University Press.

Reidenbach, R. E., and Robin, D. F. (1989). *Ethics and profits: A convergence of corporate America's economic and social responsibilities*. Englewood Cliffs, NJ: Prentice Hall.

Robertson, I. T. (1994). Personality and personnel selection. In C. L. Cooper and D. M. Rousseau (Eds.), *Trends in organizational behavior* (Vol. 1, pp. 75-89). New York, NY: John Wiley and Sons, Ltd.

Robin, D., and Babin, L. (1997). Making sense of the research on gender and ethics in business: A critical analysis and extension. *Business Ethics Quarterly* 7(4):61-90.

Robinson, S. L., and Greenberg, J. (1998). Employees behaving badly: Dimensions, determinants and dilemmas in the study of workplace deviance. In C. L. Cooper and D. M. Rousseau (Eds.), *Trends in organizational behavior* (Vol. 5, pp. 1-30). New York, NY: John Wiley and Sons, Ltd.

Roethlisberger, F., and Dickson, W. J. (1939). *Management and the worker.* Cambridge, MA: Harvard University Press.

Rosenthal, S., and Buchholz, R. (2000). *Rethinking business ethics: A pragmatic approach.* New York, NY: Oxford University Press.

Rousseau, D. M., and House, R. J. (1994). Meso organizational behavior: Avoiding three fundamental biases. In C. L. Cooper and D. M. Rousseau (Eds.), *Trends in organizational behavior* (Vol. 1, pp. 13-30). New York, NY: John Wiley and Sons, Ltd.

Sarbanes-Oxley Law. (2002). Public Law No. 107-204, 116 Stat. 745. Regarding reform legislation covering governance of public corporations, including protection of whistleblowers. See: U.S. Government, 107th Congress, January 23.

Schein, E. H. (1992). *Organizational culture and leadership.* San Francisco, CA: Jossey-Bass Publishers.

Selltiz, C., Wrightsman, L. S., and Cook, S. W. (1976). *Research methods in social relations* (3rd ed.). New York, NY: Holt, Rinehart and Winston.

Sethi, S., and Sama, L. M. (1998). The competitive context of ethical decision making in business. In B. N. Kumar and H. Steinmann (Eds.), *Ethics in international management* (pp. 65-86). Berlin, GR: Walter de Gruyter Publishers.

Shapleigh Hardware Company. (2003, August 5). Retrieved on July 15, 2003, from: http://www.shapleigh-hdww.html.

Shirom, A., and Harrison, M. (1995). Diagnostic models for organizations: Toward an integrative perspective. In C. Cooper and D. M. Rousseau (Eds.), *Trends in organizational behavior* (Vol. 2, pp. 85-107). New York, NY: John Wiley and Sons, Ltd.

Shortell, S., Zimmerman, J., Rousseau, D., and Gilles, R., Wagner, D., Draper, E., Knaus, W., and Duffy, J. (1994). The performance of intensive care units: Does good management make a difference? *Medical Care 32(5):*508-525.

Shortell, S., Rousseau, D., Gillies, R., Devers, K., and Simons, T. (1991). Organizational assessment in ICUs. *Medical Care 29(8):*709-10.

Singhal, S. (1994). *Senior management: The dynamics of effectiveness.* London, UK: Sage Publications, Inc.

Smith, A. (1995). *Adam Smith's wealth of nations: New interdisciplinary essays.* S. Copley and K. Sutherland (Eds.). New York, NY: St. Martin's Press.

Southeastern College. (2003, August 5). Retrieved on June 11, 2003 from: http://www.secollege. edu/News_Events/html.

Spector, P. (1997). *Job satisfaction: Application, assessment, cause, and consequences.* Thousand Oaks, CA: Sage Publications, Inc.

Stodgill, R. M. (1974). *Handbook of leadership: A survey of theory and research.* New York: NY: Free Press.

Synovus Corporation. (2003). Web page for Synovus Corporation, highlighting James Blanchard.

Taka, I. (1998). Contextualism in business and ethical issues in Japan. In B. N. Kumar and H. Steinmann (Eds.), *Ethics in international management* (pp. 323-339). Berlin, GR: Walter de Gruyter Publishers.

Tharenou, P. (1997). Determinants of participation in training and development. In C. L. Cooper and D. M. Rousseau (Eds.), *Trends in organizational behavior* (Vol. 4, pp. 15-27). New York, NY: John Wiley and Sons, Ltd.

Time Magazine. (2002). Persons of the Year, The Whistleblowers. Cover story by Richard Locayo and Amanda Ripley. December 160 (27):30.

Treviño, L. (1997). Ethical decision-making in organizations: A person-situation interactionist model. In T. Donaldson and T. W. Dunfree (Eds.), *Ethics in business and economics* (Vol. II, pp. 601-617). Aldershot, UK: Ashgate Publishing.

United States Sentencing Guidelines Manual (1993). %8A1.2. Amendments as of November 1, 2002. http://www.ussc.gov/GUIDELIN.HTML.

Velasquez, M. (1990). Corporate ethics: Losing it, having it, getting it. In P. Madsen and J. Shafritz (Eds.), *Essentials of business ethics* (pp. 228-243). New York, NY: Meridian Publishers.

Velasquez, M.G. (Spring, 1983). Why corporations are not morally responsible for anything they do? *Business and Professional Ethics Journal* 2:1-17.

Victor, B., and Cullen, J. (1988). The organizational bases of ethical work climates. *Administrative Science Quarterly 33:*101-125.

von Bertalanffy, L. (1968). *General system theory.* New York, NY: George Brazillier Company.

Walsh, K., Bartunek, J. M., and Lacey, C. (1998). A relational approach to empowerment. In C. Cooper and D. M. Rousseau (Eds.), *Trends in organizational behavior* (Vol. 5, pp. 103-126). New York, NY: John Wiley and Sons, Ltd.

Werhane, P. (1985). *Persons, rights, and corporations.* Englewood Cliffs, NJ: Prentice-Hall Publishers.

Wholey, J. S., Hatry, H. and Newcomer, K. E. (Eds.). (1994). *Handbook of practical program evaluation.* San Francisco, CA: Jossey-Bass Publishers.

Woodstock, Theological Center. (1995). *Ethical considerations in the business aspects of health care.* Washington, DC: Georgetown University Press.

Worthen, B. R., and Sanders, J. R. (1973). *Educational evaluation: Theory and practice.* Worthington, OH: Charles Jones Publishing Company.

Index

accountability, as ethics advocate 180; *see also* leaders
advocates 168; *see also* ethical advocates
  characteristics of 168-181; *see also* actions of 168-181
  leaders as 167
Affholter, D. 115
affirmation, ethics 173
Agich, G. 73, 83, 84
Aguilar, F. 2, 9, 32, 168
Allied Holdings, Inc. 152, 169, 173, 174
Allport, G. 152
American Society for Bioethics and Humanities (ASBH) 63
analysis, ethical decision making 22
  unit of 23; *see also* data
Andrews, K. R. 133, 181
Applebaum, E. 89
appraisement; *see* evaluation
Argyris, C. 18, 34, 80, 83
Arnetz, B. B. 3
assessing, ethical environments 97; *see also* evaluation
  considerations in organizations 32-34
  effectiveness 103
audit, defined 105
  designs for 110
  distinguished from program evaluation 106
  goals for 105
  qualities for good 106
  types of 105; *see also* evaluation

Badaracco, J. L., Jr. 42, 181
Baier, K. 19
Baumeister, R. 84
Bayley, C. 54
Beauchamp, T. 19, 20, 32
Bebeau, M. 43
Blake, D. H. 42, 52, 105

blame 47
  assessing for 48-52
  assigning of; *see* assessing
  collective 49
  individual 48
Blanchard, J. 9, 171, 173, 178
Bok, S. 45, 69
Boumans, N. 3
Bourbonnais, R. 3
Brown, M. T. 88, 90
Buchholz, F. 7
Burke, J. 171, 180

Callahan, D. 43, 45, 69
Campbell, D. T. 115, 116, 117, 125
Campbell, R. 9, 25
Carr, A. Z. 170, 181
Cartwright, D. 29, 30
cases, for ethics 123-124
  limits of 123
  reliability of 123
  testing with 124
Cathy, T. 47, 176, 180, 181
CEOs, role of 47, 49, 51, 69, 167 ff
Chadwick, R. 20
Charns, M. 18, 19
Chick-fil-A, Inc. 157, 176
Childress, J. 19, 20
Churchill, L. 2
client focus 33
Coca-Cola Company, The 4
Cohen, R. I. 86
committee, access to 83
  advisory to ethics program 143
  ethical deliberations in 82-85
  ethics 82; *see also* structures
  functions of 129
compliance, benefits of 63, 74
  critical thinking in 69
  debate regarding ethics 63-64
  defined 62
  development in US 61
  discretionary actions 66